Real
Cardiff

The Flourishing City

Other Titles in the series:

Real
Cardiff

The Flourishing City

Peter Finch

SEREN

Seren is the book imprint of
Poetry Wales Press Ltd
Nolton Street, Bridgend, Wales

www.serenbooks.com
facebook.com/SerenBooks
Twitter: @SerenBooks

ISBN 978-1-78172-469-9

A CIP record for this title is available from
the British Library

The publisher works with the financial assistance
of the Welsh Books Council

Cover photography: © Peter Finch, 2018

Printed by Latimer Trend & Company Ltd, Plymouth.

CONTENTS

INTRODUCTION

Cardiff – The Flourishing City

Boom towns stimulate. Living in them we get a sense of excitement, of furiously going somewhere, of being something. Cardiff has felt like this quite a few times in its long history. And today it's feeling like this all over again.

I'm on the harbour front in the Bay seeing some of the best of it. Europe's most liveable capital city[1], and, year on year since 2016, the one with the greatest increase in popularity as a destination[2]. It's here all around me. New build still happening in all directions. Following the impounding of the waters by the Barrage and the opening of both the Senedd and the Wales Millennium Centre, I asked a developer if the Bay was now complete. Not for another twenty years, he told me, there's space and opportunity enough here for at least that.

Booms arrive at places where opportunity presents itself, where money can be turned, where great fortunes can be amassed overnight. All you need is the suggestion that this is happening and the rush will begin.

Before the Romans arrived here in AD 55 to build their fort on the Severn shore the locals, the Silures, had a couple of huts, some fishing henges, and a place to launch boats. But the needs of the invaders presented opportunity. First a village and then a town accumulated as natives learned to offer the services that the Roman garrison commander did not. Food, drink, entertainment, women. Cardiff blossomed.

Not that the place was called Cardiff then. The Romans knew it as Tamium, a name they also used for the river. However, the *Antonine Itinerary*, the third century survey of the Roman Empire's roads, lists this thriving fort and village as Bovium. Nomenclature is unclear. The twelfth century *Liber Landavensis*[3], The Book of Llandaff, suggests that the river might have at one time been called the Tâm. Plenty of fog, then. I love that.

The whole habitation, of course, could have been called Roath, a village a short distance east of the Taff estuary. I suggested this to much derision in the first *Real Cardiff*. It's an idea that legendary Cardiff historian and compiler of the *Cardiff Records*, J. Hobson Matthews, proposed back in 1901[4]. I see from my latest council tax demand that the idea has not caught on yet.

Cardiff's booms of the Dark Ages, if it had any, go largely unrecorded. By 1262, almost two hundred years after the Norman invasion and more than seven hundred after the Romans had left, the population of Kardivia[5] had climbed from the few hundred who must have lived in Bovium to a dizzying two thousand and twenty. The Black Death of 1348 and the rampaging of Owain Glyndŵr then knocked that back to around twelve hundred. This was a collapse, a great shrinkage, when Kerdif's early High Streete, East Streetwardee, West Streete and South Streete[6] between them could only house as many as walk round Roath Park Lake on a hot bank holiday.

By 1801, the date of the first census, the population of market traders and sheep skin exporters at what had now become known as Cardiff had crawled up again to one thousand eight hundred and seventy. If you included outlying villages such as Roath, Lisvane and Llandaff, however, then the figure would hit three thousand four hundred and twenty seven[7]. Not a huge number by contemporary standards but it was a new clustering of people. The Glamorgan Canal, which had first reached the sea near the present Clarence Road Bridge in 1794, had a lot to do with this fresh and soon to become unstoppable burgeoning.

The root lay with the industrial revolution and the manufacture of first iron and then steel at the heads of the south Wales valleys. This was closely followed by the mining of coal, on what turned out to be an epic scale, right down those valleys. Without these newly flourishing commodities the prospering of the town just beyond the valleys' southern extremity would never have happened.

By 1851, with the Glamorgan Canal full of barges, Bute's first dock functioning, and the Taff Vale Railway bringing down ceaseless trucks of steam coal and iron ingots, the Cardiff population had risen by more than sevenfold to 26,630. This was what former First Minister the late Rhodri Morgan calls the heroic period. The rocky path to Welsh supremacy, in terms of population numbers anyway, had now become a rolling road. By 1901 that population had swollen to 172,629. By 1951 it had reached 267,356. From a village where everyone would have known everyone else to a city where you could have an affair and get away with it in less than a hundred and fifty years. I made this suggestion to a group of local citizens gathered in Penarth a few years back. There was a small silence and then a woman at the back put her hand up. "Oh, no you can't," she said.

Population growth since the nineteen fifties has continued. Perhaps not at the scale witnessed during the great industrial age but in fits and great bursts nonetheless. In 2001 Cardiff was 292,150. Six years later, just before the financial crash, it had risen by more than 10% to 328,200[8]. Certainly a place big enough to get lost in, but still eminently knowable.

More recent population figures are harder to settle on. Estimates put the city at 358,400 in 2016 with continuing growth at well above the national average projected for the decade to come. Cardiff's Local Development Plan[9] for the period is predicated on a population that will top 412,801[10] by 2026. This figure does have an element of elasticity about it, however, and has been challenged a number of times. But whichever way it's looked at Cardiff's population growth will continue to flourish.

Ambition

Cardiff's ambition, ever since the Normans first arrived and put the plan into action, has been to take over the surrounding countryside. Through the post-Norman centuries, and with the exception of a brief time in 1851 when iron town Merthyr significantly overtook it, Cardiff's position in the south east of Wales as the leading centre of trade, wealth and governance has been unassailable. In charge, yes, but as an exemplar of who we all are, maybe not. Cardiff's long relationship with its backcountry has always been difficult.

The idea of Cardiff as dominant force, capital of something, a hub, a headquarters, a focus for aspiration, an outlet for national exuberance, a thriving heart of created wealth with all the trappings that attend has long been with us. First the Butes' nineteenth century empire building, their grand battles with rivals, their construction of the greatest coal docks in the world[11], their transformation of the town's fabric with a nineteenth century Disneyland castle at its core. Then the town's elevation to city at the turn of the twentieth century and its clamouring rush to beat the rest of Wales as the home for the new national institutions. The white Portland stone civic centre in Cathays Park would provide the backdrop. The National Museum, The Temple of Peace, Board of Health, National War Memorial, the largest of Wales' local authorities and then UK Central Government's Welsh Office all duly arrived. More recently Cardiff won the marathon battles to have the National Stadium, opera house and new Assembly Government Senedd all built here.

Cardiff is like France insisting that everything of European significance gets headquartered on French soil. The National Maritime Museum slipped to Swansea, but that was a minor matter. Almost everything else of Welsh consequence is here. Our national broadcaster, bent on leaving leafy Llandaff, ended up not in Wrexham nor in Carmarthen but in Cardiff's very centre.

Despite these attractions, most of which aid Cardiff's ambition and certainly help it punch above its weight in the European big city stakes, relationships with its surrounding penumbra of habitation are often strained. As with most cities those who do not live there harbour resentment. "You're from Cardiff, see, you don't understand Wales. You're not really Welsh anyway."

Unlike most city regions, conurbations as they once were known, Greater Cardiff's dense central core is not surrounded by a periphery of slightly less compressed habitation, as can be found in, for example, the cities of Manchester, Copenhagen, Stockholm and Gothenburg. Instead, at about five or six miles out, there is a more sparsely populated ring of woodland, hill, mountain, and farm. Outer Lisvane, the Cibwr Ridge, Peterston, Rudry, the flatlands on the far side of Marshfield. Beyond that, where other greater city regions have an extra-urban area of population decrease, Greater Cardiff locates further dense suburbs and ex-industrial towns – Caerphilly, Pontypridd, and the once industrial valleys themselves. And we don't relate well. There are seemingly intractable suspicions. Sophisticates vs hillbillies. Haves and have nots. Heartless townies vs loving woolly backs.

When in 2007 the European Capital of Culture bid team visited Cardiff we were told that we did not relate to our hinterland. Liverpool, which won the contest, clearly did. Cardiff instead had turned its back. Despite providing the city with all it needed to grow, sending down a huge work force daily to staff its enterprises, to use its shops and then to party all night in its flourishing drinkeries Cardiff regarded the valleys as second class.

The Capital Region

The Cardiff Capital Region City Deal[12] which will put paid to all this suspicion and separation forever, so the planners say, aims to combine core and hinterland into one entity. This it will do by simultaneously solving the region's transport problems and ushering in a single, equitable, and very influential administration. As Prof Brian Morgan[13] told me, this new entity will have power devolved to it from both Welsh Government and local authority. It will start small but end up big and powerful. Some existing government agencies may well feel threatened.

The deal continues to solidify as I write. There is churn in the air. When Ken Skates, the Welsh Government's Cabinet Secretary for Economy and Infrastructure took up his new role in 2016 he complained that he had now inherited 48 advisory panels dealing with various aspects of the proposed City Region. What is it going to be and how will it work? No one appears to quite know. The Elizabeth Haywood *Report on City Regions* of 2012[14] is famously silent on how governance will operate. Who will give way to whom is not spelled out.

The idea for an interrelated economic entity in south Wales has actually been around for a long time. It was a component of economist Hilary Marquand's grand plan[15] of the 1930s which proposed a recasting of the industrial framework all the way from Tiger Bay to Merthyr Tydfil. The late Rhodri Morgan suggested that if you combined the three mini-regions of urban centre and attendant valleys – Cardiff, Newport and Bridgend – into a single entity you would have half the population of Wales under one roof. "It's not a matter for governments to create this," he told me. "It's there anyway."

Knitting it all together with a combined metro[16] system of interlinked and interdependent tram, bus and rail services will be a huge economic and cultural driver. The Metro system, which has been sold as something reminiscent of London's tubes, will actually be more like Frankfurt's mix of surface trams, trains and buses. It will run everywhere. Cardiff, which needs space for its ever-burgeoning population, will be able to spread northwards with impunity.

We will have come a distance. In 1966 it was suggested that Wimpey should start to build for a Cardiff-overflow in Caerphilly. "We don't build houses in mining towns," was the response. In business eyes Caerphilly was irretrievably part of the coal-rich valleys. Although eventually the builder did respond to pressure and the new Caerphilly districts of Watford Park and Hendredenny were created.

Yet the road to the new regional power centre remains long and littered with difficulty. Money is out there. Private, public, regional, UK central. All it will take is for one of the Cabinet Secretary's 48 bureaucratic assemblages to be given genuine teeth, for power and responsibility to shift, and a City Region Capital Western Powerhouse Authority with its own operating departments could come into being. Transport first then housing followed by training. New towns will be built. Visiting St David's Two for a browse in John Lewis will become as easy for Merthyr residents as it is for those of Roath.

We need what happened in Greater Manchester with its elected mayor and unity between 10 constituent local authorities to happen here. It will be like joining a mini-version of the EU but without a referendum. It will take political will and an amount of vision, qualities Wales has often lacked. But this time the worm may have turned.

Are We All The Same?

We may have the ability to fuse local infrastructures and provide central services but will we ever become one people? Of this I'm not sure. The barrier of that Caerphilly massif remains, the hills north of Cardiff forever hiding the city's backdrop of valleys from view. While many valley people visit Cardiff on a regular basis and almost all have done so at some time in their lives the same cannot be said in reverse for Cardiffians. North of the city does not exist. Between the Bay and the Beacons is a worm hole that takes you from bustle to national park green. The valley lands in between are rarely engaged with. Cardiff finishes at the roundabout just south of Castell Coch.

Population pressures, however, are on unity's side. Despite the dissolution of almost everything that originally drew people to these dozen or so valleys[17], a slow native population decline and the failure of most attempts to provide new sources of employment this landscape remains essential for Cardiff's survival. Continued city growth requires an ever-enlarging workforce and dormitory suburbs, schools and hospitals to support it. Once the city has finished high-rising, brown field infilling and green belt abandonment it will still need more space. A cultural meld is certainly in the offing.

Where next?

Taking a group of undergraduates around the centre on a psychogeographic ramble intended to offer some introduction to what this city is and how it works I've been struck by how many failed to see the connection between Cardiff and the sea. It was as if the port had sunk into insignificance and the sounds and smells of water had been relegated to a decorative fringe. That the city lacks unity with its waterfront is self-evident. Work is not down there. The main rail line remains a Mason-Dixon. When we visit the impounded flat-water Bay its leisure yachts appear disconnected with the tidal seascape beyond.

These young newcomers that I'm walking with through Cardiff's Norman past see the place as full of green space and light. As yet the city lacks a dense high-rise skyline (although one is coming) and the dazzling white of its administrative centre still impresses. It's a comfortable place to be in. You can enjoy yourself here.

After the dip following the 2008 crash change is now once again rolling. Construction cranes are everywhere. With the exceptions of Cardiff University's controversial[18] demolition of Victorian buildings in a conservation area on Park Place in order to develop an enormous new centre for student life, the construction of a new Museum of Military Medicine opposite the station in Cardiff Bay and the Council-backed proposal to create a new £110m, 15000-seater city centre arena there's not that much that involves the establishment of new millennium centres or vast shopping malls. There are no great engineering projects incorporating barrages or towers on artificial islands. Few major road systems. No great tunnels. The distant possibility of a power-generating tidal lagoon offshore if the proposal for a smaller lagoon at Swansea goes through and if that structure works.

The BBC is, however, moving to Three Central Square, a tight Foster & Partners designed office block opposite the main rail station. In its wake arrive other institutions and commercial operators. HMRC is deserting Llanishen to establish a new super region tax centre on the one-time site of the *Western Mail*'s printing machines. The UK Government Property Unit which looks after accommodation for non-devolved government agencies is also working towards the creation of a new public sector hub[19] nearby. Joining them will be the re-sited Cardiff University School of Journalism. Into this confined yet significant development, where Russell Goodway proposed the building of a great conference centre linking rail station with stadium, the local authority has also promised to shoehorn a replacement bus station. It will be called The Interchange. The never exactly loved Marland House[20] has been demolished to make space.

Out in the wings are the wilder proposals to resite County Hall, to build a high line linear park along the route of the present Queen Street to the Bay rail link, to put a contemporary art gallery at the Graving Docks next to Techniquest, a science park to be established off the north Cardiff M4, an innovation park at Maindy and a new home for Cardiff Blues somewhere in the sporty reaches of the Ferry Road peninsula.

As ever, most proposed new development involves accommodation although this time with emphasis on Purpose Built Student Accommodation (PBSA) in tower blocks. Cheap to erect and subject to fewer building and planning controls than regular apartments and usually considerably smaller these are now everywhere. Further education is a city growth area with the universities and colleges all enlarging their facilities. Money is being made offering undergraduates new sky-scraper apartments with great views, integral gyms and industrial strength Wi-Fi. Come down the lift and you'll be right where the action is. The days of sharing converted workers' terraces in the deeper reaches of distant Cathays are in retreat.

Wales' tallest building, a PBSA proposed for Custom House Street, opposite the Golden Cross, will offer 450 new student rooms. At 132 metres and 42 storeys the structure will easily see off the previous height holder, Swansea's 107 metre Meridian Tower. The same developer, the Watkin Jones Group, is also responsible for the 24-storey student accommodation development at the end of Charles Street. Just along from the site of Cardiff's highest high-rise where the old York Hotel and the Custom House stood, Premier Inn plan a 248 room hotel. New build, naturally, but existing facades will be kept.

Despite all this apparent accommodation success there are a few cracks showing. A couple of speculatively-constructed students blocks have already found it difficult to let their quota of apartments. Applications have been made for change of use. Brand new students lets now available to non-students – singles, and even families. Could the whole deal simply have been a ruse to get us all living in smaller and smaller spaces? Time will tell.

Cardiff's Local Development Plan (LDP) has agreed the creation of at least 41,400 regular-sized new homes during its twenty year period. Many have already been built but of those remaining at least half are now under construction on a band of new greenfield sites encircling the city. Cardiff's new districts are significant in number and they are planned to dazzle. However, because they will generally be built before the transport links that will serve them, they will inevitably be difficult to get to and from. New Cardiff runs in an arc tracking the M4. Former farmland on both sides of the motorway is being filled with dormitory estates replete with clinics, schools, shopping centres and bright community centres.

In addition brownfield infill is taking place on every city site possible from the old Ely Paper mills (800 new homes at The Mill) to the site of the Ty Mawr farmhouse at the end of Southminster Road in Roath. Porth Teigr in Cardiff Bay will get Box City, an innovative, low-cost hotel, shop and office complex constructed from hundreds of shipping containers.

In the inner city, or are near as you can now get, Cardiff and Vale College have opened their large Dumballs Road city centre campus. The former industrial area between the road itself and the river has been jointly acquired by Cardiff Council and Ikea's property development arm, Vastint. The 30-acre site, a considerable slab of river-facing land, will include the building of a large number of affordable homes. Just further north land occupied by Brains Brewery and surrounding tenements is soon to become Central Quay, a mix of apartments, offices, bars, restaurants, shops and hotels. Brains' brick chimney stack will be preserved as a link with what used to be. It's another new quay in a city that only ever really had one original and is being marketed as a place with a Covent Garden vibe targeted at creative craft traders, bars and restaurant operators. At 16 acres and with easy walking access from the to-be-redeveloped Cardiff Central Station, Central Quay will considerably enlarge Cardiff's inner-core.

There are other things, a few. The Royal Navy are building an £11m new training and warship docking facility on Roath Dock near Porth Teigr. The A4232, the Peripheral Distributor now named Ffordd Ewart Parkinson, has been extended as far as the Ocean Way roundabout. Good, but not as far yet as the place where we all want it to go, the M4. There are Government-backed proposals to build Cardiff Parkway, a privately-financed rail station, the first of the modern era. This will be Cardiff Capital Region's transport hub and shopping complex along with hotel and business park out on the eastern fringe at St Mellons. But such plans have been floated before.

We are not doing much preserving. We are losing our old place names, dropping our ancient connections, abandoning habitats. The city, famous for knocking things down and filling things in, continues to redevelop its Bay. There are far too many new "units of increased density" as one critic complained. Never enough street facing human scale houses. But that's how the future usually is.

South Wales needs a plan, as Hilary Marquand said all those decades ago. We have one now. Dramatic, difficult, and divisive it may be but when the component panels, boards, committees, councils and governments have finally agreed to agree, then deliverable. Cardiff, after years of hunting for world status is a real city at last: it will be that.

Notes

1. Cardiff Council's current promotional slogan.
2. Data from travel search engine Kayak shows that Cardiff's popularity as a holiday destination has more than tripled since 2016 with an increase of 223%.
3. *Liber Landavensis* or *Llyfr Llandaf*, the Book of Llandaff, a mainly Latin compilation of 500 years of Llandaff diocesan records and is one of the great early books of Wales.
4. *Cardiff Naturalists' Society Reports and Transactions*, Vol 33, (1900-1901) Matthews, J Hobson, *The Place Names of the Cardiff District.*
5. *Liber Landavensis.*
6. Williams, Moelwyn I, *Cardiff – Its People and its Trade – 1660-1720, Morganwwg – Transactions of the Glamorgan Local History Society*, Vol 7, 1963.
7. Williams, Moelwyn I.
8. Source – Office of National Statistics
9. *Cardiff Local Development Plan 2006-2026 Deposit Plan.*
10. *Cardiff Local Development Plan Background technical Paper Number One – Population and Housing.* Updated May, 2014.
11. Although the docks built by David Davies and John Cory at Barry were deeper.
12. The Cardiff Capitol Region City Deal of 2016 between the UK Government, the Welsh Government and the 10 City Region constituent authorities provides a £1.2 billion investment fund for regional development which will include among other things provision for regional transport, skills and employment and the development of capabilities in compound semiconductor applications.
13. Professor of Entrepreneurship at Cardiff Metropolitan University, former Chief Economist at the WDA and member of the Cardiff Capital Region Advisory Board.
14. Haywood, Dr Elizabeth, *City Regions*, 2012. Report of a task and finish group established by the Welsh Government in 2011.
15. In 1930 Hilary Marquand was appointed as Prof of Industrial Relations at Cardiff University.

In this capacity he wrote a series of reports for the Board of Trade dealing with depression era south Wales. These included what the National Library describes as the magisterial *Industrial Survey of South Wales* (1931) and then the famous *South Wales Needs A Plan* of 1936. He became Labour MP for Cardiff East in 1945. He died in 1972.

16. The unitary city already has a metro of sorts, although it fails to coordinate even itself with other forms of transport. See p.210 for a tour around its twenty stations.

17. How many there are depends on how you define valley and where you start. Beginning in the west at the Llyfni and finishing at the Llwyd in the east Wikipedia counts 14.

18. Almost all development proposals are to some degree controversial. They represent change and it is a human trait to resist this. Some developments, however, are more controversial than others. Cardiff University have demolished a line of existing structures on the east side of Park Place facing the University's main building. This despite opposition from Cardiff Civic Society, the Victorian Society and a good many others. University consultation documents suggest that the new build will aid "the developing of Park Place as an active and vibrant pedestrianised urban environment". *Cardiff University Centre For Student Life Project Brief*, 2015.

19. Hub is the word of the decade. When I wrote the first volume of *Real Cardiff* at the start of the millennium there were none. Now they are legion.

20. Council Advice Services Hub. Facilities now transferred to Cardiff Central Library Hyb on The Hayes.

CENTRAL

THE EAST GATE

Railroad Bill are banging through 'Take This Hammer' near Boots on Queen Street. It's a favoured spot. It draws the crowds. Railroad Bill is a skiffle group complete with washboard and tea chest bass. This is the early nineteen-nineties, the age of techno pop. The band is about as unfashionable as it's possible to be. Despite this, or perhaps because of it, the semi-circle of interested passers-by that has formed around them is growing.

Out front Dan Nichols, red round face afire and wearing his washboard like medieval armour, is roaring at the crowd. The band have moved onto 'Six-Five Special', the Don Lang[1] signature tune from the 50s TV show that took skiffle to the world. Railroad Bill's version is delivered at double speed. Dan, a graduate in politics from Aberystwyth, has skiffle in his soul. He's got the bloodline. His uncle is Geoff Nichols, bassist with the Avon Cities Jazz Band, who in the fifties were known as the much celebrated Avon Cities Skiffle Group. This home-made, anyone-can-do-it music is part of his lineage. And his band is certainly doing it proud today.

The crowd, who for the most part wouldn't recognise skiffle's main man Lonnie Donegan from Kenny Everett, are entranced. Dan, who can give Lonnie a run for his high-speed money, is zooming from side to side of the band like a goalkeeper. He howls out the number's pre-Beeching lyric at an audience who have never experienced trains steaming down anything. He rattles the engine's thunder across his washboard chest plate using fingers tipped with thimbles. The band behind him, Chris Walker, Andy Baillie, Dave Jones and Geoff Haynes, rock and momentously roll on their guitars and ukuleles. "Over the points, over the points, over the points. The 6-5 special's steaming down the line. Yes. The 6-5 special's right on time".

For a brief time during the nineteen fifties skiffle was king. It was an essentially acoustic music that mixed American jug-band, down home blues and old-time country with Britain's musical hall tradition and ubiquitous Cockney humour. In 1955 Chris Barber's banjo player Lonnie Donegan took an old Huddie Leadbetter song, 'Rock Island Line', to the top round the world. Bands like his formed on street corners everywhere. The only thing there was in any of the places that youth gathered was skiffle. But by 1958 it was all over, killed off by Tommy Steel and the irresistible rise of American rock and roll.

Railroad Bill's revival is timely. There's virtually no-one around who can remember skiffle and its engaging energy is just right for performance on the city's newly refurbished thoroughfares. The Council have yet to work out what to do with these randomly organised episodes of street theatre but they will. For now the music is catchy, it's performed brilliantly and it's fun. For the next twenty-five years Dan Nichols will steer the band along an increasingly successful revivalist course. There will be forays into punk, European tours, recordings, any number of YouTube clips and a world-beater as backing band for Lonnie himself before he died in 2002. Dan, the Railroad Bill leader, doubles as Sir Alfred Street, the Roath Historian (see page 86) and helps keep the wolf from the door by working for Cardiff Council as a street events officer. The world has come full circle.

Busking, or variations on that form, is today a centrepiece of Cardiff street life. Musical acts featuring everything from rapping guitarists accompanied by backing tracks to fully-feathered south American pan pipe bands complete with incongruous north American tepees can be encountered anywhere from Cardiff Central to outside Sainsbury's at the eastern edge of the inner city. In between you'll find the richest mixture there is. East European drifters totally failing to play the instruments they use as props (guitar, accordion and in one case I witnessed something that looked like a Romanian euphonium). Badly amplified preachers who insist that it's only Christ who can save you from the moral decay peddled by the bars that line most central streets. Blokes dressed as gold, spray-painted versions of Hopalong Cassidy who make money by having you pause in wonder at them standing there like human statues. Actual statues (miner with lamp, bunch of women, Nye Bevan with his arm raised) which provide the backdrop for naff keyboard players and their poorly-maintained dancing puppets. Eight-foot tall silver robots that look like they'd rust swiftly in a downpour. A youth in Cardiff City strip who keeps a football bouncing off the ends of his toes and his knees for an hour straight. Fire-eaters, tightrope walkers, jugglers, plate spinners, unicyclists, clowns and shouty fez-wearing magicians with giant packs of cards. All this backed-up by itinerant street merchants in large number, bent on selling you the sort of plastic crap that even the Pound Shop has failed to shift. Cardiff daytime street life is as much an attraction as the super-clean malls. Stay shopping, don't go home yet.

You might expect the streets of a capital city to offer you illegal things that have fallen off lorries or dope in any and all of its street disguises: blow, crack, bump, skunk, e, huff, cherry meth, beam me up Scotty and snow. But that's not what you get. Instead it's bubble machines; your name in Chinese twisted into a piece of bicycle spoke; electronic cigarettes get them now before the law changes; fake perfume containing about as much of the original as an homeopathic medicine; sparkly phone fronts that save you the time of having to doodle the patterns there yourself; Cardiff City scarfs, hats, shirts, gloves, bags, banners, stickers, and underpants; plus long coloured balloons that can be bent and twisted to resemble dogs, hats, hammers, planes and even chairs. In short pretty much everything you don't ever set out to buy, don't actually want, haven't the space for, but somehow or other end up acquiring. Is the reason we do this pity, point of sale pressure or simply forgetfulness? Out back at my house are stacks of *Big Issues*, all of them unread. I should try the mag really, as a streetwise substitute for *Hello!*, *Punch* or the *People's Friend* it's actually not at all bad.

The place that Railroad Bill has picked to perform their stuff has a venerable history. The band are playing just down from where the East Gate to the town once stood[2]. When it was dismantled at the end of the eighteenth century the posts on which it hung were allowed to remain. They stood silent, for decades, pillars to what once was. There's a subterranean instant-eat cottage pie restaurant nearby named after them. Pillars. The folding sign out front advertises the delights within: Traditional English Breakfasts – Lighter, Super, Great & Real Value Giant. Even at the top end prices don't go higher than a fiver.

Around here youths sold *Socialist Worker* and *International Times*; Toy Mic Trevor once crooned; banjo players strummed; and Ninjah banged on bins. Much earlier, bears were made to dance for money and bets were won and lost. In the days when the gate, with its three grand arches, was known as Porth Crockerton, it opened onto a growing cluster of cottages strung out along Crockherbtown Street, the highway east. This remnant of the Roman road was renamed in 1897, the year of the Empress of India's jubilee. Queen Street it became. Its historical connection was relegated to the name of the service alley that ran along the back of the developing shops – Crockherbtown Lane. Since then all attempts to put Cardiff back in touch with its past by restoring the older nomenclature have been officially resisted.

Along the ancient Crockherbtown Street citizens sold veg from stalls erected at the edge of the unending mud. Cardiff's roads were not paved until well into the eighteenth century. Today the area has Cardiff Council Zone One priority which means that cleaning carts get down here so often you should be able to lie flat out and not get dirty. The carts do their work in the early hours. Right now the paving slabs are awash with charity collectors; a South Wales Mobile Police Station here on a PR exercise to reassure the citizenry that pick-pocketing and other rough behaviour will not be tolerated; a man dressed as Andy Pandy playing a contemporary version of a hurdy gurdy and peddlers selling inflatable Disney characters at about a quarter of the price they are in the mall-encased genuine Disney store.

The three arches of the East Gate are speculation on the part of the Council who depict them thus on their celebratory blue plaque. John Speed's map of 1610, the only piece of early evidence anyone actually has, shows the gate's arches in the singular. Which was it? The descendent of a Roman triumphal entranceway or a much more mundane single opening in a medieval wall? The Council's plaque dates from the 1980s, a time of city boosterism. The marks in the paving across Queen Street show where the gates might have stood and how thick they could have been. The past in sanitised, squared-off, easily digestible slices. The real gates were pulled down by Council decree in 1791, well before the dawn of photography. No visual records were kept. It's so often like this. The past is obliterated by the present. Oblivious Cardiff sails on into the future.

THE SHERMAN

The Sherman emerged at a time of great political change in the UK when Edward Heath gave way to Harold Wilson and the red tide rose. The theatre, a dull brick post-modernist structure sitting darkly amid the terraces of Senghenydd Road, opened in 1973. It had been built with the financial support of Cardiff Pools entrepreneurs Harry and Abe Sherman. There was a plaque celebrating this fact on the left as you went in. These were the days when the arts were a rising power. The Arts Lab Movement was in full swing. Public art was on advertising hoardings. The Castle was full of sculpture. Chapter had opened in Market Road. And now there was a new Cardiff theatre that would present work that would never be seen on stage at Greyfriars Road's Victorian New.

The architects of this dark slab were Clive Johnson and David Hughes, both working for Alex Gordon and Partners. You need to dig to find their names. Architects don't get their signatures at the bottom of their works like painters. Inside the structure were two auditoria and a maze of steps and curving stairs. When you got to the main theatre you felt as if you'd entered by way of M.C. Escher's *House Of Stairs*. For a time, a decade at least, the Sherman was cutting edge offering the avant-garde all the space it needed.

There were small press bookfairs in the foyer, cult films and performances by Moving Being, Joint Stock, and Brif Gof in the theatres. John Newman in his *Pevsner Architectural Guide* described the building as "of dark brown brick, virtually windowless, giving nothing away". It fitted the programme and the times.

The Sherman began as an on-campus theatre with financial aid from University College Cardiff in 1973. It took on independent charitable status when the University withdrew its support a decade later and the building was purchased by the Welsh Arts Council. It was at the forefront of the Council's push to see new theatres open right across Wales.

By the turn of the millennium, though, with the city in which it was situated outgrowing its industrial past and facing up well to the bright glass and apartment future, the Sherman found itself in retreat. Putting on productions using its cramped back of house spaces was proving less and less popular. Its programme had become dominated by the needs of its funders. It was in the wrong place, wrong side of the tracks, out of time. It was beyond Cathays Park and in the heart of student land. The city's focus had moved south to the blossoming Bay.

A fix was needed. How could it be made a brighter place? How could its facilities be readily updated? How could it be brought back to the centre of Cardiff's creative life? Architect Jonathan Adams was invited to knock it down and build it back up. The brief was to make it work again. The proposals would be funded by selling the building's air rights. Cardiff was now such a booming place. New residential near the city's heart could be sold for anything you like. Ten floors of apartments would be built on top of the theatre's existing structure. New entrance lobbies and car parking would be added. The slick and the financially secure would move in.

As a city Cardiff then had no tall buildings policy, preferring to deal with cases as they emerged. There was fear that despite the theatre being situated to the east the city centre's Portland stone heart might be compromised by new looming towers in such close proximity. City Hall must not be overlooked. Nevertheless the plans were approved and the future looked bright.

But the financial crisis, when it came, put paid to all that. Proposals everywhere were reined back. At the Sherman finance was sought elsewhere. It was found too, an ACW[3] triumph.

Today I'm sitting in Foxy's Kitchen in the rebuilt theatre's large and brightly lit foyer. Here ham and mustard sandwiches cost £3.75 (but only £3 if I'm willing to eat them standing up just outside in the street). Jonathan, who has joined me to explain what he's done, is telling me how he originally wanted to strip the place and re-envelope it as one building. "The fantasy of staircases and changing levels had to go," he says. As it is he has cleaned out the old foyer, levelled floors, demolished walls and staircases, provided a new rehearsal room, upgraded back of house and added an improved management suite. What was dark is now full of air and light.

Outside the silent, almost secretive shade of the frontage has gone. Access is level. The walls have been clad in domestically proportioned steel tiles. Graffiti-resistant patterned stainless are on the visible frontages. Patina smeared galvanised are out back. Window openings are diamond shaped just like the cladding. The entrance foyer has been expanded, lipped with a projecting sensual eyebrow and lit inside with a born again purple light box designed by artist Jessica Lloyd Jones. "The lighting here can be changed according to need with colours altered and projection patterns switched," says Jonathan.

The frontage is best seen from an acute angle, approaching up Senghenydd Road, rather than face on from the other side of the street. Its looks alternate between vaguely reptilian and slightly Arabian. Sometimes it's both. The back of house loading bay is a two floor Moorish arch. The eyebrow straight from Narnia. It's called Sherman Cymru now but you could be forgiven for imagining you were no longer in Wales.

Under artistic director Rachael O'Riordan the theatre is currently attracting new crowds with a mix of new writing and co-production. Its two performance spaces fill with everything from community theatre to dance and musical to political drama. Audience numbers, particular among those who have never been to the theatre before, are rising. Vibrancy has returned.

Sitting around us are a Chapter-style crop of creatives in earnest conference, their tablets and files beside them. Above the place where, in defiance of fire regs May Day poets had once hawked their books, there's evidence of a leak. Paint has flaked and stained, perfection compromised. Jonathan is worried. But it turns out to be the failed flashing on a roof light, now fixed, repaint awaited. Tension drops.

Poetry For May Day should run again. We should do it here. A replay of the revolution is always exciting.

THE QUEEN STREET ROCK & ROLL AXIS

If this were America there would have been a rock and roll hall of fame here. A place to celebrate what formerly was, the luminaries who played and the Welsh music dynamos who came to see them. A whole rock epicentre for generations. As it is there are two empty storefronts, an eyebrow threading concession with its shutters down and four vibrating armchairs. For £1 you get five minutes of coin-operated motor-driven arse and back massage, the total cure for shop-drained customers. Except there aren't any. This is the future and the future no longer works.

I'm in Cardiff's Capitol Centre looking for traces of the cinema which once was. Its five arched entrances, its steps, its uniformed commissionaires and pageboys all disappeared forty years ago. Of them and the wonders they once royally fronted there is not a single trace. The Capitol opened in the age of the talkies in 1921 and lasted until Thatcher came to power in 1979. In its fifty-eight year history it was both cinema and theatre with a seating capacity on two levels approaching 3500. At its height in 1957 queues to see Bill Haley and his Comets stretched round the corner to Churchill Way and rolled all the way down to Guildford Crescent Baths. Performances of *South Pacific* in Todd-AO wide-screen ran for twenty-six weeks while the all-conquering *Sound of Music* was shown for nineteen long months without a single interruption.

'The Rage of Cardiff', as the place promoted itself in the 1920s. The Capitol was certainly that. Through the years its small stage presented an unending run of live hot music. From Gene Autry and his cowboy guitar in 1939 through to the tartan-trousered Bay City Rollers in the 1970s the Capitol was a Cardiff focus for the music of riot and change. Chuck Berry played here in 1965. He duck walked away from the mic and because so many teds jumped on stage to jive with him never returned. Dion and Brenda Lee were here in 1963. The Beatles, The Rolling Stones, Bo Diddley, Roy Orbison, The Everly Brothers. Bob Dylan. In Martin Scorsese's bio-pic *No Direction Home* (2005) you can glimpse his fans surging around the Capitol through the troubadour's taxi window.

Back stage at the top of Edward Place is now a parking ramp into the bowels of the new Capitol shopping mall's multi-story. The front steps have been replaced with a run of bland shop fronts, empty today, where Fat Face once traded, Hobbs and Phase Eight hanging in there flogging outlet quality fashion on the side. There are no extant memorials, no sense of ground zero where fame and musical wonder once sparked.

As a harbinger of the new city and the prime reason for the Capitol Cinema's demolition the Capitol Exchange Centre has dismally failed. Opened to trumpeted magnificence in 1990 this new shopping future, faux-Victorian facades outside and imitation arcades within managed to stagger for a decade before redesign was decreed an economic necessity. The Capitol Cinema replacement, an unloved round the back multiplex had come and gone, so too had two floors of Virgin Records and the Italian clothiers Benetton.

A ten million pound redevelopment at the start of the new millennium failed to fix the rot. Substantial footfall remained an illusion.

As I write plans are announced for a possible third revamp. A 'major repositioning', as the latest developer, NewRiver, suggests, will lead to increased footfall for their proposed new mix of retail with leisure. We live in hope. The money maker hiding in the smaller print is the parallel proposal to build one hundred apartments in the air space above the centre. The city grows higher and higher.

The axis rolls along Queen Street pulling its unmarked moments from rock's past along with it. The slope into the Top Rank Ballroom once faced the entrance to mighty Woolworths. Top Rank ran from 1963 to 1982. Led Zeppelin, Freddy and the Dreamers and Alexis Korner's Blues Incorporated all played. Woolworths (1913 to 1985) sold the hit songs of the greats recorded by imitators and issued on their cut price Embassy label. Both slots in the continuum faded to grey.

I've chosen Easter Sunday to make the traverse so I should expect lack of crowds and street hawking at a minimum. The fairground carousel at the foot of Park Place remains closed and curtained like a giant blancmange. The Jehovahs in pairs announce the arrival of the Kingdom to street silence. There are no takers. No buskers. No bird whistle sellers. No men with racks flogging hats and sunglasses and scarfs. A line of excited Chinese tourists photograph Cardiff's emptiness while new asylum arrivals wander the rain-washed precinct paving like the lost they are. Up beyond the e-cigs street-seller's stall on wheels is a poster announcing the imminent arrival of The Story of the King at St David's Hall. Given this is Easter this might have been the king of the Jews but in fact it's an Elvis tribute act. Rock, or the memory of it, codices of what was.

Facing the Castle, where at least they do mount the occasional rock show (Pink Floyd, Paul Weller, Thin Lizzy), and running back to where the old town quay originally stood on Westgate Street is the lane-like thoroughfare of Womanby Street. One of the oldest in Cardiff this bent hairpin from past time has become home to a concentration of contemporary music venues. Clwb Ifor Bach, Bootlegger, The Full Moon and Fuel Rock Club have their walls plastered with street art and fly posters advertising the rocking future en masse. Hang The Bastard, Wolf Alice, The Last Vendetta, Junior Bill, Skinnyman, Rustyshackle, Bare Knuckle Parade, Jeff

Rosenstock, Plague Vendor, Dead Shed Jokers, Afro Cluster, and Madame Twisted are all soon arriving.

Womanby was the 2017 focus for an ultimately successful series of protests against incoming high-rise and other inappropriate residential developments in what protestors saw as an essential music hub for the city. The Assembly Government has now altered the law in what they term Agents of Change Planning Regulations to put the onus for soundproofing and prevention of disturbance on the developer rather than the music venue. Cardiff Council have launched their own music strategy and want to rebrand the capital as Music City. That's an idea I can get behind.

Beyond is the north end of the Millennium Stadium. This is now rebranded as The Principality Stadium thereby honouring both the building society which put up the money and the future monarch to whose regality the house-lender adheres. A super circuit of stadium rockers can be occasionally heard performing here – Justin Bieber, Tina Turner, U2, The Stereophonics, The Rolling Stones, The Manic Street Preachers.

Over the river rushing by in flood, are Sophia Gardens. These are the parklands named after Lady Sophia Rawdon-Hastings, the second wife of the Second Marquis of Bute, nineteenth century founder of Cardiff's dockland empire. Originally the fields of Plasturton Farm, these riverside lands were turned into a public pleasure ground of 24 acres in 1854. They contained an ornamental walk lined with lime trees, drinking fountains, rustic benches, a lake with islands and flower beds in profusion. Cathedral Road with its substantial and expensive villas was created at the same time. The Marchioness wanted the park to be an example for other towns of industrial import to follow. An athletics field was added to the north a few years later.

Buffalo Bill and His Wild West Show came here in 1891 and the space was a regular site for travelling circuses right up to the present day. In 1951 a permanent structure to house visiting shows and exhibitions was built on the site of one of the ornamental fountains. This was the Festival of Britain-inspired, and as it turned out quite short-lived but extremely rocking, Sophia Gardens Pavilion.

As a terminus for the east-west rock and roll axis I've been following, the site of the now demolished Pavilion is about as well marked as the Capitol at the axis' origin. From the raised, metal-pathed bund that runs along the side of the river up from the Cardiff Bridge I gaze out at a car park. In the distance are the new

National Express Coaches booking offices and coach bays. Behind me is the Millennium Bridge, a footpath-carrying steel structure that would have opened up ready access from the horticultural borders of Bute Park to the flower-beds of Sophia. If Sophia's still existed.

Of the Pavilion (1951 to 1983) there is not a trace. Built with economy in mind in post-war shortage-addled Britain the pavilion was knocked up by reusing a war-surplus aerodrome hanger taken from Stormy Down. It opened with a concert featuring Danny Kaye and then a showing of the Festival of Britain's travelling exhibition. It went on to become celebrated as a venue for fashion shows, Ideal Home exhibitions and boxing and wrestling matches. The you've-all-lived-a-past-life-but-don't-know-it spiritual hypno-therapist Arnall Bloxham who put on shows here attracted audiences by the hundred.

Rock and roll fame adhered when the building began to be used as a venue for dances and music concerts. Almost as many rock luminaries ended up singing here in Cardiff's west as they did back in the eastern city's Capitol. Among them were Duran Duran, Slade, Thin Lizzy, The Stranglers, Judas Priest, The Boomtown Rats, Motorhead, Budgie, Mike Oldfield, The Jam, Hawkwind, Status Quo, Pink Floyd, The Who, Fleetwood Mac, BB King, Bill Haley, The Bonzo Dogs, The Nice, Jimi Hendrix, The Move, The Yardbirds, Johnny Cash, The Zombies, The Searchers, Carl Perkins, The Animals, Manfred Mann, Gene Vincent, The Rolling Stones, Little Richard, Del Shannon, Jerry Lee Lewis, and Cliff Richard. Who else could have come but didn't? Elvis Presley.

Rocking stopped dramatically in the harsh winter of 1981-82 when January's giant snowfalls proved too much for the inadequate cheapo roof which duly collapsed. Rebuild was deemed uneconomic and the wrecked building was demolished and hard core removed the following year.

The rock axis went under. Its ley weakened by age and climate. Fashion shifted. Audiences aged. Can I feel anything here of the former glory? Not a thing.

Yet rock rolls on in Cardiff, how could it not? Other venues have proliferated – The CIA (now the Motorpoint Arena), Chapter, St David's Hall, The Globe, Tramshed, for a time The Point and The Coal Exchange. Minty's illustrated gig guide map shows all these venues and more. But there's nothing yet to rival how things were in rock's great formative days. UK touring shows that once never

missed a Welsh stop now terminate at Bristol. Take a look. As I write Wilko Johnson, Muse, The Kaiser Chiefs and Ginger Baker's reformed Air Force are all making their ways around the UK but none are coming to Cardiff.

★★★

To test my Rock and Roll Axis theory to destruction I walk the length of the ley with photographer Emyr Young. If the spirit still flows then the music will be here. I'll stop those with buds in their ears and ask them what they are hearing. Emyr will shoot them, appropriately for rock and roll, in black and white. Headphone wearers pass our station at the intersection of Queen Street and Windsor Place at the rate of around 60 an hour. Most are determined striders, solo walkers, earphones and hats, eyes on the future. Half won't stop, their private worlds violated by my well-meaning intrusion. But enough do. Why are you doing this, they ask? I'm tracing the music ley I say. By chance, as I'm informed by one hip hop listener, today is record shop day, a celebration of vinyl, indie corners, retailers who love what they do, driven by rock as much as profit. Spillers and Kelly's Records are our Cardiff champions. But rock, it transpires, has rolled. The ley flows with where we are going, not where we've been.

Logic – Upgrade
Bombay Bicycle Club & Lucy Rose – Flaws
Artful Dodger – Movin Too Fast
Twenty One Pilots – Migraine
Vince Staples (featuring Snoh Aalega) – Jump Off the Roof
Kiki Dee – I Got The Music In Me
Redlight – Gold Teeth
Fleur de Lys – Maria
The Vaccines – If You Wanna
Luke Christopher – Lot To Learn
Lady Gaga – Born This Way
Bruno Mars – Just the Way You Are
Paramore – Crushcrushcrush
Film Soundtrack music I've downloaded I have no idea what it is
Carole King – Tapestry
Police – Every Breath You Take
Alterbridge – Edge's Theme Song, a remix of Metalingus
Anirudh Ravihran – South Indian Classical Music
Section Boyz – Don't Panic
The Last Shadow Puppets – The Element Of Surprise
Hussain Al Jasmi – El Layl Wahsha
Christine And The Queens – Narcissus Is back
Dolly Parton – Don't Call It Love
Mohammed Abdul – Mabygali Galb
System Of A Down – P.L.U.C.K.
Hozier – Someone New
Wyclef Jean – Knockin On Heaven's Door
Taylor Swift – Love Story
Lupe Fiasco – Kick Push
Zack Knight – remix

CHARLES STREET CARNIVAL

Sprawled around the sides of a small battered room above what would later become the Grass Roots Coffee Bar the small crowd present were not really sure why they were there. This was the first meeting of the Carnival Committee. As the majority of those attending had experience of neither committees nor carnivals it was a wonder that anything happened at all.

The year was 1977 and Charles Street, at this point in Cardiff's trajectory from boom port to Euro capital, was an inner city business slum. Premises were shells held together by flyposting and buddleia. The back of the building we were in resembled Babylon's hanging gardens. The lights flickered. You got dirt on your hands if you touched anything. But no one really cared. Ian Horsburgh, a young planner recently arrived in the city, was the meeting convenor. The attendees were a mix of residents, activists and floaters on Cardiff's free thinking artistic fringe. The Council had suggested that something be done to celebrate the Queens Silver Jubilee. Ian had come up with the idea of a carnival. "So that's all agreed, then," said Ian. We all nodded. A decision to do something had been made although no one was sure just what.

The 70s were a time of alternatives, of cheesecloth and punk zips, of tie-dye and bum flaps. The world was ours to do with what we wanted. We wanted it changed. We did this with determination, dope, vibrating colour and psychedelic fonts. The Charles Street Carnival and its soon to be formed parent body, the Charles Street Arts Foundation, had little experience of management, fund raising, or actually organising anything. It nonetheless lasted for 17 years. The centrepiece was always the annual July festival. A closed-to-traffic inner city street filled with more than 60 stalls, performances, artistic interventions, live music and boundary-pushing fun.

Carnival standing orders banned anything sexist, racist, oppressive or offensive. Never be 'highbrow' or 'elitist' handouts to participants warned. Who took part? Demented Are Go, The Heavy Quartet, Cabaret 246, Diversions, No Fit State, Moving Being, Mike Harries, The Boys Brigade Marching Band, Peppermint Parlour, stilt walkers, Bomb and Dagger, Fire Down Below, The Memphis Benders and the Grace Williams Ladies Choir. Terry Chin one year with a papier maché recreation of the Cardiff Giant[4]. The whole affair was often opened by Lord Mayor Albert Huish or Radio Wales DJ Vince Saville dressed as a Native American and preceded by a performance from St Patrick's Pipe Band.

There was legacy too. Each year by dint of persistence and with an astute understanding of how to get the best out of the Welsh United Nations Association and the Manpower Services Commission Ian Horsburgh arranged a series of artistic interventions and work camps, all based in the city. The murals at the rear of Chapter Arts Centre, the Peace Garden behind the Temple of Peace and Dennis Bridge's daffodil-decorated water tower[5] at Cardiff Central were all Carnival projects.

On Carnival day the street's churches would all continue to hold services for weddings and funerals. Weddings were predictable, funerals generally not. Queen Street had been pedestrianised in 1974 so vehicular access was only possible up Charles Street. The Carnival always tried to accommodate where it could. Street closure would be set for after the hearse had gone. Weddings were encouraged to take place in the morning before the Carnival really got going. On one occasion, however, a grand wedding was booked into St David's Cathedral for mid-afternoon. The gloriously-coutured bride arrived to find the street filled with stalls, rock music and dancing carnival participants. She was duly driven through the centre of this excess and, exiting her limo with a flourish, processed up the aisle. Carnival goers, thinking this was a heat of the afternoon artistic intervention, followed her inside, whooping and yelling as they went. They all stayed for the full ceremony and loudly cheered the happy couple when the service was done. Years later Ian, raising money for the Carnival on Queen Street, was approached by a woman who turned out to have been that Carnival bride. "It was a marvellous occasion," she told him. "It quite made our day."

Did anyone make any money out this? God no. Participants were the city's entire population of fringe dwellers. The establishment, represented here by the centralist presence of Marks and Spencer ably aided by the might of the Catholic Church's St David's Cathedral resented the whole thing. Over the years they moved from mild support, putting small amounts into the donor's pot, to downright opposition and complaints to the Council. In fact it was the Diocese that eventually brought the Carnival down. In the early 90s a short-sighted organising committee had proposed siting the band stage on ground immediately outside the Cathedral's entrance. Rock Against Racism in the face of God. This was clearly not going to work. The Archbishop took his concerns at max volume to a meeting of the Council Planning Committee. Here he first led participants in prayer and then set about demolishing the whole ethos of the carnival as an activity for the public good. He wanted it banned. His complaints did not fall on deaf ears. The Carnival although never formally banned found itself mired in a swamp of health, safety and regulatory issues. The whole operation went down soon after that.

Today the street is a refurbished shadow of its former ragtag magnificence. At its entrance the clean brick façade of M&S faces the clean brick façade of Next. Beyond paintwork has been refreshed and signboarding restrained. Gone are Diversions, No Fit State, The ffotogallery, the graphic designers and the British Legion poppy manufacturers. Oriel Bookshop and Gallery with Monty's next door has been demolished. We are straight now. Once we rocked.

At the Queen Street intersection stands public artists Dennis O'Connor and Bernie Rutter's *Without Place*. This is a two-storey high chrome-framed office chair with a couple of objects sited on top. It is typical of O'Connor and Rutter's work, famous as they are for putting in chrome stanchions (trees, gateposts, towers) and then adorning their extremities with objects that have local resonance (ravens, cartwheels, boats). For Charles Street they have chosen a mortar and pestle and a can of film.

Maurice gives me his view. He's the *Big Issue* seller with the Essex accent who twenty years back flogged Christmas wrapping paper which was so thin you could stick an unpointed finger through it, but now finds the relative respectability of the charity business brings him a better income. "That bowl with the handle coming out of it is what chemists used. And the film, that's for the cinema business that used to be here." Charles Vachell, an early town house developer, gave the street its name. He was twice Mayor of Cardiff and an apothecary to boot. Mortar and pestle solved. But film? In my time working from premises in this street it was never that. Jewellers, clothing wholesalers, accountants, solicitors, lawyers, estate agents by the dozen. But no cinema. However when I check I find that in cinema's boom time of the 30s and the 40s United Artists had offices here, as did Walturdaw Cinema Supply Co (everything required for the cinema, ballroom and theatre). So too did the Phoenix Film Service, renters of documentaries and other shorts. They shared their premises with a ladies hair and skin specialists and a wholesale tobacconist.

Just south of M&S is Ebenezer, a now deconsecrated Neo-Gothic church which was constructed in 1855 from multi-coloured ballast brought in by coal ships returning empty to Cardiff Docks. It has been saved from a future life as an apartment block or a carpet salesroom by the Catholic Archdiocese. Fearful that this splendid Grade II building sited immediately opposite the Cardiff Metropolitan Cathedral of St David might compromise their sanctity (shades of the Carnival playing once again) they acted swiftly. In 2012 they bought the premises from the Welsh chapel-goers who had worshiped there since 1978. A redevelopment plan involving the Heritage Lottery, the RNIB and the Jane Hodge Foundation was put in place. Renamed Cornerstone the chapel is now run as a commercial restaurant specialising in corporate catering, a hub for heritage learning (as the Lottery puts it) and local community activity. Much stress is put on the building's 25-year history as a Welsh-medium chapel although slightly less mention is made of its earlier 141-year existence as Charles Street Congregational Chapel (English). When you apply for state funding you clearly need to press only the right buttons.

Lower down towards David Street the stuccoed town houses have lost most of their garish early twentieth century signboarding and late twentieth century graffiti. At the corner with Bridge Street only the facade remains. The block of rag-tag clothiers, designers and jewellers has been replaced with the Bridge Street Exchange, a 26-storey block offering 463 students rooms with coffee bar retail at ground level.

Street and street furniture throughout have been tidied. Character has changed once again. A cluster of gay bars have opened to supplement those round the corner on Churchill Way. The Quakers offer chiropody and shiatsu. The beat generation Cellar Grill Coffee Bar in the cellar of Regent House is a distant memory. Grassroots has been tamed. Where the Estonian Club stood solicitors now offer legal advice. Inner city sensibleness. Just as some of the residents have always wanted.

GUILDFORD STREET

At a point just south of Queen Street station the former Taff Vale Approach, now known as Station Terrace, becomes Guildford Street. It's hard to see it on the ground but it's there on the maps. At the turn of the century, the nineteenth that is, Station Terrace housed everything from the British and Foreign Bible Society and Maskell's Temperance Café to Powell Williams Electro Platers and the splendid Cory Temperance Hall. On the Queen Street corner stood the Alexandra Hotel which briefly served as the Pig and Whistle before being demolished to make way for the Capitol Exchange a century later. Alcohol and abstinence have fought a long battle around here.

Today the Terrace is almost totally devoid of attraction. Developers have rebuilt it to serve their own financial ends. Footfall is channelled swiftly from its bleak winds to Queen Street where pedestrianisation has attempted to turn the thoroughfare into a land of retail joy. Opposite Queen Street railway station, itself in its fifth rebuild since it was first opened as Crockherbtown station in 1840, is a Spar outpost housing a branch of Costa. The rest is gloomy building rears and car parks, metal grills, isolation switches, outlet pipes, and the distant cubist windows of high rise Helmont House.

Near the point where buses dwell while waiting for the Churchill Way lights to change is a pair of illuminated digital hoardings advertising Spectrum cruelty-free make up and the latest show at the New Theatre. Behind stands what could well be Cardiff's least visible listed building. This is secret central, a palace of mystery, a shimmer of enigma kept out of the public gaze for at least two centuries and still in semi-hiding. That's the perception. The reality, of course, is slightly different. This is the Cardiff home of the world's oldest secular fraternal society – the Cardiff Masonic Temple.

The building started life in 1893 as the United Methodist Church, entirely in keeping with the temperance flavour of the district at the time. Its frontage was onto Edward Terrace, later Churchill Way, where a Bath stone façade of arched windows and columns surmounted by a slate roof presented the chapel to the world. The Freemasons, who had been meeting above a potato store in Wharton Street, purchased the premises when the exponentially expanding United Methodists moved to Four Elms Road in 1893. The original chapel frontage is still there, doors and windows now blocked and with a square and compass and the words *Masonic Temple* engraved high up across its entablature.

Inside the Temple is like a tardis. This sensation is aided by the fact that when I arrive there is no power. Network Rail have dug through the cables. The Temple labyrinth is full of Masonic darkness. The sense of time machine increases when eventually the lights do return and I find myself within a building rich in the accoutrements of the past. There are cases full of engraved glasses, jewels, prints, medals, embossed leathers, stones and further Masonic detritus from down the years. The walls, when they are not displaying the grandeur of the Temple's Masonic symbolism (the celestial and terrestrial globes on their pillars, the hung G for God and Geometry, the anchor and the ark, the square and the compass, the all-seeing Masonic eye), are either draped in banners or hung with photographs of Freemason Grand Masters past and present. These austere, well-groomed men are depicted in tasselled, garter-blue edged lambskin aprons, all wearing their medals and chains of office. They remind me of blazered bowls players, or the secretary of the British Legion Club in Womanby Street who once bravely came on stage at 10.30 to tell Champion Jack Dupree it was closing time.

Most rooms have a framed photo of HMQ as a centrepiece although the bar walls are covered with black and white shots of Welsh greats. "Are all these people masons?" I ask, peering at a shot of demur era Charlotte Church. "Philip Madoc yes, Max Boyce probably not." Women, as it turns out, are absolutely not. "Females can become Freemasons but in their own order. Those in Cardiff meet in Llandaff North." Freemasons are similar to golf clubs in their attitude to gender equality.

Freemasonry, the ancient craft, has an almost antediluvian history. It's no longer much to do with putting up buildings although the first masons are sometimes suggested to be those who erected the Tower of Babel. It's not a religion either but you do need to believe in a supreme being. It's not secret although it used to be. To join you ask. Evenings are spent engaged in complex ceremony, the awarding of grades and the honouring of ritual followed by a meal, speeches and drink. Charitable works are often to the forefront. Boy Scouts for grownups someone said but that's being unkind. Do masons roll their trousers up and do people have funny handshakes? They do.

I'm being shown round by the Chairman, Andrew Davies. Andrew has a retail background and is the man who has been since 2010 largely responsible for turning the building's fortunes round. Rooms inside the complex can be rented for weddings, dinners, presentations and other celebrations. You can hire a space here and hold a poetry reading if you want to. Users include U3A, the Civil Service Pensioners Club, the local universities, and the Welsh Academy of the Voice.

In 1918 the Temple bought up the row of terraced cottages lining Guildford Street immediately to the north of the original chapel. This enabled facilities to be considerably expanded. This now includes three elaborately wood-lined temple-spaces decorated with mosaic pavements, a bar, a large kitchen, numerous meeting rooms and a car park. The valley rail lines are right next door but you can't hear a thing.

Masons come from all sectors of society. Plumbers, electricians, surgeons, ex-servicemen, the police. Often employments where ritual and ceremonial are already present to some degree. And more poets than you'd imagine. The American Masonic Poetry Society[6] lists hundreds.

Andrew is a mason, naturally, and he's also a vest frottoir player[7] with Zydeco bands such as Whiskey River, the Swamp Devils, and the Splott Bottom Boys. He's a regular accompanist to Cardiff's Sicknote Steve and once won the Tenby Busking Competition. Being told all this while standing in the elaborate and quite awe-inspiring Duke of Connaught Temple makes it hard to believe. If asked earlier what Andrew's hobbies might have been I might have suggested chess or solving quadratic equations.

Why no one has yet offered the masons shedloads of cash to move on and allow this prime site to be developed as an apartment block or, more likely, turned into a branch of Weatherspoon's has to be do with its grade two listing. The high costs of keeping its historical elements intact are a clear deterrent.

Outside I face up Churchill Way. Where the Bute Dock Feeder Canal once flowed on the surface. When the Temple was first built Mrs R. Mander Fox, teacher of music, lived opposite on the corner of Edwards Terrace. Next door was Philip Morris' loan office. The Steak of the Art restaurant now. The buildings shift, their residents move on, but the roadways and the shapes they make inevitably stay the same.

LOOKING FOR DIC PENDERYN

Cardiff Market has always had a musical focus. At the Trinity Street entrance most Saturdays you can listen to the Red Choir. Earlier it was a skiffle band and before them any one of a whole string of street musicians playing accordions, zithers, banjos, and things you blow into or bang. Today it's Kirk Morgan doing the pretty well-constructed blues. He is positioned on the iron railinged passage that divides the original St John's Churchyard from its 1822 extension that was once known as Old Troy.

Old Troy is now a park with its memorials tidied. Kirk's amplified take on Mississippi down-home seeped across its largely empty benches. Busking has come a long way since James Turburvill[8] sang his *tribanau* in these dirty streets. Kirk has a mike stand and a battery-powered amplifier. He sells CDs from a basket as his feet. 18 songs for £5. Guitar and harmonica. A bargain.

Inside the great Victorian glass-roofed metal shed that is Cardiff's covered market Ed Kelly's second-hand record retailing enterprise (last visited in *Real Cardiff Three*) has expanded right across the premises of the Cardiff Bible Depot. Allan Perkins, Ed's nephew and the current owner, has a stock of at least 25,000 seven inch vinyl singles and more than 100,000 albums. Sales are good. Vinyl outstrips the CD by a factor of five. He sells more vinyl, he tells me, than all the other record shops of Wales combined. He's got a banner advertising his stall's presence running almost the entire market's length draped over the first-floor balcony. Amid the black plastic stacks are more than a few valuable items. A Madonna picture disc of *Erotica* along with a signed-by-all-four Manics (including the lost Ritchie Edwards) single *She Is Suffering* taken from their ground-breaking 1994 album *The Holy Bible*. Are these for sale? No.

What I'm actually trying to work out is how a covered market hall, built by a town corporation in 1886, could also have been the site of the hanging to death of the Merthyr people's martyr Dic Penderyn. The history of this market, or, indeed, of street trading in Cardiff in general is a bit like the history of Billy Smart's Circus. Set yourself up and then, almost immediately, move on elsewhere. To be fair, however, the indoor market has been on its present site since 1835. It's the outdoor version that has constantly moved (the High Street, The Hayes, Mill Lane, the back of St David's Hall and now morphed into what appears to be a single stall on Queen Street.

Town fairs, which sound similar to markets, were a different operation. They are replicated today by the car boot sales of Splott and Bessemer Road and the farmers' markets at the Mackintosh Institute and on Fitzhamon Embankment. Here itinerant traders would sell their wares and offer their services on specific days of the week. In mediaeval times there were regular fairs on Wednesdays and Saturdays in the High Street with enlarged versions taking place to coincide with the festivals of St John the Baptist and the Nativity of St Mary. The retail operations of traders and packmen, as they were known, would be supplemented with jugglers, acrobats and singers. These events would often take place in the yards of

Cardiff's two great churches, St John's and St Mary's, the dead and the living carousing as one.

Things then, as they are now, were much regulated. Town bells would be rung to announce the start of trading. No transactions were permitted beforehand. Transgressions were remedied by a special Piepowder Court which offered immediate settlement of disputes. The powers of this court were limited to the period of the fair. It was an easy way of coping. 'Piepowder' is a corruption of the Norman French 'pieds poudrés' which translates as 'dusty feet'. We could use them again. How else to get your money back when the cut-price drill you've just bought fails to spin.

The town gaol once stood at the St Mary Street entrance to Cardiff's indoor market. That was before the predecessor of the present building occupied the site in 1835. What's in place now is a 1886 rebuild of Solomon Andrew's 1884 market building. That one was completely destroyed by fire in 1885. Cardiff's current gaol in Adamsdown, which most people imagine to have been there since time immemorial mainly because of the sheer ancient look of its walls, was actually built in 1833. The much smaller operation it replaced on High Street was where Dic Penderyn was brought to meet his end.

Dic, actually Richard Lewis, had killed no one. In the Merthyr uprising of 1831 a mob had marched on the Castle Hotel, Merthyr. Crowd control in this early nineteenth century commotion was not in the hands of truncheon-bearing police as such events usually were during twentieth century mining disputes. It was in the hands of the armed military. Soldiers had been drafted in by the severe to draconian Home Secretary, Lord Melbourne. The soldiers fired. In the commotion which followed hundreds were injured and sixteen died. Richard Lewis and his cousin Lewis Lewis managed to stab a Southern Highlander, Private Donald Black, in the leg with a bayonet. Deliberately or by accident? We are still not sure.

The two Lewises were the example that the Home Secretary was determined to make. They were tried, found guilty, and both were sentenced to death. Lewis Lewis, the agitator and organiser of the riot, had somehow managed to help an injured special constable during the insurrection. In recognition of this his sentence was commuted to transportation. Richard Lewis, however, was to stay the course.

Despite a petition of Jeremy Clarkson proportion proclaiming his innocence and appealing for clemency Dic Penderyn was hung by the neck at Cardiff Gaol on 13 August, 1831. The hanging place was in the gallows yard in a court off St Mary Street. The platform was twelve feet high and had ornamental ironwork on three sides. A crowd gathered to watch and drew their collective breath in, as crowds do, when Penderyn swung.

The City Council have a blue plaque on the St Mary Street exterior of the Market celebrating and marking the spot. 'The County Gaol stood on this site for over three hundred years'. The actual site of gallows would have been back a little. Thirty yards in, according to William Luke Evans as quoted by J. Hobson Matthews in Volume Five of his *Cardiff Records* of 1905. That would put them underneath the old H. Samuel Everite Time clock (no longer working) and next to the Market Munchbox, sausage bap £1.80, black pudding 50p.

When Penderyn's coffin was taken to his birth and burial place in Aberavon thousands lined the route. He was 23. Penderyn's case continues to be raised by politicians and historians. Alexander Cordell said he was innocent. So did historian John Davies and poet Harri Webb. Recently politicians Ann Clwyd (in 2015) and Stephen Kinnock (in 2016) have called for an official pardon. But nothing gets done.

Outside in the pedestrianised street another market has opened. Antiques and Pontcanna-desirable knick-knackery, posh cakes, artisan goodnesses, vintage clothes. The St Mary Street flea market is pretty near where the Shambles once was, the ancient meat and corn market, half stuffed under the town hall. What goes around comes around. But not Dic. Someone has tried to remove the phrase 'alleged wounding of a soldier' from the plaque. Wales revising its history once again.

NORTH ROAD'S PSYCHIC CENTRE

Where was this place? Ask a psychic and they couldn't tell you. Madame Romany, fortune-teller with crystal ball operating out of Cardiff Market, did not advertise among her services the finding of gateways into other worlds[9]. TV medium Sally Morgan told the *Daily Mirror* that Cardiff was the fourth most psychic town in Britain (after Eastbourne, Torquay and Norwich, which gives you the range). This should have filled the streets with shape-shifters and the air with ectoplasm. But it didn't. How these things are decided I have no idea. Does someone visit the city to count the ghosts? Does talking to the dead sell newspapers? Apparently it does.

Finding the real psychic centre was clearly a matter for the poets. In the seventies, a psychic time if there ever was one, poetic interest in megaliths, stone circles, alien landing sites and places of immense spiritual power was widespread. The literary magazines were rich with poems about primordial stones guiding the spirit, of the truth shimmering between seats of ancient power, and of gateways to wonderworlds opening if you could only find the right spot in the soft supernatural air. Ley-hunting was what a lot of this was called. Leys were alignments of ancient monuments, megaliths, cromlechs, natural ridge tops, water fords and wayside crosses. They had been discovered by Alfred Watkins[10] in the 1920s. His *The Old Straight Track* was a new age best-seller.

Chris Torrance, king of the south Wales verse shamans, lived in a wildman's cottage, deep in the Pontneddfechan reaches of the Brecon Beacons. A Watkins aficionado he had discovered his home to be in mystical alignment with both the Roman grave marker Maen Madoc, and with Maen Llia, the fat female stone that stood between the Senni Valley and Ystradfellte. If extended, this line of power would roar across the south Wales coalfields to eventually slice right through the centre of Cardiff Castle. The Castle, ancient and latter-day modern all in one, was once seat of the Butes. According to new age druid and blogger Chris McDermott, it was "a hot-spot of energy and masonic and magical design". It was a node. The city's psychic centre had to be here.

In the early 2000s, still hunting for the precise spot, I found myself standing just outside the North Road entrance to Bute Park. And I could sense something. Could this be it? Here the Bute West Dock Feeder and the Glamorgan Canal, two watercourses, had once crossed. The Roman road north from Cardiffium had come out of the fort to intersect. Torrance's ley, full of literary power joined it. It was the mid-point between Bute's rebuilt-by-Burges Castle and the Turner-built City Hall. Pretty much the city's geographic middle. A locus, a fulcrum, a spiritual lens through which a whole world radiates. The Psychic Centre, at last. I felt the power radiate and then I moved on.

Years later on a sun-filled Saturday afternoon I reach the spot again with a walking group in tow. I'm the guide. The Psychogeography of Central Cardiff. An easy sell. We track around the sites of the lost (Blackfriars) and the hidden (the Feeder, still visible between wheelie bins in Park Lane). When we come up out of the underpass to gather around the Bute Park gates I start to explain.

"This is the city's Psychic Centre," I say. You can sense the mystic crackle. I explain about the intersecting lines of energy, the canals and roads and leys. I bring in the proximity to the seats of power at both Castle Keep and City Hall Council chamber. I invent something about the mid-day shadow of the glowering Pearl Building on Greyfriars Road pointing right at this spot.

Emboldened I tell the tale of Dave Reid, blind poet, who would, when he'd run out of money and in thrall to pissedness, get the police to give him a lift to his bedsit on Cathedral Road. He'd do this by lying on the ground right in this place. He'd flail around with his white stick until someone from the Police Station opposite sent a car round to collect him and drive him home. You had to look after your disabled. You couldn't put a blind man in the cells.

Actually though, you could. On one occasion Reid, fully bevvied, played his stick flailing trick, got the lift, was bundled successfully into his Cathedral Road back room only to find himself unable to stay put. Like Whac-a-mole he came out again and started waving his stick around at the sober traffic passing The Halfway. He was part way through reciting a poem about life, love and death to anyone who would listen, no one was, when the police returned. This time they took him back to the cells and locked him up overnight. Apparently he continued his verse chanting there. Right opposite the Psychic Centre. This spot is full of wonder.

I tell the audience. They cheer. They've grown in number too. This particular Saturday is also, it transpires, Armed Forces Day and there have been shows and parades and tank demonstrations in the Park. The crowds mill by. Kids in cardboard helmets, blokes who go to the gym, dazzlingly blonde soldier's wives. Quite a number have stopped to listen. What is this guy standing on a waste bin on about?

I tell them all that the spirit flows right here and that they can feel it too. If they want to. They can. "Put your hands up," I command. They do. Most of them. "Hold them there a few feet apart, palms facing." There is a sea of smiling, expectant faces. They all have their hands raised. "You can sense it can't you?" I shout. "Feel the spirit move between your hands. You can. Holy heat." I'm a revival preacher now raising hwyl, pulling the mystic from out the ground and throwing it into the air. I can see their beaming faces. "You can feel it, can't you?" I shout. "Yes," they say, and we all laugh and cheer.

On we move, 80 strong now, hell this is quite a company. I plough into the park against the Armed Forces Day swirling tide. Lady Bute's Bridge[11] next. Here Mrs Bute would cross to check her horticulture. It was the place where the tanneries and waterwheels were when the feeder was a mill leat. Beyond was, in her day, the end of Cardiff, the boundary, just west of the ever moving river.

THE BATTLE FOR THE VULCAN

Vulcan – say that word and most likely people will tell you that it's the home planet of *Star Trek's* Mr Spock. He was the Vulcan with pointed ears. Some might mention that it's a process for modifying rubber and also the name for Britain's best known nuclear bomber. Retired now, one stood on the skyline at Rhoose for years. Most, however, won't recall Vulcan's origin as the Roman god of fire and volcanoes, and the name then given to countless iron foundries that sprang up the length of industrial revolution Britain.

Cardiff's Vulcan, the Victorian pub on Adam Street at the back of Cardiff prison, was built in 1853 to quench the dry throats of Cardiff's iron and steelworkers from what became the East Moors works nearby. The works have long disappeared now and it's hard today to imagine that shiny Cardiff once possessed of a fire breathing filthy giant right at its heart. The Vulcan dispensed pints by the thousand to workers coming off shift, to working class locals from the nearby and now vanished Irish district of Newtown, to stragglers from Splott and off-duty prison warders. A sawdust-floored mix of working men wearing working clothes, sat on rough benches around the pub's open coal fires, drinking Brains from tall, thick-sided pint glasses.

The pub (or hotel as it liked to be known) had been extensively remodelled by architect F.J. Veall in 1914. An art nouveau tiled façade had been added in 1901. These pre-war alterations were significant. When canvassed for support against demolition CADW, the Welsh heritage organisation with the power to list structures, pointed out that these turn of the century improvements had totally removed any 1853 flavour from the structure thereby rendering it insignificant as an exemplar of Victorian drinking culture.

The Vulcan outlasted the heavy industry which once supplied its main trade. When the steel works closed the Vulcan continued, more quietly now, as a haunt for local drinkers, dart board, crisps, splendid Victorian urinals, cards games, more Brains beer. And when the nearby terraces were eventually slum cleared (although none would use that word now, slum, when the local residents were rehoused in improved accommodation, they'd say), when all that happened the Vulcan hung on. Stranded now at the end of the late nineteen nineties, the pub stood in isolation in the centre of a hard-topped car park. Opposite was the expansionist University of South Wales' Atrium built on the site of former BT buildings. Next door was student accommodation in non-prize winning tower blocks on Pellet Street. The arrival of St David's Two, the city centre shopping paradise just round the corner, sealed the Vulcan's fate. There was a fervent need for the city to expand everywhere it could. The Vulcan was in the way.

In 2009 Brains announced that they would terminate their lease. Marcol Asset Management, the ground landlord, had development plans. More student accommodation could be built here. Apartments could be erected. The car park could be turned into a multi-story giant. All options that would bring a financial return.

Keeping the Vulcan on as a cramped pub serving beer and peanuts was just not an attractive enough option.

Meanwhile the pub's clientele had again changed. With the original local population now rehoused elsewhere the Vulcan began to attract beer connoisseurs, bohemians, linguists, artists, writers and later students and lecturers from the nearby university. The tavern's one hundred and fifty year old charm still worked. With its cranky darkness, irregular furniture and misshapen rooms the Vulcan was the perfect antidote to the city centre's glass and aluminium bars housing hundreds of vertical drinkers in shot-fuelled swarms.

The writers gathered here. Centred around author and beer devotee John Williams the contributing cast of John's local short-story anthology *Wales, Half Welsh*[12] plus others met to enthuse and decry the literary world.

A popular and well-publicised campaign promoted by Rachael Thomas and Graham Craig to keep the pub open attracted some high profile signatories. The Manic Street Preachers' James Dean Bradfield and actor Rhys Ifans, who you rarely actually saw at the pub itself but whose hearts were clearly in the right place, smiled for the cameras. Fortuitously the campaign co-incided with the west's great economic crisis. Brains' building development went on hold. With a license to carry on for another three years, The Vulcan was temporarily saved.

CAMRA listed it among its top fifty UK pubs. Brains put in a new tenant and trade temporarily continued. The end eventually came in 2012. The brewery quoted lack of profit as the main reason for the pub's demise. The writing had been on the wall for decades.

Cardiff is a young city. Its shape and size is based almost entirely on the dock and steel trade developments of the nineteenth century. Beyond the Castle and St John's Church it has very little that's old. Cardiff is no Bath or Edinburgh or Dublin. It is not very good, either, at keeping hold of such past as it does possess. When things are in the wrong place the city wipes them away. It did that to most of the pre-St David's Centre townscape, to the Glamorgan Canal, the old town halls and walls, the skating rink on Westgate Street, the zoo at Victoria Park, and the cinemas that once crowded Queen Street. All gone.

We are good at being new, being an administrative capital and a tourist destination, but pretty hopeless at preserving what once made us different. Yet unlike the Red House, the Railway Hotel, another fashionable but now demolished Victoria pub that once

stood facing the sea on the Ferry Road peninsula, the Vulcan will not be completely lost.

Where the Red House was deemed as not of enough significance to preserve by everyone the Vulcan has been carefully unbuilt, photographed, annotated, and boxed by the National Museum Wales. It is currently being re-erected at the St Fagans National Museum of History. The reopening of the preserved pub, fixed in time forever as it was in 1915, will be around 2020. There will be sawdust on the floors again. Historic ales brewed to nineteenth century recipes will be served from the pumps. Alcohol, the real stuff. Teetotal Iorwerth Peate, the St Fagans founder, will spin in his grave. Beer on the sacred site, how could the world?

It's an artificial solution and not what campaigners really wanted. It's a loss to the city's historical fabric. It gives south Cardiff yet another beerless gap. It feels like we are giving in to mammon. Yes, all those things. But a St Fagans rebuild is better, certainly, than just letting it go.

ST JOHN'S SQUARE

Clive and I are smoking Solent in St John's Square. Menthol cool, just like us. It's 1962 and we're in our parkas, fur along the hoods, worried about the future. We are festooned with CND badges, *Make Love Not War*, *Scrap Polaris*, *Ban The Bomb*, and are selling news of how the world might be saved to anyone who wants to know. Clive holds a stack of CND's *Sanity*. I've an armful of the Committee of 100's *Black Paper*. The old order has to go. Lead dissenter Bertrand Russell has been on TV promoting mass civil disobedience on an industrial scale. Demonstrations will involve thousands. This is a time of utmost peril. We'll change things by our sheer mass and the irrefutability of our points of view. Our weekly meetings at the Friends Meeting House on Charles Street are ram packed with enthusiasm. All smiles and chanting. We will prevail.

But so far today it's only Clive and me. Warning the world. In the past hour I've sold one *Black Paper* and given someone change for the phone. Clive draws the cool Solent smoke deeply into his lungs. His stack of *Sanity* remains undiminished. But he has hope.

Officially St John's Square doesn't exist. It is St John's Street. Originally, according to Speed's map of 1610, there were two streets here: St John's on the western side where the Wimpy Bar stands and Working Street on the east. Between them were houses, demolished last century to let in light and air.

Today it's a square, a public space, an open plaza; it would be if it were not for the cars. St John's Square – wide enough for meetings, markets, concerts, and the putting to death of those whose beliefs you don't agree with, as happened in 1555 to Rawlins White. This was a time when the country under Queen Mary had returned its spiritual allegiance to Rome. Those who still espoused the Protestant cause were regularly hunted down. Rawlins was burned at the stake in a spot somewhere near the Church of St John.

White was a fisherman with hang-nets on the foreshore south of Splott farm. He was reciter of scriptures from the Cranmer Bible who would not retract. *Foxe's Book of Martyrs*[13] published in 1563, eight years after White's death, has him as an unlearned simpleton who couldn't read. He had his son teach him Bible passages which he would loudly recite to anyone willing to listen. In his monumental *The Book of Welsh Saints* author Terry Breverton suggests that White had a house near the Taff at the end of Womanby Street. Jon Manchip White, a direct descendant, disagrees. In his *Rawlins White, Patriot To Heaven*[14] he makes Rawlins a little more superior as a shipowner with property in Llandaff.

Once restrained by Catholic forces Rawlins was confined in the notorious Cockmarel, a prison below one of the watch towers in the eastern section of Cardiff's town wall. This was once, as I recount in the first *Real Cardiff* book, under the staff room at the back of The Complete Present on Hills Street. Redevelopment on redevelopment – The Complete Present itself is a place lost now in the depths of St David's Two. Rawlins' ghost rambles there, promoting his case still.

His burning was a sorrowful affair with the martyr allegedly repositioning the straw beneath him so that it would burn the faster. There's a commemorative plaque in the trouser department of House of Fraser (ask the assistant just where). It would be better on the outside wall of St John's Church but it's no doubt too late to move it now.

Today, before Christmas, and in crisp air, there's a German Sausage seller in Rawlins' place. Here you can buy a meaty Krakauer or a gluten-free Käsearainer along with a further range of delicacies of which German friends of mine have never heard. The staff are entirely Polish.

That Christmas is now regarded in the Welsh capital as a German affair shows, Brexit notwithstanding, how European we have all become. A branch of Spar, the Dutch cost-cutter, stands on the corner where Cardiff-Italian café Asteys once sold tea and cake. When Clive and I were street-selling this would have been known as Little Asteys to differentiate it from Big Asteys nearer the rail station. Today, deeper into what's proudly proclaimed as Cardiff's Festive Quarter, they are selling Dusseldorf Burgers, French pancakes and foot-long Frankfurters. Owain Glyndŵr's pub stands on the Church Street corner where the Kemeys-Tynte Arms (later known as the Tennis Court and then the Buccaneer) once were. Owain Glyndŵr burned most of Cardiff down in his ridding Wales of the English raid of 1403, the last Welsh War of Independence. He gets celebrated as a railway engine on the Rheidol railway and again as Owain Glendower in Shakespeare's *Henry IV, Part One*. There's a statue of his supposed likeness by Alfred Turner at City Hall[15].

Opposite the sausage seller on the corner of the High Street Arcade stands a place where the Whoppa rules all – Burger King. The building has been a lot of things through the years: a branch of Wimpey, Gas Showrooms, the original Techniquest. In the eighteenth century it was the Green Dragon. It was rebuilt at the turn of the twentieth as Fulton & Dunlop's Wine and Spirits Vaults. Its first-floor Mahogany Room was lavishly appointed in William Burges-style: mosaic freezes, stained glass, rich wood panelling, leather furniture. Here councillors, merchants and shipowners met and deals were done. When they re-routed the trams the decision as to where was taken in this spot. Frozen in time the room still exists. It's used for flame-grilled burger servers staff meetings now. Public access nil.

Across the square near Greggs is a branch of Coral the bookmakers. In the early decades of the twentieth century the Lynn Private Institute of Physical Culture ran a gym here in which boxer Jack Petersen, British and Empire Heavyweight Boxing Champion, used to train. There's a commemorative plaque outside, ignored by almost everyone. Boxing only thrills when it's on TV.

Today Clive has vanished into the fog of the future. We lost touch decades back. But there's still something of the spirit he stood for hanging on here. Protests still happen and agit prop is still sold. Round the corner at the Aneurin Bevan statue the socialists have gathered and are haranguing passers-by with Sandinista rhetoric and calls for local Labour Party reselection. Copies of the *Morning Star* are pushed with gusto. Nye himself, hand raised, stands proud with a traffic cone on his head. It's what city statues of great politicians usually do.

THE BUTE PARK GORSEDD

I am in Bute Park hiding from the Kidney Foundation annual 10K road race. Before me is the stone circle built by the Gorsedd of the Bards in 1978. Eisteddfodau are announced annually at such sites with an ancient ceremony involving robe-wearing druids, the unsheathing of great swords and the dancing of nubiles bearing flowers. The rings, reminiscent of the stone circles of antiquity, litter Wales in increasing number. Cardiff has two. This one at the southern end of Bute Park and another in front of the nearby Museum. Portals into the otherworld right in the heart of a capital city. But totally fake.

The creation of these circles by the Gorsedd and the ceremonies surrounding their annual declarations was invented by Iolo Morganwg in 1792. Iolo claimed to have uncovered a druidic past to the whole Eisteddfod shenanigans. He began to agitate for the re-establishment of a Gorsedd of the Bards of Ynys Prydain along with an appropriate pageantry to go with it. Pure fantasy but he nonetheless managed to convince organising officials of the probity of his discoveries. His fabricated ceremonials were *reintroduced* at the 1819 Eisteddfod in Carmarthen. Two hundred years later, and despite being exposed as the fiction they clearly are by Prof G.J.

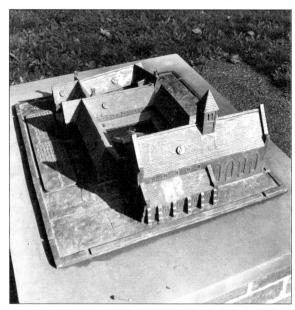

Williams in the nineteen fifties, the ceremonies continue. They have been practised long enough now for Iolo's creation of a sparkling ancient past for his nation to have entered the collective consciousness.

Unlike its perfect fellow in Bute Park the circle in front of the Museum is half-wrecked by misplanted trees. Its Radyr breccia uprights are worn and cracked. Its portal and altar stones are missing, unaccountably removed for reasons of safety. The inner ring of white alabaster slabs from Penarth are almost totally dissolved. The circle itself is no longer where the druids put it in 1899 either. Then it stood much nearer the feeder but was uplifted and rebuilt in what was at the time called Druidic Gardens to make space for development. The past has always been a moveable feast. City fathers embellished the circle with a German First World War howitzer on one side and a stone coffin dug up in Bath on the other. These illustrious objects have long been moved on. Today the Gardens have a tea hut and a bronze sculpture of a sullen looking girl by Robert Thomas.

The road race has filled the city centre with lycra-clad runners and jet-fast Paralympians in racing machines. Street running is a component of national life but so far the park remains clear. I step back to view the stone circle through a giant wooden frame, created in 2012 by Mark Folds. It's the best of the Bute Park creative interventions. Elsewhere the park is littered with well-meaning wooden carvings, frogs, flowers, fish, like oversized garden gnomes. The land here also holds the abandoned foundations of what might have been a city art gallery. This was a plan of the fourth Marquis from 1937. But war intervened. On damp ground behind the Animal Wall all we are left with are concrete slabs. This southern end of the park subsequently became part of the estate the fifth Marquis of Bute set aside in 1947 for the building of a Roman Catholic Cathedral. That didn't happen either.

I walk north to the scant remains of the Dominican Blackfriars monastery. Reconstruction here has been limited to a cast metal model on a plinth, created in 2014 by Rubin Eynon. Floor tiles salvaged during excavation have been re-laid in the nearby West Lodge's Pettigrew Tea Rooms. Blackfriars was the second of Cardiff's two medieval monasteries. The other is the Franciscan Greyfriars, vanished below the high-rise weight of what was once the Pearl Building, now Capital Tower.

Blackfriars dates from 1286. It met its end in 1538 when Henry VIII took its lands and reallocated its building stone for projects elsewhere. The last monks, all with typical Cardiff-sounding names, are commemorated by an inscribed stone bench on the current site. David Thomas. Richard Llewelyn. John Lewis. Thomas Davies. Richard Nicholson. In 1887 the Third Marquis of Bute excavated and marked the lines of the original buildings with low brick. In 2013 this restoration was itself restored, courtesy of aid from the Heritage Lottery. There are graves, marked and unmarked. That of Bute relative, Dame Lelgarde Harry Florence Bellingham, for sure. Then the Bishop of Bethlehem, allegedly. And if you go in for speculation, those of various saints, and, amazingly, Joseph of Arimathea.

Cardiff, land of Avalon, flying saucers buried at Blackweir. Wherever you look reality is challenged. Leaves blow, early autumn, across the place that was once so holy. Here in the heart of Bute Park. Real enough.

TREDEGARVILLE

In the street I'm surrounded by the transient: a cultural mix of students and wayfarers, biddies and businessmen, skivers and

skateboarders, the ambling and the purposefully striding, all bound
for somewhere or perhaps now coming back. Ask any of them
where they are and they won't tell you Tredegarville. This place is
just one more of the city's lost districts along with Newtown,
Southey, Old Troy and Endless Farm. Where are these Cardiff
places? No one is quite sure.

Blankminster, The Bulwarks, Cibwr, Glaspole, Hams, Knap,
Nishton, Pensarn, Sokeshay, Spittal, Westhawe, and The Moors.
They've all been wiped. Developers reworking the brownfield or,
come to that, the green, very rarely hang onto history. The old
names are let go to seep down into the clay. In their place bright,
new, pronounceable and sellable alternatives bristle up in the
brochures. Corporate builders are the worst. The ones who create
new city plazas and grand avenues and then fill them with high rise
offices for the financial sector or for the departments of
government. Not much better are the apartment stackers, racking
up gain from serviced and undercrofted residential gleam or
student flats by the hundred. Get out the map of the city and put
your finger straight on these places: Capital Quarter, Cardiff Gate,
Cardiff Pointe, Bayscape, Prospect Place, Porth Teigr, Chapel
Mead. Names shimmered out of the hazy air. Can you find them?
You can't.

Tredegarville was an early beyond the town walls development to
house the already wealthy. As it morphed from market town with
quay to one of Europe's leading ports, Cardiff's 1850s boom had
fuelled demand not only for tight workers' terraces but for the
generous residences of the managers and owners. Charles Morgan
of the Tredegar Estate employed architects Habershon & Fawckner
to build four new streets – The Parade, The Walk, East Grove and
West Grove – and to fill them with substantial villas. In the 1870s
the Rhymney Railway added a passenger station. The Mansion
House, then known as Grove House, was completed for James
Howell in 1896. This linked the district to Richmond Road and the
group of lesser streets – Northcote Street, Bedford Street, Penlline
Street – built on Homfray Estate land to the north. Tredegarville
became Cardiff's eastern burgeon until the building gallop of Roath
overcame it as the century closed.

Tredegarville today remains a largely Victorian cityscape. Wide,
tree-lined streets, arched gable frontages, space. It has an extant
Victorian red post box. Attempts have been made, via designation
of Tredegarville as a conservation area, to keep original Victorian

building features intact. There is a mix of Classical and Gothic Revival, some properties with a painted stucco finish, others showing rock-faced Pennant sandstone. There are lanes and grand mansions. Some have fallen down to be replaced by present day almost replicas, replicas enough in spirit to get themselves through planning although never ever an actual replica with an identical skyline. Developers will always squeeze in higher rooflines or a wall that steps back just that bit further. If they can. More square footage to sell.

Many of the properties have become private clinics housing the city's best at implanting new teeth or repairing old ones. There's an air of post-NHS with an add-mix of solicitors and multiple education establishments broadening the scope. King's Monkton independent is here as is Coleg Glan Hafren, the latter now merged with Barry College and rebranded to form Cardiff and Vale College. The place is full of the newly emancipated, swinging their bags through the Tredegarville streets.

The welfare of the spirit has always hung heavy in the minds of Tredegarville developers. The YMCA stands in a northern corner with the one-time convent of the Rosminian Sisters of Providence next door. St Peter's, the Catholic Cathedral, was built on the

district's fringes in 1860 when City Road was still known as Plwcca
Lane and the arrival of housing on Homfray land had yet to begin.
The Cardiff Buddhist Centre stands next door.

But Tredegarville Baptist is the one at the heart. And it is still
baptising the faithful. It was built by Lord Tredegar's architect,
W.G. Habershon, in the early 1860s as a mother church for a whole
rash of Baptist chapels opening across the town. Coal magnates the
Cory family paid for it. Ballast from their ships reaching Cardiff
from Galway was used in its construction. Cruciform ground plan,
as insisted on by the ground landlord, Lord Tredegar. Renowned
for its arcaded stone baptistery and the quantity of its stained glass.
A spinster aunt of mine had played the organ there for decades.

She made Baptist 78s privately using a company who'd do this to
order at 93 Albany Road. You recorded the track in a single take.
The disc cutter produced a single copy. She did 'Mortify Us By Thy
Grace' and 'Jesu, Joy'. I'd never taken her to be that devout although
I should have worked it out. In the late 1970s she came into the
bookshop I ran and ordered book on religious plants. Her garden at
Bryn Goleu off Whitchurch Road, she'd decided, would from that
point on consist entirely of plants mentioned in the Bible.

Near the church you'll look hard for pubs. They cluster further
off on City Road and down towards the tracks in Adamsdown. On
the corner of Newport Road and Glossop Road stands the 1890s
Anglican church of St James The Great, successor to an iron
building that served Tredegarville residents when the district was
first built. St James is widely regarded as architect E.M. Bruce
Vaughan's masterpiece. It has a landmark spire, Swelldon limestone
and Bath stone dressings. When it closed in 2006 its fate, most
thought, would be similar to the now demolished Free United
Methodist Church that once stood on the corner opposite. But not
yet. There are plans – stalled when I pass in 2017 – to fill the church
with apartments including one that rises for seven floors right up
the tower. Here church architectural features will have been
retained. Everything high end, imbued with God-endowed class.

For decades I'd always considered James Howell's first house on
The Walk, with its replica of the Lytham St Annes megalithic tomb
made from Radyr stone standing unaccountably in the front
garden, to be the district's highlight. Its *Croesaw* in wrought iron on
the canopied front is not the expected misspelling, so often the fate
of Welsh as used by the unfamiliar, but a formal version of the
interjection. I'm drawn now, though, to the gashed and slashed

Ham Hill stone exterior of what was originally West Grove Unitarian Chapel. The Unitarians sold up and decamped to the Friends Meeting House, Charles Street, in 2005. By 2007 their building had been bought by evangelicals, UCKG. Smiling faced helpers were seen standing outside distributing leaflets that offered advice for those stuck in a rut, taken a wrong turn, drinking too much, wasting their lives or otherwise uncertain. God and prayer was only mentioned in the small print.

UCKG is the Universal Church of the Kingdom of God. It is a Brazilian neo-Pentecostal operation that majors on divine healing and violent body-shaking prayer. Clouds of suspicion, invariably unproven, have persistently followed the Church around since it was founded in 1977. There have been accusations of brainwashing, money laundering, and cultism. As with many other churches, members here pay their leaders a tithe, 10% of income. The church is bold. In its homeland of Brazil it is a major political force. It has twelve million members and a new £130m, 10,000-capacity, larger than the original replica of the Temple of Solomon in São Paolo.

There are not that many ten per cents reaching the redevelopment of the West Grove structure however. Nothing appears to have been spent recently on upkeep. Around the edges the building is crumbling. The main church on the first floor is locked. "There's a leaking roof," James White the young Portuguese in charge tells me when I visit. He's been in Wales for five months and thinks the Welsh are more friendly than the folks back home. On the door is a notice alerting attendees to potential risks with the Church's Strong Prayer sessions. These take place on Sundays and Fridays. "We strongly advice people of a nervous disposition and anyone with a pace-maker or heart problems not to participate as this type of service can be challenging or disturbing for some people."

From evidence elsewhere, mainly via the web's Mystery Worshipper[16] who attends services surreptitiously and then reports back, UCKG congregations are "predominantly black, and there are more women than men". The church fits the new world model, especially here in Tredegarville with its transient population of students and incomers. How many private dentist or sports injury therapists attend is another matter.

Outside the buses power past. The Cardiff that ended here when Tredegarville was first constructed has long since moved on and on and then on again. The University has occupied the land where the Rhymney Rail station originally was. The Lord Mayor no longer lives in the Mansion House. And Tredegarville, the district, is now part of Roath.

Notes

1. Don Lang and his Frantic Five, *Six-Five Special*, HMV 1957. Don Lang died in 1992.
2. A description of a walk around the course of Cardiff's town walls appears in *Real Cardiff Two* (Seren, 2004). Herbert E. Roese's *The Town Wall of Cardiff* (Carek, 2011) is an excellent academic guide.
3. From its Lottery funds ACW, the Arts Council of Wales (successor to the Welsh Arts Council, one of the founding programme funders) provided nearly three quarters of the £5.4m redevelopment costs.
4. The original Cardiff Giant was a scam carried out in 1869 on William Newell's farm near Cardiff in upstate New York. Nothing to do with our Cardiff, naturally. The American settlement was named after the local grist mill owner John F. Card.
5. The Water Tower at Cardiff Central is a disused GWR Grade II listed structure situated at the end of Platform 0 and dating from 1932. It was originally painted in GWR brown and beige. In 1984 artist Dennis Bridge and a team of youth workers decorated it with a mural of daffodils. By 2012 these had faded at the present owners, Network Rail, returned the tower to its original GWR colours.
6. http://www.mpoets.org/
7. Also known as a rubboard this is a washboard-like breastplate across which the wearer,

skiffle-style, beats a rhythm.

8. James Turburvill as Iago Twrbil was a disciple of Iolo Morganwg. He flourished between 1751 and 1781.

9. Although I am sure that if you crossed her palm with enough silver she'd have a go.

10. Alfred Watkins, 1855-1935, photographer and author. His *The Old Straight Track – Its Mounds, Beacons, Moats, Sites and Mark Stones* was published in 1925. It was the first attempt at mapping the ley lines of Britain.

11. Lady Maria North, the 2nd Marquis' first wife (1793-1841) had the bridge across the feeder built in order to gain access to the gardens beyond. She was also responsible for the sinking of the nearby well "to preserve a spring of water".

12. Williams, John (editor), *Wales, Half Welsh*, Bloomsbury, 2004.

13. Foxe, John, *The Acts And Monuments Of The Christian Church* – more commonly known as *Foxe's Book Of Martyrs*. First published in Latin in 1550 and then in English translation much expanded by the author in 1563.

14. White, John Manchip, *Rawlins White, Patriot To Heaven*, The Iris Press, 2011.

15. OWEN GLYNDWR / OWEN GLENDOWER / 1359 - 1415 / ALFRED TURNER R.B.S. / SCULPTOR – Unveiled by Lloyd George in 1916. This is one of a dozen statues at Cardiff City hall in the series Heroes of Wales.

16. http://www.ship-of-fools.com/mystery/specials/london_05/reports/1064.html

EAST

NEWPORT ROAD

I head east, into the sun. This is a trip I've taken thousands of times. Coming away from the shining glass, high-rise, skateboard boulevard, Portland stone, Edwardian echo, and drunken playground that is the capital's beating heart. Through the decades I've watched it rise and its lights come on. The unstoppable rush of sodium vapour, architectural flood luminaire, shop-front LED, lamps on poles, on brackets, in boxes, in recessed strips, on walls, let into ceilings, sunk in the ground. Our windows are forever sheets of brightness. The dark of night never arrives.

Newport Road – for that's the road I'm taking – is a traffic dense, grit-embalmed conduit that once stood as a symbol of industrial muscle and commercial success. This was the route that coupled the city with the world. It was filled with dumpers, high-siders, flatbacks, coal trucks, car loaders, coaches, bulbous vans, limos, Ford Anglias, Morris Minors, motorcycles with sidecars, Austin Sevens. No colour anywhere. Everything in utility black.

Newport Road has always done this. It connected things. It followed the line of the ancient causeway that crossed the eastern flood plain, headed for the climb of Rumney Hill. This was the stage-coach track that navigated the mudflats that filled the eastern half of the Cardiff delta. The route was a rough passage. Wheels came off carts. Things stuck and sank in the mud. Wagons and their cargos were often lost.

Before 1794, the year the Glamorgan Canal from Merthyr first opened, the town of Cardiff ran no further east than the end of Queen Street. Beyond were the remains of the leper hospital and the broken preaching cross at the southern end of the mud track that would eventually become City Road. Further out the farmhouses of Ty Draw, Ty Mawr, Upper Splott, and the village of Roath with its blacksmiths, mill, white country church and manor at Roath Court all stood in a green landscape of tree, field, hedge and light.

Today Cardiff runs the whole way to Newport, *Wales' First City*, the first one you come to arriving in Wales from the east, an appellation emblazoned proudly in the Newport bus depot, read by half-asleep visitors rolling here at cut price from London's Victoria Coach Station or Heathrow. Newport, forever Cardiff's weaker brother, begins on Newport Road. Somewhere up east of Cardiff's outer suburb, St Mellons, the signs start to appear. *Welcome to Newport*. Fields, steak houses, speculative suburban new build, golf club.

The roads here have all been renumbered in the style highway authorities use when they want traffic to take a different route. The original A48 has lost its status to become the B4487, a suburban link, a minor track. Real traffic flows on the Eastern Avenue, the new A48(M). A slow speed dual carriageway that begins almost at Cardiff's centre. It's the city's first attempt at removing the heavy stuff from its pedestrianised heart.

But I'm on foot, slogging up past the site of the first medical dispensary, now the University School of Engineering, just east of the Valley rail lines that flow into Queen Street station. It's the late 60s and I'm walking up here with Adrian Henri. Painter, Liverpool poet, avuncular outsize man. There's a club here that opens late. A place where we can get a drink now that the poetry reading I'd organised at Frederick Street's Marchioness of Bute is done.

Adrian, thick Liverpool-accented to the point of being a parody, a Beatles-era fellow traveller, has the ability to walk the line between pop and passion with alacrity. Back at the pub Adrian wowed them. Thrilled the girls, rocked the boys. His poetry with its tantalising references to panties, body mist sprays, face cream, alcohol, beat music, and school days is the perfect antidote to Walter de la Mare and Tennyson (Alfred Lord, not a Welsh bone in his honourable body) taught in the capital's schools that year. To Adrian Cardiff is just another city on a circuit that makes no distinction between Wales and England, that takes in anywhere and everywhere there's a university or a literary presence that'll invite him in. Penguin, his new mass market publisher, are amazed to see poetry selling in large quantity, for the first time this century. It has come out of the intellectual doe-eyed intelligentsia closet and sprawled itself across the terraces, council estates and working-class heartlands that make up most of the post-industrial British world. Poetry. Stuff of the effete no more.

We don't find the club. In these episodes we rarely do. The Numismatists, a late-night drinking den that was to evolve into St Peter's Rugby Football Club, and then into flats, half way up the road way beyond the re-sited Infirmary on Glossop Terrace (opened 1883, land leased by the Marquis of Bute) might have been our destination. But we don't get there. The walk is just too far.

I did get there once, though, with Vernon Scannell, poet and onetime professional pugilist. He was old then, when he visited, and dead soon after. He was a poet who could command his audience just by walking into the room. We made it first to the Numismatists and then on to the distant Royal Oak. The Oak, up beyond Roath's funeral home, with its Brains Beer, boxing memorabilia and connections with Peerless Jim Driscoll and its one-ring gym on the second floor. Scannell felt completely at home.

But today I'm on my own, walking that straight line on the wide pavement along which cyclists silently race and on which cars park, full four-wheels cracking the paving slabs, oblivious to women with push chairs and old men on sticks. In all the decades I've been tracking along it the road's essential nature has not changed. Financial services and four star hotels near the city, the UK Border Service, the offices of architects, the hospital district, sheltered housing, facilities for the deaf, sexual diseases clinic, churches, schools. Further out apartment blocks, scruff hotels, boarding houses, Vacancies, Contractors Welcome, En-suite, Car Park at Back, Satellite TV In Every Room.

The Blue Dragon Hotel has now gone. Its name boards vanished into Cardiff's past. It once boasted the worst ever reviews in the history of Trip Advisor: "My wife caught impetigo from the pillow." "Used condom found on floor at reception." "Two of our party slept in our minivan rather than put up with the room." "Mould found in the bottom of the kettle and pubic hair in the shower." "A dump." It was the cheapest hotel in the city and within walking distance of the centre. It hung on for years.

Further out, the cityscape shifts again. There's a subtle move towards old people's residential, immigrant hostels and migrant reception centres, recovering alcoholics half-way houses, Dom Polski, bedsits, on benefit b&b, traffic fume thrashed hedges, worn front gardens, no Starbucks, no cafés, not a shop in sight. The Victorian city teeters, red brick stumbling eastwards until the prefabricated roofs of Mothercare and the Dunelm Mill hove into view.

Out here Cardiff's American-style drive-in super-store suburb begins. Could be California with drizzle, feels like Akron, Ohio, Syracuse, New York State, certainly not Wales. The Welsh Refugee Council with its curious protective wrought iron work trapped behind glass is here on the district's fringe. A stream of applicants walk daily towards it. Two hundred a week, says their web site. Drawn here, in a dark wet world, by the promise of sustenance, support, and money.

I'm still walking. I'm surrounded by forecourts, car lots, vans selling hot sausages, Burger King, KFC, McDonald's, bathroom warehouses, self-storage facilities, Castle Bingo last home of the smoker although even here the wrinkled poor-chest aged have to do it outside, tv and computer supermarkets, carpet stores, instant car exhaust fixers, change your suspension spring also sir they look corroded, pet food, ceramic tile monster suppliers, car showrooms, M&S food outlet, the only place in the entire eastern city along this road where you can buy a Gastropub Cottage Pie and Cheese Mash ready meal plus a copy of *The Times*. A super pound store called What! specialising in half price fireworks, tools in profusion and aisle upon aisle of craft materials. This is the new age knitting. You no longer buy your greetings cards you make your own. Beyond where the horizon should be, the land rises. Rumney, the Monmouth village Cardiff annexed in 1938. For centuries the river here marked the county boundary. For many the country boundary. Monmouth, the only place to vote no in the 2011 extension of Assembly powers referendum, still undecided about its Welshness, not real Wales, no.

Before me is Rumney Bridge, streaming with heavy traffic. This river crossing was originally a ford on the Roman road. It acquired a wooden bridge in the twelfth century. That and its successors in both wood and stone were sequentially worn and washed away by the snaking river. The Rumney Bridge was forever in 'a dilapidated, ruinous and decayed state'. Until the present construct was opened, that is, in 1912. It's lost inside a growing city. Yet it still feels like the edge of something. This is the far eastern reach of Cardiff's alluvial flood plain. It's a place where boats once landed and fisheries flourished. Behind it Newport Road transmutes into Rumney Hill, its speed cameras and traffic signs blossoming.

There's something about this place, that once was salt marsh, flooded by the Severn at high tide, crossed on with bales of brushwood, tide fished by local henge fishermen using nets strung between poles, dug into for its clay, for bricks and for pots. The whole flat landscape once regularly alternating between sea and land. You dig down into it looking for burned bones that were once in jars hidden below cromlechs. You hunt for the jewellery lost by fleeing Celts, the remains of boats used by Viking raiders, for King Arthur's sword and crown, Roman chariots, the skeletons of horses, microliths, axe heads, flints, coins, pins. You do this and you find nothing. The sinking mud has taken them all, pulled them down towards the earth's centre, dispelled their power.

ROMPNEY

I cross the congested river bridge and enter Rompney, which is what this place used to be called in the days before mass literacy. Scribes wrote down what they thought they heard: Remni, Remne, Rempney, Rumney. The Rhymney River, in brown flood today, was once the Afon Elarch, the Swan River. This morning the birds have sensibly migrated to the reens of Wentloog and Lamby Lake south of the rail track. Rather than climb the hill I turn onto New Road, a twentieth century creation that crosses the once lush farmlands of the southern village. I want to see how far the district goes and what it feels like to cross.

Rumney Quarry, used for roadstone until the early 1920s, is now a park. In a brilliant act of political correctness the fossil-bearing strata of Silurian rock have been declared simultaneously a Site of Special Scientific Interest and a play area. There are swings at the quarry's entrance and a great slide runs from its lip. I imagined I might see fossil hunters with hammers mixing with kids on skateboards but today there are only mothers with their prams. The quarry itself is filled with the brown of cut back vegetation, a lone abandoned shopping trolley guarding the way in.

The old village of Rumney, a scattering of cottages lost in a hilly landscape, is long gone. Infill has progressed to maximum. Houses line car-choked streets. Yet the sense of an older community remains. Structural style is as disparate as it's possible to be with random self-builds next to early last century houses in twos and threes, bungalows, semis, rows of stepped terraces, architecture uncontrolled, like an allotment plot on a grand scale. In its midst the old village remains, cottages refurbished, farmhouses with new windows and clean slate roofs.

Near the green, the site of Romney's great preaching cross and a clustering of still extant churches and chapels stands the Rompney Castle. This venerable public house was once called the Pear Tree. In the nineteenth century it was bought by the first American Consul to Cardiff, who changed the name and added a sort of mock-Tudor baronial hall as an annex. This is now used as one of the bars.

Ty Mawr Road, which I've traversed to get this far is, of course, known to me. Felicity Jenkins, my partner in the great Caer Castell School twist contest of 1962 (as reported in *Roots of Rock*) lived here. I'd walk her back home lunchtimes and never get invited in and nor did anyone else, apparently. I was a baby boomer sent to a

GCE stream secondary modern as the city's grammar capacity had maxed out. Can't say I enjoyed much of this experience. The daily cycle ride from Roath to distant Rumney usually soaked me when it wasn't freezing my hands. School itself was a never-won battle. Locals vs incomers. Wrong clothes, wrong attitude, endless suspicion. The dance contest was the only thing that ever went my way. You'd think I'd get a cup of tea and a half hour in Felicity's front room at least but I never did.

Beyond the Rompney and the village green the extensive orchards of Paradise Gardens are now built over. The roads rise east-west along the hillside, contrasting infill giving way to congruous lines of semis, terraces and low-rise flats. There are still-extant pre-fabs stepping up Manobier Crescent, outlasting their sell-by dates by decades. The sense of community shifts. More kids on the street. Broken beds in front gardens. Worn grass. A white-hair, smoking, passes me at speed on his mobility scooter. The roads roll on.

No longer am I traversing the older village but instead am among matured 60s housing stock, purpose-built community centres, roads with Grand Avenue style grassed verges and central islands, space, light and deprivation, all edging in. On the heights above me are Eastern High, St Illtyd's Catholic High School, and the Quarry Hall Care Home. Ahead are the edges of Trowbridge and new St Mellons.

Newport Road, my return route, is the northern ward boundary between diverse Rumney and the newer-build monoculture of Llanrumney, its northern and much grittier neighbour. The dual carriageway of the B4487 is crossed by pedestrian bridges, although now that Eastern Avenue carries most of Cardiff's vehicular arrival Newport Road is a less fearsome place.

At the St Augustine's Church Hall back in the heart of old village Rumney the monthly folk club is getting under way. As these events go this one is predictably stocked with an enthusiastic older audience sitting around candle-lit tables before a formal stage. The 'folk' of the title refers to the people who attend. Elaine Morgan, founding organiser along with her Welsh kilt-wearing husband Derek, tells me that it's more a music club than a folk one, where almost anything goes. Punk acts follow Mozart-playing violinists onto the stage. Eleven year-olds sing the national anthem. On the night I'm there we get Beatles-retreads, contemporary French ballads, Irish jigs, singer-songwriter piano pieces and an amplified acoustic band of some power playing under the name Sea Fall.

"We once had a Italian bloke turn up with a squeeze box who sat out front, played flight of the bumble bee at the highest speed I've ever heard, and then left." Derek tells me. He's keen to emphasise the part members of the local community play in the running of their monthly show. There is an extensive committee who manage everything from door takings to a real ale do-it-yourself bar. Derek and Elaine started the club in 2005 when they discovered that the local vicar was keen. You can see the Church Hall from their cottage's kitchen window. The club is almost exclusively a come-all-ye event although you do have to book a slot and these are in some demand. "We have an annual guest act," says Derek. "It's always Gigspanner[1]."

Both Derek and Elaine have long musical backgrounds. Derek was in Linda and the Willbeez, managed by his dad and playing 60s Cardiff and the valleys when he was eleven. Elaine, who sports Joan Baez folk-era long straight hair, was a session singer making TV commercials and radio indents for Cardiff's Music Factory on East Moors. Together they formed Rose Among Thorns, a successful folk-rock band in the Fairports / Jethro Tull tradition. Elaine, however, transcended everything in 1996 when she found herself singing on the French entry for the Eurovision Song Contest.

She met Breton musician Dan Ar Braz while recording with Rose Among Thorns at Dave Pegg's Oxford studio and he'd recruited her as the lead-singing Welsh component for his new supergroup, L'Heritage des Celtes. Celtic music had been on a rising popularity curve by then for two decades. The band did a number of albums and their Breton song, 'Diwanit Bugale', taken from their second album recorded in Dublin, was inexplicably chosen by the normally French-language obsessed French as their Euro Song hopeful.

Elaine whose French, never mind her Breton, is non-existent was forced to learn the ballad parrot fashion. On Eurovision night it was placed 19th in a field of 23. Watching the YouTube clip of that performance today I'd say the song has stood the test of time better than it should have. Both Rose Among Thorns and Dan Ar Braz's L'Heritage are currently quiescent. Just about. "Although there might be a reunion, you never know," says Elaine with what might be a hopeful twinkle.

Elaine and Derek's cottage, Beili Bach, across the graveyard and over a stile from the church, goes back at least 300 years. Originally a thatched farmhouse it was reputedly used to store smugglers' contraband. Rumney's past is full of such tales – secret passages running from the long lost manor house at the head of Ty Mawr Road to the river, two Norman castles both now reduced to pretty much nothingness, a Roman road through its centre and Bronze-age spear heads discovered in the mud of its now-drained levels.

All that disappears on my return trek past a hugely active Newport Road car wash and the throngs at the lines of shops that show little sign yet of suburban decay in the face of supermarket plunder. Eastern Leisure Centre has been privatised and the new owners, Better, have a bi-lingual board on the roadside telling the world. Ahead of me, where the Carpenter's Arms was and now Sainsbury's stands, Rumney breaks free of its Newport Road restrictor to occupy both sides of the hill as it loops back towards that urban gateway at the River's edge. The bridge tollgate has been demolished and turned into a sort of lawn fronting Rumney Pottery. Ahead is the Penylan fringe-land of big box shopping, cars and bustle, saving the economy forever.

THE ENVELOPING OF ST MELLONS

Garry Evans would have loved this place. Hendre Lake: entirely artificial and full of carp, created from a mesh of reens and waterlogged soil. On the 1875 OS survey this spot is a field. Today it's reed-filled blue water. Garry, whom I went to school with, favoured a surrealist approach to learning. He once successfully managed an entire day's copying off the black board with a sharpened stick dipped in ink while the rest of us had to get by with standard-issue pens. Why? Because he could. He began his career selling fishing reels to men squatting along the edges of the newly-stocked Roath Park Lake and then progressed running his own specialist shop. While the rest of us wasted time and pondered what to do in the world Garry was already making money.

I'm in edge territory, much further east than my Rompney walk, in one of those places where Cardiff runs out. This one where it faces the wind-filled fens of the Gwent Levels. We are way beyond the city proper – beyond Roath, beyond the climb of Rumney Hill, the rolling expanses of the Llanrumney housing estate and beyond even St Mellons. As the city had grown this was

once the final frontier. But no longer. St Mellons was absorbed
into the city in 1974. Out here, below the village, on the flood plain
where the farms used to be called Pwll y Plwcca, Trowbridge
Fawr, Wern Gethin and Hendre Isaf there's an air of indecision.
City bumps against country in a green lap of field, hedge and
overgrown path.

These flatlands are where considered design has been jettisoned
in favour of frantic build. Whole new estates at the city's edge have
sprawled across the flood plain. All it would take would be a high
spring tide and a breach in the once Roman sea walls and there'd
be waterlogged carpets in the streets, desperate people crying on
television, and families noisily trying to sleep in the community
hall.

North of the lake park, information panels, reed beds and picnic
tables behind me, the housing begins. This drained land of Gwent
is now a place where the estates of Trowbridge feather into those of
new St Mellons. The forgotten estates as the residents call them.
The city's housing need fixed in a rush of thin, three-story town
houses, new decade terraces and a flush of cheap and vandal
armoured boxes that look for all the world like abandoned

containers, felt roofed and, with their tiny windows, proof against any attack.

Attack seems a way of life. In most of the places I look are signs of urban distress. There are cans, a wrecked television in a hedge, hoodies on bikes that are too small for them. Youths loping along paths in a no-man's land of trees. Along Vaendre Lane are signs of fight back. A large hand-painted sign glows behind an ivy-topped wall – BURGLARS CARWRECKERS BEWARE. Rolls of razor wire have been unwound along fence tops as if they were party streamers.

Mixed development has seen clumps of aspirational middle-class housing with their Harvester-style décor merge softly against the encampments of the less well provided. There are no tower blocks. This district is filled not with graffitied walls but green lane and open space. Unlike the inner city walking working-class suburbs

there are few alleyways. Front doors do not line the pavements. The corner shop has been replaced with the bus stop. The ever-present ditches and drainage reens remind you that even if this is the city it's also a nature-filled place.

I walk north where the ground so slowly rises, putting Trowbridge and new St Mellons behind as I enter the old. For years, most of the decades of my youth, the county boundary exerted its magic here.

In that cluster of four taverns that forms the heart of old St Mellons village licensing laws have always flickered. When Glamorgan was dry on Sundays along with the rest of teetotal Wales, Monmouth was not. Later when the pubs all shut in the city at 10.30 those over the county line stayed open for 30 minutes more.

If you are the right age then there will have been times in your life when you will have experienced that warm glow of discovery as you fought your way to the bar at 10.29 to order a final pint. In place of the expected rush there will have been calm, time in which to drink stretching out, on and on. So it seemed. Last orders in this special place were not the tight rush of most of your younger days. You were not in the city but somewhere else.

The White Hart, the original coaching inn on the road east, has been renamed the Coach House and gentrified into a full dining experience. Around it the three others compete for attention. The Star with its Ye Olde Pie & Mash Shop faces down the chip shop opposite. The Fox and Hounds in Chapel Row shines next to the massively overgrown Bethania Chapel graveyard. Out back is a huge car park. The Bluebell ancient among the ancient, stands hard at the junction of today's Newport Road with where the Via Julia Maritima once ran up the hill to Druidstone. All four still trade. Despite the coming of the motorway passing custom has remained vibrant. And then, of course, there's that new customer base in the estates to the south.

Old St Mellons fights its corner as a place apart. Old school house, winding streets, St Mellons Parish Church atop the hill. 1360 AD but with suspicion that its origins were earlier. There's talk in the histories of a wattle and daub structure once standing on this site. The churchyard is round, or more than irregularly square, and it sits high with views of England and down the channel America, if you could gaze that far. The hill and the roundness are sure signs of it being built on an earlier encampment, a Saxon church or a fort. There was once an illuminated cross on the tower, visible to shipping for miles. Like many of the churches on Greek islands, Christ was used as a talisman against the barbarians beyond.

The saint in the district's name was actually Saint Eirwg, a sixth century monk and doer of good deeds. According to the local historian Stan Jenkins, Eirwg adopted the Latin name *Melonius*, no great step from *Mellons*. In Welsh this St Mellons place was called *Llaneirwg*. On the other hand where I am could have been named

after a French Saint called Melanie with the Welsh *Llaneirwg*
coming from Meurig, a fifth century king of Gwent. No matter.
Developers, with their usual concern for history and place, have
chosen to name many of the new roads after trees and birds.

From my vantage point, staring north across Bluebell Drive, I
can see the end reaches of Llanrumney and the motorways that
encircle the city. Further out is open country. But not for long.
This is one of the places where new Cardiff is appearing at a
furious rate. St Mellons, the old heart, already pressed on three
sides by the expanding city will now be finally encircled on the
fourth. A whole village built round, its age and dignity engulfed by
brash new construction. Brick and speed rather than the slow
sureness of stone. Cardiff, the inflated city, expanding like a
balloon.

I cross back south, walking down Cypress Drive, Cardiff's
aspirational IT business park where the roads have already been
named for their never quite achieved future – Fortran Road, Cobol
Road, Pascal Close. This is a place of margins. It's a frontier
business development with the wetland wilds of the levels beyond
its metal shed sides. Dwr Cymru are here. Healthcare providers.
Surgical tool suppliers. Van retailers. Architects. Office furniture
traders.

Further, below the rail line, is the sea. In this permanently
waterlogged landscape crouched below ocean defences you don't
see it, you sense it. You know it's there because, despite whirling
clouds of pigeons, urban nature's new dominant bird, the sky is
emulsified with gulls.

THE LOST MANSIONS

Up here the city, like everywhere else within its boundaries, has lost
its past. But on Penylan Hill, which is where I now am, that act of
vandalism happened decades ago. This is Cardiff suburban
country, planted laurel taken over from native bramble, woodland
cleared, detached houses erected, roads in climbing curves and
swooping bends.

There was once a railway. The Taff Vale Railway (TVR) opened
a mineral line in 1887 to service the power station at the bottom of
Colchester Avenue and the Roath and Queen Alexandra Docks.
Hauling lines of coal trucks it ran until 1968 by which time the coal

trade had collapsed and the power station was no more. The twin concrete cooling towers which had stood on the Roath skyline like giant teeth since they'd been erected in 1942 were demolished in a spectacular cloud of dust in 1972.

The cutting, deep enough to hide a full steam-dragged train but not its rhythmic panting, was filled in and built on. Boleyn Walk, Clos Derwen, and Pant yr Wyn are there now, new brick semis, town houses, detached five beds, aspirational structures with the sound not of trains but traffic thrumming in their back gardens come balmy summer.

On the north side of this rail track was the nineteenth century Convent of the Good Shepherd. At the time when I lived in the solid-walled terraces of nearby Ty Draw Place, back in the black and white fifties, I was forbidden from going near. The Convent had been paid for by the charitable and newly Catholic John Crichton-Stuart, the third Marquis of Bute. The great man, acting like a Norman Knight, wanted to leave things on this earth that would salve the heavenly passage of his soul. The Convent was established in 1870 when Bute donated a barn and the Ty Gwyn farmhouse which sat on part of his Penylan estate. The incoming nuns felt the house to be unsuitable but declared the barn to be of pleasing ecclesiastical appearance. Duly assisted by Bute's architect William Burges and Bute's builder and clerk of works J. Barnett, it was converted into a chapel.

The Sisters of the Good Shepherd had looked after the Third Marquis during his conversion to the Catholic Church in Southwark in 1868. John Crichton-Stuart was now paying dues. Their Convent at Penylan would be a refuge for fallen women, supporting itself by the operating of a laundry, Cardiff's own Magdalena, with all the distress and misery for the inmates and their children that implied. This was an unhappy place, Matthew my companion on this ramble in the rain looking for traces of the lost tells me. We pass along Ty Gwyn Road where the Convent once was. It closed in the 1960s and was demolished without record, Burges architecture and Bute artefacts bulldozed. Heathfield House for Girls (which became the Roman Catholic sixth form St David's College) was built on the site. The present pupil intake is a multicultural melée, mostly bussed here from across the city. God has changed shape again, as he often does.

Of the Convent there is no trace bar the shape of the road bend. Matthew tells me that the sites of lost houses can sometimes by discerned by the trees that remain. The district is rich in tall and aged Scots Pines which would have stood in the gardens of the great houses. Saplings for their owners to enjoy. Giant champions now.

The road climbing from the distant town was once called Welshmanshill[2]. It led then to the farm of Llwyn y Grant and the ancient track east now metalled as Llanederyn Road. It's Penylan Hill today and, until you reach the Garth, Cardiff's highest place. Nob Hill, Matthew calls it. A late nineteenth century version of Lisvane's Druidstone Road, a place where those with money went to escape the insanitary and industrial dirt of the burgeoning town.

Matthew Williams is an obsessive for lost places, where things once were but are now no more than empty air. He started out as an antique dealer with a shop in Llandaff but soon became immersed in the history of the objects he was handling, the traces they had left on time, where they came from, why they were created. It was a small step sideways to an interest in buildings and, in particular, great houses. His present day job is Curator of Cardiff

Castle, a great house if there ever was one. There's something about the look of Cardiff, he tells me, the stone and brick it is built from, its architects and land owners that is so attractive.

His lecture series on the *History of Cardiff Castle, Cardiff the Georgian City* and allied subjects regularly sells out. *The Lost Houses of Cardiff*, an interest sparked when a friend of his, Thomas Lloyd, published *The Lost Houses of Wales* in 1986, is a current offering. "You should make a book out of it," I tell him. He appears reticent. "I'll leave a record of my researches with the Archives," he says. Maps, plans, details, photos. "The photos are the hardest to obtain. Dozens must exist in private collections, shots of strangely dressed early relatives playing croquet on lawns, standing outside grand doorways, holding the reigns of horses. Their owners are unaware of the history they own."

The Hill, north of that ubiquitous but lost TVR rail line, was for a brief period wood and farm dotted with grand houses. That brief period started in the middle of the nineteenth century. At that time Cardiff's boom was just beginning and rich new shipowners and merchants were seeking great places in which to live. The boom continued until the 1920s after which great draughty residences with only 45 years left on their land leases became somewhat less than desirable prospects.

Penylan House would have been the first, built on freehold land around 1860 and occupied by glass and hardware merchants, the Primavesi family. It was demolished after the 1920s to be replaced by a Jewish old people's home. That home itself has now been replaced to become the much larger Penylan House Community Nursing Home. It stands tight against Eastern Avenue which blows right through its grounds. There is only a small white fragment of boundary wall that might recall the past. Check the southern edge of The Retreat. Care home assistants stand next to it and smoke, an activity forbidden inside.

South of us are the remains of three great houses. 'Remains' is a massively overdone word here. Matthew is pointing out the boundary walls which once surrounded the mansion of Oldwell. Here the brewer John Biggs, father of international football player Norman Biggs, once lived. So, too, did potato merchant William Young. It was built in 1887 and lasted until 1987. Then it and a second great house, nearby Wellclose, once owned by Thomas W. Jotham, woollen merchant, were demolished. In their place the retirement flats of Redwell, Oldwell and Stonewell Courts were constructed. Nurse on duty. Gardens mowed for you. Early gateposts and Scots Pines.

Over the road, now occupied by an architecturally challenged set of flats that sit back from the road like a student's first attempt at sorting the city's social housing, is Hillside Court. This was the site of a three storey and nine bedroomed Hillside, a grand house from the 1880s that did time briefly as a 1960s hotel before being demolished as the decade closed. The line of its drive remains as does its stable block, now converted to gentrified mock-Tudor housing.

As we climb rising Ty Gwyn, Matthew is enthusing on his subject. The lost houses all had viewing platforms right on top. We turn to look back out at the emerged view of the city and the channel spread below us. In the time of the great mansions it would all have been smoke from the chimneys of workers' housing with further smudges and smears from the docks themselves. Today there's new white-sided high-rise and an air of Cardiff actually being something again, like it once was. Making money, doing its residents well.

Up here, on the hill's higher reaches, were Shandon, Linden, Graigisla, Fretherne, and Birchwood Grange. Some changed their names as they passed from owner to owner. Others were demolished and replaced by new builds with new names in a welter of history rebranding itself. What remains? At the junction of Ty Gwyn Road with Ty Gwyn Avenue there's a lintel in a garden wall that was once part of a Fretherne outbuilding. Outside a drive leading to the present Cardiff University Penylan Campus you can see the half-moon bends in the wall that once formed a space in which horse-drawn carriages could turn. And there are trees of course, Scots Pines everywhere, towering.

Shandon (later known as Penylan Court), just down from Graigisla (renamed as Tal y Werydd and then Ty Gwyn Court), was the home of shipowner W.J. Tatem. In its Tal y Werydd incarnation Graigisla was home to Tatem's friend and fellow shipowner Daniel Radcliffe. Tatem later rose to fame as Lord Glanely, ennobled after making a large donation to Lloyd George's Liberals and signing the cheque simply Glanely. "But your name is Tatem," complained Lloyd George. "Why sign as Glanely?" "Because that will soon be my name, and if it isn't, then you won't be able to cash that cheque," was Tatem's reply.

Bronwydd, half way up the Avenue of the same name, was demolished by the same thing that removed most of the grounds of

Penylan House – Eastern Avenue. Bronwydd, built in the 1850s, had extensive grounds. Near their northern edge was the Holy Well[3] of Penylan. After it had been donated to the city by its last owner, former Mayor of Cardiff, Sir Alfred Thomas, Bronwydd did time as a children's home. In what would have been the grounds today stands a nursery. History repeats.

At the top where Ty Gwyn empties onto Cyncoed Road stands one of the few great houses to survive. It's small by Penylan's lost mansion standards. Cornborough, named after one of his shipping lines, was the home of one-time freeman of the city of Cardiff, benefactor William Reardon Smith. Being made a freeman is a great Cardiff honour. In the nineteenth century only the great and the good were so rewarded. In more recent times these distinguished souls have been joined by a more varied collection of recipients. These include the Pope, the National Union of Mineworkers, and the Daring-class Destroyer, *HMS Dragon*. The honour once gave recipients certain privileges including the right to carry a naked sword through the streets, to drive sheep through the confines of the town, and to be hung with a silken rather than hemp noose, should one of those turn out to be necessary. Under the fun-dampening Local Government Act of 1972 such enjoyments have been curtailed and the honour is now merely ceremonial.

In the distance is Birchwood Grange, once home of architect Charles J. Jackson and now subsumed by the University. Just below, behind the walls of a newly gated community off Ty Gwyn Avenue, stands White Lodge. Built in 1924 this latter-day arrival was the one-time home of Welsh banker Julian Hodge.

Matthew reels off facts as the rain pours into my notebook, blurring the ink to illegibility. Greatest of all the lost houses, he tells me, was Green Lawn. This was constructed, 'regardless of cost' in 1874 to a French design, and situated right at the top of the hill. It was surrounded by five acres of grounds, two lodges, multiple flag staffs, and a whole set of further springs and ponds. It was built by George Parfitt and Edward Jenkins. In 1935 it was knocked down and used the site for new housing.

The hill downsizes. Great houses are removed to make way for smaller buildings. Today those smaller buildings themselves are being demolished to make space for even tighter redevelopments. A house on Bronwydd Close is being knocked down in order to build flats on the same site. This has already happened further up Bronwydd Avenue itself. Great gardens shrink and vanish. Apartments, which give the greatest financial return, march into their place.

We drop back down passing the end of Melrose Avenue, the housing stock there built in 1931 by Charles Hoare. He wanted to call the road Hoare Avenue but was persuaded by the Council that this might not be the most appropriate of names. Instead he called it Melrose, named after the small town on the Scottish borders where he had just holidayed.

The rain changes tempo. We stand in front of Halewell House, the latest new build, the final addition to the space revealed after the TVR Roath branch cutting had been filled. It could have been called Ty Penylan (but that was elsewhere). Instead the name has been created from the surnames of the owners.

This is a future house, insulated to arctic standards and built on a thin and difficult plot right next to where hill climbing cars change gear. Below it seeps the water that once sprang from the rocks in the fields near Greenlawns and, no doubt, from the Holy Wishing Well of Penylan lost to redevelopment, flattened to make space for cars. Around here there is god in everything. He rolls down the hill curing everything in his wake.

THE MUSEUM OF ROATH

In the old library in Trinity Street where some of Wales' greatest books were once housed and a meteor that fell on Cardiff in the nineteenth century was kept in a cupboard. Things have changed. Upstairs is Yr Hen Lyfrgell, the city's Welsh language centre. In the basement is the people's museum, The Cardiff Story. Here are housed a ceramic souvenir of the 1927 FA cup, a 78 record of Frankie Lane singing 'Jealousy' in a Spillers' sleeve, a brass Bute Dock police belt, a tram bell, and the figurehead from *HMS Hamadryad* along with a rolling series of exhibitions that take in everything from the highs of Cardiff sport to how the city faced the fury of the many floods it has coped with in its two thousand year history. It's a unique experience and a fine collection. But it pales into insignificance compared to what exists in Roath.

In painter and social worker Geoff Reynolds' shed at the rear of a terrace in Werfa Street stands the Actual History Museum of Roath. In this small structure Sir Alfred Street and Dr Glenn Roy, aided by Dame Shirley Road, have assembled a unique collection of objects pertaining to our shared Roathian past. Here is a photograph of *RNS Albany*, a dreadnought, docked at the Roath Navy's base near the prom at Roath Lake. It bristles with guns ready for the forthcoming war against Splott. The Mappa Maindy, salvaged from a pigeon loft in Cathays where it had been in use as a roof tile, shows the world as it was once thought to be. Flat Holm is twice the size of Afrika, Walles is as huge as Amerika, with Roath at its centre. The Elm Street marbles, recently rescued from a fire at the carpet warehouse on City Road, are now once again in their jar for the Roath world to see.

On a side shelf is a fragment of a Roman frieze from the time of Emperor Claudius Rhodus. It clearly shows the arm of a Roath peasant standing near the rising ground of Penylan Hill. In the peasant's hand is a fragment of what is almost certainly a Clark's pie. The Museum possesses a rare film of Lake Roath Monster with its distinctive giraffe neck swimming past the Lake islands. In a glass case is a desert boot with the toe section bitten off, a souvenir of a Lake Monster encounter.

During a recent visit Dr Glenn Roy took time out from his detailed research into the Long March of Chairman Moy in the 1940s to talk to me about how the Roath world had been at the turn of the century. Back then the 100 year war with Splott had finished, the corridor to the sea along Clifton Street had been agreed, and Roathian peasants had happily returned to their 90-hour working weeks. They manufactured brass hip replacements, and cheque cashing machines that were proving so popular among the population at large.

Dr Roy's fellow academic, Sir Alfred Street, wearing a tweed jacket and brown Penylan trilby, explained to me that this year is the centenary of Roald Dalcross. Dalcross is author of such enduring classics as *The Enormous Carpet Tile* and *The Fantastic Mr Splott*. As he was born in Roath and lived here for two years the Museum is actively promoting *City Road of the Expected*. For this celebration a man will come out of the chip shop eating a small chips and people dressed as characters from *Charlie and the Sweatshop Factory* will pass by in cavalcade. "Although," as Sir Alfred points out, "they could be anyone".

In the 2014 Roatherendum the district voted overwhelmingly for independence. The campaign was hard fought with hustings at the Roath Park Pub and other local centres. Today Sir Alfred fronts the Rexit movement. In response to the criticism that little has changed since the vote and that Liberal Democrats are still appearing in photographs pointing at bin bags he has told voters that "Rexit means Rexit". "Our bananas are whatever shape we want them to be."

The Roath Museum is a hidden gem worthy of inclusion in Trip Advisor's top ten Cardiff attractions (although regularly beaten by clear Cardiff fakes such as the Castle and the Codfather Fish Bar). It opens annually at the time of the Made in Roath Festival. In 2016 it attracted a record 250 visitors with some coming from as far as Fairwater and Cathays.

Made in Roath is an arts festival like no other. It encompasses the entire city district pushing the boundaries out to where they well might have been back at the time of Cardiff's origin. Outer Penylan, lower Cathays, Tredegarville and Upper Adamsdown all return to the Roathian fold. Roath where it's cool. Cardiff's new cultural epicentre. Beats Pontcanna into a tin hat.

The Festival is now into its ninth annual manifestation and has stretched out from a long Saturday and Sunday to more than a week. It is run by a group of artists including Gail Howard, Helen Clifford and Becca Thomas and began as a sort of painters open house day. Much in the style of the National Garden Scheme's open gardens weekends, you could tour the district visiting the back rooms, basements and lofts of Roath's growing crowd of painters, makers and sculptors. In the first year ten studios opened their doors. That number has now topped thirty and is supplemented by more than two hundred events.

These includes pop-up galleries, strolling players, poets, peddlers, street food sellers, commissioned creatives, concerts, performances, platforms, innovations, interventions, installations, improvisations, broadcasts, publications, dance and diving, multi-cultural workshops, films and touring vans, knitting, cooking, brass bands, guitars, digital doodling, and, of course, the Actual Museum of Roath.

Dan Nichols, the washboard waistcoat wearing front man for the street skiffle band Railroad Bill (already encountered in *The East Gate* on page 20), became Sir Alfred Street in 2013. He was joined by Geoff Reynolds as Dr Glenn Roy and Claire Davies as Dame Shirley Road. Dame Shirley gives popular Roath cake making demos in the Werfa Street back garden. Currently the team are uncovering the thoughts of Chairman Moy. These contain many unalloyed truths: "Wellfield has many restaurants, all are filled with teachers", and "Mynachdy is a distant land, with few pleasurable surprises," something Mynachdy residents might dispute.

At the Museum of Roath lecture I attended recently music had been moved front stage. Recent Museum acquisitions have included the sheet music of George Roathby, the 'Monarch of Merriment' and include water-coloured examples of his songs 'At The Lido At The Alder Road', and 'I Made An Oath To You In Roath'. Resident practitioner John Liepins, earlier seen demonstrating use of an original Roath brass hip-replacement, serenaded us with a couple of songs from the Paul McClarksie repertoire. 'All You Need Is Roath' and 'Penywain Is In My Ears And In My Eyes' had never sounded so cool.

EATING MY WAY DOWN CITY ROAD

I'm sitting in the Codfather trying to explain chips to Sue. This staple of British cuisine for more than a century has to be judged on the size of the portion. You don't visit a chip shop for the thrill of fine dining. You come for quality, quantity, crispness, aroma. The Codfather Fish Bar & Kebab House at the town end of Cowbridge Road East delivers all of those. The original plan had been to eat in every restaurant from here to Victoria Park but I've been won over instead by the charms of City Road. Cardiff's "multicultural melting pot of independent retailers" as the BBC describes it[4]. And much nearer home.

City Road has form. Lloyd Robson based his *Sense of City Road* project here as did The Sherman Theatre with their 2017 piece of community theatre, *Love: City Road*. Performance poets Cabaret 246 began life in City Road's Roath Park Pub. It's also where I almost bought my first car – a tangerine low-slung three wheeler called the Bond Bug brought out by Reliant in the late sixties. The big plus was that you could drive this unstable futuristic go kart solo on a motorcycle licence. That and the fact that you could get one no money down on hire purchase. The minuses were almost everything else. My girlfriend at the time told me that she wasn't going to be seen being driven around the streets of Cardiff at 70 miles an hour in a reclining position two inches from the road. So that was the end of that relationship.

City Road is a stretch of total multi-culturalism that runs from Death Junction where Albany, Crwys, Mackintosh and Richmond meet to the former site of the Longcross opposite Cardiff Royal Infirmary. It has 51 eating places. Cowbridge Road East, a thoroughfare that is at least three times longer, can only muster 42. I've traversed City Road many times. Most recently this was as leader of a psychogeographical tour of Roath for the Local History Society. They were a game group of mainly retirees who willingly listened to my shouted poems delivered from the middle of the road and to my portrayals, delivered while standing on benches, of the artistic and historical wealth the district holds. Walking past the graffitied frontage of what was once the Gaiety cinema someone asked me just what made this walk psychogeographic. "We'll be traversing the streets in alphabetical order," I replied. Arabella Street was in the other direction. No one said a thing.

Restaurants in City Road are a growth industry challenged only by the rise in the number of barbers. Men getting their hair professionally cut is again in fashion. There are eleven men's hair stylists along City Road, a product as much of the needs of the local, transient population as of the transferable skills of many of the immigrant hair cutters. Hot towel shaves and beard trims are as popular as full-on haircuts. Service is offered with style and runs late into the night.

But these things don't concern me. I'm here for the food and it seems to be available everywhere. As an element of control I've decided to define a restaurant as a place where you can sit and be served at your table. Space to stand in the corner eating a kebab from a bag doesn't count. What confuses things has been the rapid rise in take away operations. Food previously only ever obtainable by sitting down in a restaurant can now be enjoyed at home, delivered in a polystyrene insulated box on the back of a push bike. Everyone along the Road offers such service. Customers don't home cook anymore, if they ever did. Ovens have been jettisoned and hotplates sold on. Why bother when your mobile can do all the work.

We begin at KBS near the lights. Kebabs, Burgers and Sausages. It's all those. Kurdish staff serve mixed shish and chips in huge quantity and at a very reasonable price. This is a place to come when you are bladdered. I've been told that by friends at the allotment. There's a notice on the wall advising customers that KBS represented Cardiff as one of 10 cities in the finals for the WKD Golden Kebab Awards of 2010. There's no mention of how the shop did. When I look it up I discover that Zulfi's of Leeds won.

The following evening we try Chunky Chicken, 'the Peri Peri masters' who have a halal certificate proudly displayed behind the counter. Chunky Chicken is done out in Macdonalds-style bright plastic with illuminated wall menus, bench seating and tables secured to the floor. It looks a little like an intergalactic space liner might have looked in the age of Flash Gordon. It's a chain with

more than twenty-four branches the cheerful Pakistani serving behind the counter tells me. Does he like it in Cardiff? Better than London from where he's come, and easier to understand the accent. I order the house special of steamed and flame grilled chicken basted with olive oil and served with rice, fries and salad. The rice is Indian style, the chips Welsh-reconstituted. The peri peri comes in various strengths but even the mild is hot.

Next we're in CN, named after China's internet domain. This is as far eastern a restaurant as they come, windows steamed, Chinese clientele, Peking Pork, MaPo tofu, free Wi-Fi, karaoke upstairs. As an antidote to the Road's obsession with kebab and chips the place is superb. My tofu with red and green chilli is spicy enough to have me deliriously walking up and down the pavement outside in order to regain my breath.

As we proceed along the kebab highway Sue's nerve begins to crumble. At the prospect of having chicken burger and chips three nights in a row she disallows Miss Millie's on the grounds that despite the metal tables out front this is entirely a take away. The tables are there simply for customers to rest at. I am overruled when I spot someone actually eating and drinking coke while seated. They are not using cutlery so it still doesn't count.

Further down the Lebanese, Turkish, and other middle-eastern brands begin to merge. The Indian restaurants could be Pakistani but are probably Bangladeshi. Asian fusion operations offer everything at once. In addition there's Pepe's El Paso, run by a half Iranian, half Mexican born in California and offering the full enchilada dining experience complete with sombreros and inflatable cacti.

Nearby the Taco Express, a poorly illuminated fellow Mexican traveller, turns out to be a Kurdish operation in disguise. The tacos arrive with naan bread on the side. There are no burritos but you can get Turkish tea. The owner talks rapidly in Kurdish to a group of men clustered at the top table. There is no sign that they have come here to dine. Beneath the dismal lights there are no other customers. I feel as if I have strayed into an episode of *Breaking Bad.*

Behind a bus shelter facing the site of Cardiff's first piece of automatic shopping, a 1960s machine selling milk 24/7 for 6p a carton, revolutionary in its day, stands Alwali. This is branded as Cardiff's first Omani restaurant. Until recently it was the Lana Persian but cultures shift with rapidity in this road. I'm peering at the menu when a bloke from the bus queue, looking over my shoulder, tells me that this is actually a great place. The lamb shewa is wonderful. "You recommend it?" "I do." We go in and he follows. "I thought you were waiting for a bus," I ask. "Oh no, I'm the manager," he replies. The staff are a mix of Syrian and Tunisian with a waitress from Mauritius. It's the owner who is Omani, but he's not here. On the wall are pictures of a man in military uniform. This is Qaboos bin Said Al Said, the Sultan. We follow the manager's suggestions and, to be fair, the food isn't bad, although I do have the impression I've eaten similar elsewhere.

So which are the best places? In a road where restaurants open and close like market stalls that's hard to say. Take your choice. Do you want intimate, such as Chilli Basil's 16-cover Burmese masquerading as Thai? Or maybe the 120-diner, industrial cafeteria-sized Spicy Village where you can sink into an armchair and get a mixed-platter of kebabs served with disco lights as a backdrop.

For me it might be Troy, with pictures of Abdullah Ocalan, the PM of Kurdistan on the wall. A full on charcoal grill which offers dishes worth returning for. Or Oz Urfa, another Kurdish operation billing itself as Mesopotamian but whose hummus, sksoka, yaprak sarma, antep ezme and haydari are the genuine article. Moved on, by the time you read this, relocated. Thus it is on Arabic Street, Sharie Al Arabie, centre of Cardiff's multiple worlds.

In a taxi sometime later, driven by a Yemeni, I ask where in Cardiff he goes to eat. "City Road," is the firm reply. "Abo Ali, maybe, or the Beirut Grill House. But, you know, after a while they all begin to taste the same." I know what he means.

PENYLAN QUARRY

The Romans came to Cardiff. We know this, most of us do. I'd known since I was a child. I'd had the original Roman stones along the bottom edge of the Castle pointed out to me many times. Enthusiastic parents, teachers, uncles and others keen to underline the city's respectably ancient origins all knew. Our Roman past was important. The stones showed the extent of the Roman's fourth fort, built on the site of earlier wooden structures in about 290 and abandoned 80 years later. It was occupied in its ruined dark ages by the Mabinogion's king Ynwyl, the Romans having fled back home to leave these lands of Ynys Prydein to the wild Celtic winds. The Roman walls run three, four and five feet high around the Castle's base. They are distinguished from Burges' later additions by a course of red stone. Other than that, though, of the Romans and their great coliseum, aqueduct and hard-paved dead straight marching roads there was nothing.

The reality is, of course, different. There are the two big Roman sites: the villa at Ely racecourse (marks in the turf, visited in *Real Cardiff Three)* and the Courtyards building at Cold Knap where I'd been given a fragment of Roman roof tile as a souvenir. After that there are scores of further sites. Local archaeologists have banded together to create the mellifluously titled Research Framework for the Archaeology of Wales. This makes them sound like a government guideline. Their directory of local sites, however, runs to fourteen pages. They have identified so many Roman remains in the south east of Wales that you'd imagine this place to be Rome itself where history still litters the streets. There are hoards of Roman coin, weapons, inscribed stones embedded in church walls, battle stations, mines, field outlines, farmhouses, store rooms, temples, kilns, forges, representations of the Gorgon's head, memorials, grave markers, coffins, altars, boats, roads, paths, steps, floors, walls, abutments, bridges and wharfs. Beneath the twentieth century sludge of street and suburban garden lies the Roman past. It's everywhere. Stick your hand in the soil and you'll come up with a sword.

They'd visited Penylan. At the top of the hill they'd dug a quarry, cutting sandstone for their fort and their roads. The Iter XII, the great Via Julia Maritima to Carmarthen, was down the hill from here. It ran along the causeway from the Rumney river crossing and on to the fort. The line is preserved by the present Newport Road. A metalled surface of Roman origin was uncovered during work constructing the riverside roundabout to provide a link to the then new motorway. Around the quarry itself pottery had been found and evidence discovered of wall foundations. Romans lived and worked here. Gazed out at the channel. Took a stroll in the Llanederyn woods. You'd imagine this would lead to multiple archaeological digs and tourist board promoted interpretation boards. There'd be busloads of Roman fanaticals arriving to sop up the ancient motes and mystic early air of Cardiffium and Peniolandium squatting here near the Tatum Saxon shore. But no. It took me several decades to work out that the quarry was Roman at all.

When I grew up in this district before roads had been cut and, indeed, back when much of the housing now covering the hill like suburban armour was still a future speculation in builders' minds, the quarry was a recreation destination. You'd come up here to spoon, sitting on the bench on Llwyn y Grant Road, looking out at the sun setting over the distant Channel. Well, I didn't. But I was told by my aunt that others did. The quarry was a mud hole in the hill with water and a few tench and frogs in its bottom. You could slide down the banks. There were blackberry bushes and a weakened by years of rationing local population would be here annually with their baskets and their cloth bags.

Rumours about the water were many. Jean Challenger, a 32-year-old housewife, was beaten to death near the quarry in 1956. She'd been out blackberry-picking. Attempts were made to drain the pond by police seeking the murder weapon. But the spring was too strong and they failed. The stories surrounding this event, however, were many. Down in the dark depths they'd found bikes, cars, carts, unexploded bombs, medieval gold plate, inscribed stones, chariots, swords, javelins, a Welsh plesiosaur, and a whirling route on down to King Arthur's mystic world.

What was there, and in abundance, were fossils. Amid the Silurian mudstone layers have been found shelly faunas and graptolites and other remnants of that ancient time when this hill was at the bottom of the sea. During my schooldays while I and my friends went there to engage in primitive gang warfare the studious tidy boys did different things. They turned up with small hammers and, hanging themselves out from the crumbling layers, proceeded to knock those strata about. Clear champion collector was Cardiff High School pupil Robin Old who, with two friends, formed the official-sounding Penylan Geological Society. This was actually an ancient cabinet housed in his attic and in which he and his mates displayed and labelled their specimens. In 1964 he presented the National Museum of Wales with a box containing more than a thousand fossils, flora and fauna from pre-history, once preserved in the Penylan mud.

Today there's not much left. In fact there's nothing left. Arriving in 1971 the new motorway grade dual carriageway connecting Western Avenue with the roaring M4 opened. The Queen did the honours, unveiling a foundation plaque at Heath Hospital, the University Hospital of Wales, at the same time.

This new Eastern Avenue ran in a cutting right through the city's north eastern sector. It threw up noise and dirt. Grants were made available for the installation of soundproof double glazing. This turned out to be only partially successful. The worried and the sonically challenged held meetings. Houses in the road's path, and there were many, were demolished. Compensation was offered. Local residents reached for their paying-in books. What else could they do?

My mother was convinced that the new traffic overload now streaming along this inner city motorway was decimating the insect population. Cars in our street would show up mid-summer with fly-blown windscreens. If you want proof there it is, she told me. If we carry on like this there won't be any flies left. The new game was standing still in the street to see if you could hear anything. If the slightest whisper of distant traffic intruded then a letter went into the council asking for reparation. If we got any then I never heard about it. We did not have new windows. The old leaky ones with their sticking wooden sashes were still there right up to the day I moved.

But the quarry, what of that? It was gone, the new road cut right through it. Except it didn't. Not quite. The northern wall went, taken away in the dumper trucks to be replaced by tarmacadamed highway. But the rest was simply abandoned, nature was allowed free reign. The site was fenced. Access was removed, there wasn't even a gate. To the quarry's south ran the semis of Dorchester Avenue, to the east a great earthen bank and then the Colchester Avenue allotments. To the west the former Edward Nichol Children's Home redeveloped as a quiet, almost gated community of residences and garages, walled and fenced and tight.

To see what remained meant getting in. Using binoculars to peer through the leafless winter trees from the far side of Eastern Avenue had revealed tantalising glimpses of sky reflected off water. I briefly toyed with the idea of getting someone to drive me along the dual carriageway. Opposite the quarry site we would feign a breakdown. From the hard shoulder I would climb the motorway fence and disappear from view in the bushes. But then the AA or the police might turn up and that would be that.

In 2008 the now taken-over Countryside Council for Wales[5] had commissioned a brief report into Cardiff Sites of Special Scientific Interest. Penylan quarry, the lost and abandoned, was included. "The richest and most abundant source of fossils from the Cardiff Silurian rock strata" the author concluded, echoing young Robin Old's conclusions of 1964. He then explained that, as I'd discovered, access was more or less crap, although he didn't quite use those words. He suggested scaling an iron spike fence and following a path that runs along the A48 bank and then crossing the highway fence. Failing that he offered climbing a brick wall and then crossing very dense scrub. Both approaches, he suggested, would raise "a number of Health and Safety issues". Indeed. The fact that the paths he'd identified now seemed to have vanished compounded the problem.

I peered down in the quarry's direction from Penylan Hill bridge and wondered. I already had one failed attempt under my belt. A cousin of mine who lived near the allotments had suggested that I could climb her rear garden wall and stroll along the top of the bank. This exercise had been doomed from the start. I fell off the wall, landing in a world of unrestrained bramble relieved occasionally by the thrusting barbs of hawthorn. There were no paths nor ground that could be crossed without first attacking it with machete. This dense underbrush was the result of forty years of unfettered growth. A better barrier than any amount of anti-vandal paint and coiled barbed wire. They should surround vulnerable warehouses with this. You'd need a tractor to get through. I pushed forward to find myself first facing the reported iron spiked fence behind which was an unscalable breeze block wall. Beyond this the motorway zoomed. Scratched to buggery I gave up.

But then, by chance, I found it. A way in. There was a garden fence with a hole in it and beyond a stretch of ivy clad but not yet totally brambled ground. It didn't take me long to get through. Thirty metres in was the pond that had filled the old quarry. Overhung by trees and full of weeds but still open water. Of the much-prized fossil bearing cliffs of Penylan mudstone, however, there was no sign. Their layered mud brown sides had gone. They were now densely overgrown, green and tumbling, choked with bush and bramble, the highest mound of unrestrained blackberry visible anywhere in Cardiff. This was a land unmarked by animal track, path, or discarded hardcore. There were no abandoned cars, broken bikes, bust pushchairs, or dumped MFI kitchens, fractured white in all their melamine-faced chipboard splendour. Nature had returned.

Could I remember any of this? I'd been here so often years back. But no memory stirred. I might as well have been on Mars. I left, quietly, but not before a great bramble, the great grandchild of the bush from which my mother had once collected berries, managed to scram me right across my face. I retreated, disfigured, hoping I wouldn't be challenged and have to explain myself. The lands of Llwyn y Grant farm lay behind. Below were once the fields of Ty Draw. Let the past go and it vanishes. In front of me, laid out like Sim City, is what we've done with it.

THE MILL PARK

You could hear the scratch of Bob Dylan all around you. He was in everyone's heads right then. Everything was changing and we were there at the forefront. This was not going to be the same world it started out as, not when we'd done. Alan's approach was to begin by dressing himself entirely in purple. He'd been to the launderette, ignored all the signs forbidding it, and thrown his entire wardrobe in with a can of Dylon. He was now the colour the rainbow rarely gets to, a dappled purple smudge from head to toe.

Alan, my fellow explorer of the new world, lived on Westville Road, facing the Mill Park, a quiet suburban stretch of grass and tree. A central green reservation of ex-Tredegar land between the Edwardian terraces which had been transferred to the people in 1906. It opened in 1912 as a Pettigrew-designed parkland complete with 95 varieties of trees and shrubs, drinking fountain, a rockery, a children's paddling pool and a summerhouse.

By the time we'd got to be standing there, 1963, Harold Wilson PM and the Beatles heading for world domination, most of those things had gone. The paddling pool was controversial from the start with locals fearing that it would attract a class of children who would lower the tone of the neighbourhood. Echoes of this appeared at the time of the recent millennium when proposals to establish a children's play area on more or less the same site were similarly rejected. The pool had been filled in during the thirties after a diphtheria scare. The summerhouse ended its days being vandalised to death. The trees at this time still stood, however. Alan, the photographer, wanted to use them as backdrop.

We'd been inside his house rifling his father's vast collection of science fiction, double-banked across the shelves: Eric Frank Russell, Isaac Asimov, Olaf Stapleton, Ray Bradbury, August Derleth, H.P. Lovecraft. It was Lovecraft's Cthulhu Mythos which preoccupied Alan. This was a fictional universe where mankind had proved irrelevant in the face of cosmic horror, a place populated by the Great Old Ones, the Elder Gods and the struggle between good and evil. SF at the edge of fantasy where it was often best.

Cardiff's SF connections have always been strong. We host Trekkie conventions at our hotels. There's a fracture in the fabric of space time that runs through *Torchwood*'s secret base down the Bay and then there's the buried giant saucer. This landed millennia ago resulting in the formation of Penylan Hill. Parts of the saucer's rim now form the edges to Roath Park Lake. The force field from its motors can be felt when standing in the queue at Morrison's. The Actual Museum of Roath (see page 86) has a broken fragment from the saucer's main propulsion unit which they'd be happy to show you if you ask.

My own preferences in all this, however, centred not on SF but on the guitar slung round my neck, the harmonica in a harness in front of my mouth and the single hanging earing I had purloined and was wearing defiantly from my left ear.

Alan took the shots. These were mostly me standing before the Forest of Dean stone coping of his front garden wall, the Mill Park suburbanising the background. After that we went to the folk club on Charles Street, fingers in the ear, "it's not the leaving of Liverpool that grieves me", and boys in caps toting Dylan smiles. I'd left my guitar at home, of course, I could never really play.

Today, decades later, Dylan is still there but making records of Frank Sinatra songs, his voice blown, not that it was ever, as a voice to hold a note, that good. But the Mill Park rolls on. It's lawns restructured and the river that flows through them – the Lleici, the Licky, the Roath Brook, the Nant Fawr, the Nant y Dderwen Deg – given new flood defensible sides. The park has somehow always been central to my life.

The grist mill from which the park's name derives would have stood at right angles to the present stream. Its big wheel turning in the water. Records show a mill on this site going back a thousand years. According to Hobson Matthews' *Cardiff Records* the mill was demolished in 1897. The last miller was George Burfitt in 1894. How something that had been in existence for a millennium could have been swept away without record or marker is beyond me. In the days of its origin when the manor of Roath took in most of Cardiff this was the Molendinum de Raz[6]. It stood where Trafalgar

Road meets Sandringham, near the plaque to the poet Dannie Abse at number 66. The road would have been laid right next to the miller's bedrooms.

Cardiff then was a radically different place. Housing did not reach the Lleici until the end of the nineteenth century. Roath had its parish church, its green, its manor house (now Summers Funeral Home), its farms and a couple of cottages. No pub until the Claude arrived in 1890. There was a centre, clustering near the present roundabout at the bottom of Albany, Marlborough and Waterloo. But it wasn't much. Villages mostly weren't. The bulk of the mill's flour went to the castle. If you get down into the stream's water, or hang precariously on the sloping bank, you can see where the wheel spun, it's housing still visible.

We know the names of some of the millers: Edward Phillips, George Burfitt, Maurice Griffiths, John Evans, William Morgan, James Rowe. A number are buried at St Margaret's Church. In 2012 the Cardiff Archaeological Society carried out some excavations and made a geophysical survey of the site. Teams operating assemblages that looked like lawn aerators with wiring attached prowled the park's greens. Local excitement was high. But the results confirmed only what we already knew. The mill has been demolished and there's not a lot left.

Following its destruction the mill's stone was taken to places unknown. The millpond and much of the nearby land's natural declivity were levelled by filling with refuse using a labour force drawn from the otherwise unemployed.

Recent and, it has to be said, mightily controversial flood prevention work by Natural Resources Wales has seen a complete transformation of these parks. Tree after tree has been felled. Saplings will be planted to replace them, lawns dug and returfed, flood walls installed, new bridges constructed and a cast bronze sculpture of the mill in its heyday created by Rubin Eynon will be sited near the river's bank. Eynon's tasteful model reproductions already successfully adorn Blackfriars and Caerphilly Castle. Soon locals will kick balls again across the refurbished green pastures of Waterloo Gardens and the renewed Mill Park will fill with summer frisbee players, local all-night bench-sitting youths and walkers with dogs. No millers, no Dylan, my H.P. Lovecraft forgotten and Alan emigrated. But the river will still flow.

Lake Myths (revised):

Atomic
Lost gold
Horse and cart buried at centre
Tunnel to the Castle
Big bivalves
Bass
Bream
Bloaters
Cyncoed house drains
Soap
Money
Snakes
Nightclub in Lighthouse basement
Signet Ring Jimi Hendrix
Lady of Lake and silver sword
Floaters

THE EASTERN FLATLANDS

Northmore came here for the shooting. So he insisted. He had a bowie knife, a great six-inch blade thing, which he unsheathed to gasps of admiration. "For skinning," was what he said. We never saw the gun. We're beyond St Mellons out on the flatlands that stretch all the way east from Cardiff to Chepstow and beyond. The Welsh Netherlands, drainage ditched and turf green. We'd been down on one of the bridges which crossed the Cardiff to London main line. Looking at trains, collecting numbers, marvelling at the roaring leviathans which went past engulfed in steam.

For most of us the number collecting thing had little depth, figures ordered in a book. They could have been car registrations or airline logos. Someone we knew collected pub names. Didn't go in, wasn't old enough, but he had a book of Jolly Sailors and White Harts that was a thick as your arm. Northmore was a bit like this although he could discourse on the Star Class, Castle Class, Kings and Halls. He was also good at explaining why the diesels were coming and how, despite the railway's inevitable reduction in usage of coal the miners would still be okay. "They'll just need to dig out less," was what he said.

To add to this Northmore was also a fan of buses, something which hadn't reached us, his otherwise one for all, all for one mates. In his post-school years he would travel the country in order to hang around the car parks of great international venues. He would do this in order to observe the variety of coaches that would arrive from all over Europe. He'd take photographs of these grand buses and write their details down. For now, though, this being the about to start swinging sixties, Northmore confined his number taking obsession to those of vehicles which passed outside the school along Newport Road. Lunch times we'd be inside trying to twist to the honking rock of the Gary Edwards Combo. He'd be out in the drizzle writing *Bristol Royal Blue Long Distance* and *Bedford VAL Single Decker* in his spongy pad.

The trolley buses, or their numbers, which also interested Northmore, didn't run as far as our school at the top of Rumney Hill. Their eastern terminus was at a roundabout in Pengam. For twenty-seven years from 1942 the backbone of public transport in Cardiff had been the almost silent six wheeled double-decker electric bus. If they'd operated up Rumney Hill, Northmore would have been ecstatic.

Public transport in Cardiff had begun in the mid-nineteenth century boom years as the city incessantly expanded. Horse-drawn cabs and carriages were superseded by horse-drawn trams which could carry more passengers. One of the earliest was operated by Solomon Andrews, the gutsy entrepreneur responsible for Cardiff Market and a string of shop and office premises right across the town. Andrews was an aggressive operator, given, on occasion, to driving his horse-drawn buses in the paths of the trams of rivals in order to slow them down.

In 1902, having compulsorily purchased all horse-drawn opposition, Cardiff Corporation launched a city-wide electric tramway network. There were two depots: west of the centre at Clare Road; and east on Newport Road, Roath. Power came from the Corporation's own Roath-based power station which also contributed to the running of the street lighting system. Initially a wonder of the age, trams were soon perceived as being both slow and noisy. They went only where their rails directed them. They blocked other traffic. And when you journeyed on them you got shaken to death. Luckily nothing lasts, by the mid-30s they needed replacing.

Here, by one of those bends of local logic that was second nature to a person like Northmore, the Corporation opted not for a new fleet of go-anywhere diesels but for replacements to be driven by electricity. The decision was not made from any early green sentiment or concern for the environment, but because the generating of the power the new transport fleet would need to operate would help keep Valley miners in work. This was an early and often forgotten act of Cardiff engaging with the concerns of its hinterland. Although perhaps not entirely altruistically. On Valley day, Thursdays, when the shops of the Rhondda closed and Welsh mams would flood to the big city it would be coal money they'd spend.

New electric trams were rejected as being uneconomic and noisy. Electric trolley buses were chosen instead. In the years they ran the Corporation operated seventy-nine[7] of them. Liveried in maroon and large, they were often the only way to get into town. Their power supply came from double overhead wires along which the buses would slide their spring-mounted roof-top booms. At junctions there were great meshes of cable with points, poles, posts and supporting brackets everywhere. Until 1970 when they were withdrawn Cardiff trolleys were omnipresent.

Would we want them back? Some of us might. They could be ponderous but when needed were capable of ripping it up at speed. There's an apocryphal tale of an early hours maintenance fitter at the Roath depot needing milk for his tea and hitting 72 mph, sparks and all, while going to collect some from City Road. The booms never left the overhead wires. Contemporary regulation and the obsessive European need to double protect everything would, no doubt, make reintroduction impossible. Live six hundred direct volt electricity, up there flowing along bare wires and with the rain pouring through? You must be joking.

Today on the flatlands my destination is a barn near where the Environment Agency Wales are well ahead of themselves with their replacement of threatened sections of the sea wall. Down here, literally down too, we are below sea level, building is progressing at an industrial scale. Beyond the huge white wind turbine of the former energy park that now marks the Welsh base of Pinewood Studios are scraped fields in the process of being filled with foundation hardcore. There are trucks and mud and men in hi-vis yellow everywhere. Big boxes by the score will be built. Logistics and warehousing will flourish all the way to Newport.

In a barn that appears to be marooned in the centre of a working stock farm are the workshops for the Cardiff and South Wales Trolleybus Project. Hidden behind a potch-repaired facade of fractured corrugation stand two Cardiff trolleys. A standard side-entrance double decker (no 262) and a doodlebug single decker (no 243). Whereas most of Cardiff's fleet went for scrap, many to Bill Way's metal yard at the top of the East Dock, these two have magically been saved.

The Project is fronted by Keith Walker who shows me round. Our conversation is punctuated by the bleating of sheep and agricultural smells are everywhere. Keith is a retired engineer, as is Bob Heatley, who is repairing the doodlebug driver's door on a makeshift bench. Keith worked for GKN, then as a marine engineer for the British Indian Steam Navigation Company and later at the Royal Ordnance bomb factory in Llanishen. Bob was once a foreman at Ely Paper mill and then a fitter and a driver for Weadon's Travel. In the way that writers never stop, neither do engineers. Retirement is no end to labour. They simply continue milling, machine fixing and getting their hands stained by oil elsewhere. Their Project is small with a hardcore of around half a dozen activists. They work ceaselessly, attempting to bring the time-ravaged buses back to life.

It's a long and slow process. The materials needed can be hard to find. Deals need to be managed with panel beaters, metal casters and suppliers of cable. Everything takes eternity to fix. The Project took delivery of their vehicles in the nineties and despite two decades of repair still have a way to go. Keith tells me the complicated stories behind each vehicles' survival. Of Cardiff's originals only four survive. One is in the National Museum of Wales's store at Nantgarw, one is at the Trolleybus Museum near Doncaster. The other two are here. They were found dumped on distant farms and airfields, rusting to uselessness, falling to pieces, collapsing into the soil. They have been brought here, lovingly, by suspended tow.

Inside the passenger saloon of the single-decker Bob proudly demonstrates the working bell and functioning lights. The seating is ragged but being replaced. I am hugely impressed at the lengths the small team go to simply to get the detail right – to fit the same rubber edging that once existed on the back running boards and the same pattern on the bulkhead metal work. Bob tells me that in any given repair he likes to end up with 70% original and 30% replacement but that can't always be achieved.

On the upper deck of bus 262 which shows No 4 Roath Park on its entirely original destination blind, I stoop. Clearance between floor and ceiling is 5 foot 6 inches, a height I hadn't achieved when I first travelled. In a container in the barn's corner are bus parts. There's a set of trolley wire points, known as a frog. There's a trolleyhead and there's a money collecting box as used for the original Pay As You Enter system operated by the Corporation when the buses first came into service. There are bus stop tops and Corporation signboarding. Keith talks about the great Heath Robinson trolleybus-washing machine which was situated in the Roath depot and how they had their own foundry there making spare parts and bus stop poles.

On the running board of the double-decker is a Bruce Coach Works, Pengam, nameplate. No 262, it turns out, is an entirely Welsh manufactured vehicle. Ah Wales, you have the zippy Gilbern car and now, in addition, you have the double-decker maroon trolley bus.

For the trolley future Bob tells me of a plan they have to set up wires across the barn's roof so their buses will look more realistic. But they won't actually put electricity up there. You'd need an act of parliament to get a real system up and running again, says Keith. When the Cardiff Bay Development Corporation was in its early days and the Industrial and Maritime Museum still stood there was a proposal to build a circuit from the museum right out and along the Barrage. Came to nothing. Same thing happened to the Vale of Glamorgan Council's proposals for a Trolleybus-utilising Transport Experience on number one dock at Barry.

On the Project's promotional DVD which Keith has got running in the heated inside of the single decker Frank Hennessey is talking about the distinctive noise the buses made as they pulled away. It was an unmistakable sound. Check it out, it's here: http://www.soundsnap.com/tags/trolley_bus

GOING HOME

This is Queen Street again. It's 1970 now and I've the longest hair I'll ever have. I'm wearing a t-shirt covered in stars bought mail order "for those who want to be one jump ahead". This is the future, after all. Woodstock has had its four days half a million strong. We've been golden, we've been stardust. We've been the time of man. A music festival to end all music festivals. And now we are glorying in it. Ritchie Havens, CSN, Canned Heat, and The Who all on the Queen Street cinema split screen. And then three huge versions of guitarist Alvin Lee blazing through *I'm Going Home*, his band, Ten Years After, exalting behind him.

The 1969 Woodstock festival was three days of love, peace and music held at Max Yasgur's Catskill Mountain dairy farm in upstate New York. It had been a defining moment for pop music and its consumption. Rock had moved beyond foot tapping to embrace the whole culture. You no longer just listened, now you lived.

Ten Years After, a white blues band from Nottingham with ideas on how to move the form a bit beyond the harmonica twelve-bar promoted by Alexis Korner, had found themselves in the right place at the right time. Michael Wedleigh was filming, Martin Scorsese would edit, and TYA would find themselves thrilling the world. Lee, looking like an exotic Fagin, his hair thrashing the sides of his head, would take the music to new heights. Bass player Leo Lyons would be beside him underpinning the climb. What might have started as a simple blues riff, 'I'm Going Home', in this version at least, took in everything from 'Baby Please Don't Go' to 'Blue Suede Shoes' and 'Whole Lot of Shakin'' to 'Dimples', washing the chorus through 'Baby Let's Play House' complete with Elvis bluesman mumbles. It was the kind the King might have managed himself if the Colonel had only let him.

We might have wanted this Woodstock excitement live in the city and threw our collective arms open in welcome but its living anarchy never came. This wasn't the place, there wasn't the space. We got Pink Floyd inside the Castle walls followed by Andy Fairweather Low, Queen, Hawkwind and Status Quo. Much later we got the flower show in Bute Park, horticultural rather than peace and love. A few of us blew bubbles along that Queen Street rock axis, Gentlefolk sold embroidered denim from their redoubt on High Street, but generally Cardiff's embracing of the great wide musical yonder was not what it could have been.

Ten Years After rode the wave for a few years laying the foundations for a whole generation of blues rockers with maniacal fiery leads and a way with riffs that owed more to Marshall amps than Blind Lemon. They disbanded in 1974, reformed a decade later and then, fracturing and restructuring as they went, rode the nostalgia circuit until Lee died in 2013. Leo Lyons and guitarist Joe Gooch, who'd been with TYA since 2003 formally threw in the towel in 2014. The two formed Hundred Seventy Split (named after the junction of the two main highways in Nashville). HSS – a blues rock power trio with an eye to more than revival.

Despite five decades of rocking and Johnny Cash-style black clothing Leo's eyes still sparkle. He has retired, if you can call what he now does that, to an Edwardian terrace in Penylan. It's been restored to perfection, and, when I visit, looks today much as it might have done when it was first built in 1904. The district was originally part of the great Tredegar Estate which ran from Splott Farm, south of the present railtracks, to the summit of Penylan Hill. On the lower slopes Tredegar's agents developed a middle-class suburb of terraces. 'Middle class' was not a term the early developers would have used. These houses were 'respectable'. Lesser properties were 'artisan'. They named their new streets after Boer War battles, Crimea victories and campaigns engaged in by Lord Tredegar himself. Sir Godfrey Charles Morgan (1831-1913), Baron and Viscount, was one of the six hundred who rode into the Valley of Death with the charging Light Brigade. Check the road names: Balaclava, Harrismith, Alma, Kimberley, Mafeking, Ladysmith, and Westville all have their origins in the Empire military experience. Once obvious Russian and South African locations had been exhausted Tredegar's agents turned to British glory elsewhere: Agincourt, Waterloo, Trafalgar, and Blenheim all get a showing. The build, four up three down plus conservatory, high ceilings, bay windows, Bath stone surrounds, is classic turn of the century. In the mushrooming new city's suburbs the houses were designed to accommodate a class of professionals: managers, teachers, doctors, merchants, bankers, and their families. These were people with a penchant for gramophones, cycles, bamboo furniture, floor tiles, linoleum, telephones, high school education, indoor bathrooms, respectability, etiquette, health, cosy homeliness, picture rails, dadoes, leaded lights in many colours, pleasure gardens, India rubber plants and hanging baskets. They flocked to Penylan.

The norm in the Edwardian times when these houses were built was to rent. Home ownership and death defying mortgages were a phenomenon to come. Renting was respectable. The great Cardiff estate owners – Windsor, Bute and Tredegar – all followed the same pattern of operation. They leased their land in ninety-nine year tranches to local builders for speculative development. Each appointed their own Estate architect to police quality and progress. Bute's man, E.W.M. Corbett, insisted on the provision of window bays and small gardens, even for the most artisan of properties. Tredegar's architect, W. Scott, ensured the homogeneity of most of Penylan. Houses would reflect each other with grace and style. On the way there would be few architectural surprises and there would certainly be no sign of the avant-garde.

Music runs in Leo's blood. By now he owns 23 basses and has Jet Harris' original Vox amp upstairs. One of his uncles, former miner Morgan Kingston, had become an operatic tenor. In 1913 Kingston sang at the White House before President and Mrs Woodrow Wilson. The President liked what he heard enough to present Kingston with a statue of an American eagle holding a Welsh harp in commemoration of the singer's Welsh connection. It was the name Morgan that had done it. A stage name in reality. Kingston had been christened Alfred Webster and had been born in Staffordshire and brought up in Mansfield. Despite those sixteen signatories of Welsh descent on the Declaration of Independence America has always had trouble locating Wales.

Before Cardiff Leo lived largely in Nashville, plying his trade not as a rock bass player but, amazingly, as a country songwriter. He began, as many songwriters do, by hawking a homemade cassette of his wares up and down Music Row. Unlike most, however, he turned out to be good enough to become a staff writer at Hayes Street Music, green card and cowboy boots included. That was in the early nineties when country was still country and the vinyl record was still king. Until recently Leo maintained a house in the city but says the place is not what it was. It has grown toxic and become full of swirling, intersecting roads. Like Cardiff could have been if Centreplan with its motorways on stilts right into the heart of the city had succeeded back in the seventies.

HSS tour a lot but don't play in the UK as often as they might. Down the road, near enough almost to shout and be heard, is the Globe. This heritage and tribute band emporium opened in 2008 on the site of the Penylan (later the Globe) Cinema. HSS haven't gigged there yet nor at the more recently arrived Tramshed, a slightly larger operation on the other side of the city. But given Cardiff's new status as a twenty-first century music city and with venues to match there's every possibility.

Notes

1. Gigspanner are a post-Steeleye Span folk roots trio led by fiddle player Peter Knight.
2. *Walschmenhull*, according to a minister's account of 1392 – as reported in John Hobson Matthew's *Cardiff Records Volume 5* published by Cardiff Records Committee in 1905.
3. Holy wells at which believers could connect with the spirits predated Christianity. When faced with entrenched pagan beliefs the new religion simply took them over, attributing their curative and divination powers to Christ. Bent pins or coins were offered. Votive strips of cloth, usually from the believer's own clothing, were tied to the branches of nearby trees and bushes. If the wish or prayer was for the curing of a disease then as the fragment of cloth disintegrated so the disease would leave the body of the believer. Penylan Well on Penylan Hill (not to be confused with the curative Ffynon Bren at the hill's base) was reported as always choked with bent pins and the bushes near it as full of fragments of cloth. The imprint of Christ's knee was allegedly on its lip. The well existed into the age of photography and a shot can be seen in the *Reports and Transactions of the Cardiff Naturalists Society* from 1903.
4. *City Road*, a three-part mini-series covering the Road's sex shops, gyms and tattoo parlours, broadcast on BBC One during 2016.
5. In 2013 a new body, Natural Resources Wales, was formed by merging the Countryside Council with the Environment Agency and the Forestry Commission.
6. See Diane Brook's excellent and very comprehensive *A Short History of Roath Mill* in *Morgannwg* Volume LVII 2013.
7. Six were single-deckers. Prior to their arrival, and as a stop-gap, Cardiff bought 7 single-deck vehicles from nearby Pontypridd. With their distinctive motor whine and ponderous performance they were nicknamed *doodlebugs*, a name which stuck on their superior successors. They were in use for about 18 months.

NORTH

WALKING IN FROM CAERPHILLY

Moving away from the station with its *Gwlad Gwlad* painted road bridge and a chiropractor with premises built right over the rail tracks I began to marvel. The train operator had for once co-ordinated things with Cardiff Bus and seamlessly got us here in about 40 minutes flat. Door to door. The Cardiff world did not used to be like this. For most of the twentieth century city public transport meant standing for hours at a bleak bus stop in the rain and then getting left there when the bus finally arrived, full. The task of public transportation was getting the buses from A to B. Simultaneously taking passengers and following a timetable were secondary considerations.

In just about every recent research report, demographic study, development plan and economic strategy Caerphilly has come out as a vital component of the urban massif that is the capital. This was Cardiff dormitory. You shopped, drank, dined and worked over the hill, down there, in the whirling metropolis. In your red brick house you slept. Caerphilly was just a name. It was Cardiff really. Except that it wasn't. It had the wrong accent. It was the wrong shape in the wrong place. It had the wrong history. It had the wrong castle. It was not the city.

The mountain, centrepiece of the Caerphilly ridge, made the difference. Despite its modest height, 271 metres max at the trig point, and its non-threatening nature – you did not die of exposure if you got lost here, you did not fall to a bone-crushing finality if you slipped from its crest – this was a real and present barrier. Although actually crossing it was an easy matter. In the long past mule trains loaded with panniers of coal or iron had trekked its paths. More recently drinkers out for a good time in the city and missing the last bus home had found themselves staggering slowly over the mountain's top.

The path to Cardiff goes up the mountain through trees. I'm trying to follow the route of the Rhymney Railway. It's beneath me in its 1870 tunnel. I zig. I zag. The track far below rolls straight as a die. I can hear its trains as they rush. Their sound erupts among the hillside trees from the brick ventilation shafts, bored through the rock to vent steam and smoke. Caerphilly was once a Rhymney Railway stronghold. The company's locomotive and carriage works were here, east of the fractured castle on that land that is now the Caerphilly Business Park but was once, gloriously, The Harold Wilson Industrial Estate. Harold, the politician we all thought was going to save the world, with his Gannex and his eternal pipe. He would have been proud.

According to the council-installed interpretation boards the hillside here was once an employment hotspot. In the past there were clay pits, brick works, coalmines and quarries. Today there are only trees. The ridge itself is brief, slipped across in an instant, only the path's inclination lets you know it's been passed.

Unlike the boundaries between Cardiff and Newport, rival city states and battling ports, the border is also unmarked. There are no signs saying *Welcome to Cardiff* nor *You Are Now Leaving Caerphilly, Land of Cheese*. Instead the path falls anonymously into the city passing the sloping greens of Llanishen Golf Club to skirt the railway's re-emergence from the dark depths of the mountain. You can hear the rail operator rocking but you can't see it. The trains clatter below, covered by a blanket of industrial buddleia and rapacious Himalayan Balsam. Down there, where they are, was once Cefn Onn Halt. First city structure on the route south. For much of the twentieth century trains stopped here by request. You stuck your hand out. But now you can't. The Halt has been abandoned, left to the ghosts of golfers and picnicking families and all those others who now reach the park, if they come at all, by car.

CEFN ONN

From the platform edge John Briggs is photographing the two carriage Pacer unit heading north to Bargoed. His best shot is the one taken just as the train disappears from view into the mile long tunnel. We're standing on the overgrown and now crumbling platform of the former halt. It opened in 1910 and lasted until it was replaced in 1986 by Lisvane and Thornhill Station. That's 500 metres to the south. Road access, car park. Cefn Onn had neither of those.

It's 2003 and we are here on a whim, satisfying our interest in industrial history. The adventure we are actually bound for, as research for *Real Cardiff Two,* is the walking of the Glamorgan Canal from the place where it entered the city to where it discharged into the Severn at the Sea Lock in the Bay. The canal was once the town's lifeblood. Its start and finish are now both hazed by the fog of the past. A field north of Coryton Asda. A spot on Penarth Terrace, west end of Windsor Esplanade. The canal is now gone from both: built over, memory a shimmer, soon to be washed from the air.

As we climb back up through the massed growth and tangled ivy of what remains of the ferro-concrete footbridge to access the fence and the gate into the park John suggests that we should not encourage untrammelled public access to the workings of the railway. "If you trespass on the tracks you can die," he says. "Why not just mention the park?" In the end I write about neither[1]. Just the canal, north to south.

The public park at Cefn Onn and the golf club beyond it were once both served by the steam trains of the Rhymney Railway and it's soon to be master, the Great Western. How else could an urban population hobbled by lack of horse, car, or for the most part even bicycle, get here from their terraced suburbs miles to the south? In the early part of the twentieth century when the sprawl of Cardiff was still relatively limited and districts like Cyncoed, Llanishen and Lisvane were no more than villages, Cefn Onn was deep country. Half a day's walk for a coal trimmer. Refreshment stops sparse. Nothing when you arrived either.

Cefn Onn park, a great tree and pond-filled undulation of mystery and fabrication, is one of the city's best. Exotically blossoming north of the M4 it pushes Cardiff on towards the mountain. It was originally the project of Ernest Prosser. He was General Manager of both the Rhymney and the Taff Vale Railways (TVR). Running railway companies earned Prosser a good income. He invested in land setting himself up as an estate-owning country gentleman. He bought Cwm Farm as well much of what has today become Llanishen Golf Club. He also purchased a large slice of the woods of Wern Fawr or at least that part of it known as The Dingle. Here he damned a tributary of the Nant Fawr to create a pond for use as a swimming pool. He was about to build a great house to go with it when his son, Cecil, contracted TB. A century back this disease was usually fatal. The cure, if such could be obtained, involved fresh air and sunlight. Copious amounts. Prosser constructed what was later to be converted into the park's summerhouse in an attempt to help his son convalesce. Two rooms, balcony, veranda. All to no avail. Tragically Cecil died in 1922.

Prosser lost the will to go on. He retired from the railways, and retreated to a lonely life in a dark house on Fidlas Road. He left the Dingle Estate uncompleted and in the hands of a gardener, Tommy Jenkins. Prosser himself died in 1933 and the estate was eventually put up for sale. Showing speed and perspicacity not normally associated with city fathers Cardiff Corporation dithered for four days max and then purchased the 169 acres for £7500. To make doubly sure they had enough space the Corporation then went on to buy more land to the Dingle's south. The Parks Committee named their resultant estate Parc Cefn Onn. This was 1944 and the war was not quite finished. Cardiff was a bomb-sited wreck and the country was a land of shortages. Plans for post-war rebuild had not yet commenced. The Parc's development as a facility for the leisured future is nothing short of a miracle.

Cardiff Corporation planted the exotic, and the rare, majored on rhododendron and azalea, improved the trails, preserved oak and beech woodland, created a picnic field and added public outbuildings – toilets, cafes, shelters. Over the decades Cardiffians came.

In 2017 I return to find little has changed. Disused Cefn Onn Halt is still there. The aged green diesel units continue to vanish into the mountain's side. The park that surrounds is still lush and mysterious. Grade 2 listed. A Cardiff masterpiece.

From Lisvane and Thornhill Station, unmanned but bustling, I catch the diesel down the overgrown, green tube of track back to

Queen Street. There are no small boys cheering the trains. What's to see? This is all repetitive diesel stock that has been in use for decades. Buses on rails. No goods trucks. No clacking engines. No sign of the coal that once came through by the waggon load. The mountain marks the southern rim of the south Wales coalfield and there were working pits just a few miles north of here. Silent now. The landscape has been homogenised for tourism, sign-boarded, covered with waymarked trails, benches and hard-topped tracks.

Despite the encouragement of TV's *Trainspotting Live* and a push to get young people interested in mail trains and banana yellow track repair units the spotters are gone. Vanished the way of balsa wood aeroplanes and pig's bladder footballs. Instead there are families out for a city fun day along with late-shift call centre operators all joining the rattling bucket down from the Valleys with its load of pushchairs, briefcases and backpacks.

Cardiff is a green city of endless dimension. From its railways it looks so soft and careful. It's safe to live here. That sense stays with me the whole ten minutes of the journey back.

CORYTON GYRATORY

I could tell that the green lung was nearby the moment I got out of the car. I sneezed. My eyes started to itch. I sneezed again. Hayfever. It had taken most of a lifetime to discover that I was susceptible. Years of unhindered rambling across fields and now this. Here I was walking up Northern Avenue suffering and not a field in sight.

'Green lung' was a term a planner had come up with to describe Cardiff's superabundance of open spaces. This was largely parkland originally donated to the city by the great landowners in a fit of munificent benevolence and added to as compulsory components of subsequent developments. Free space for city citizens, all full of invigorating, oxygen-rich air. Up here in the northern reaches the city's great green arc which began at Bute Park had become truncated. It was reduced to a scattering of lesser grassy splashes – Parc Caedelyn, Hailey Park, Parc y Pentre, Moundfield Recreation Gardens. The city lists 137 such spaces, but the grandest was not among them. That lay ahead.

The Coryton roundabout didn't exist when I came up here with Cobbing[2] on our great Welsh tour in 1973. The A470 banged north unhindered by interchange and over bridge. Cobbing wanted to stop at the Lewis Arms in Tongwynlais, Tripp's last outpost of the Cardiff accent, the place where the Welsh one began. But we hadn't the time. Cobbing instead had to put up with my Cardiff imitations, ark ark the lark in Cardiff Arms Park and all that. That plus my stories of how those living in the older western city (Ely) are supposed to sound just that little bit different from those living in the more recently built east (Llanrumney, St Mellons).

Today the roundabout certainly does exist. It's a vast oval mesh of intersecting roads cut through across its centre by the A470 and the M4 in from London and still heading west. For many changing direction here that essential roundabout sensation of driving *round* in a circle is missing. The road lopes as it loops. Its outer edge surrounds a 35 acre grassed and undergrowth-specked expanse that is rarely trimmed and never gardened. No shrub-filled borders. No flower-beds. No champion trees. Officially it is not a park nor a reserve but merely a space. The public are not banned from entering, the gyratory is peppered with walkways, pedestrian access underpasses and foot bridges. The Cardiff Naturalists Society, botanising across here in recent years has identified 287 species of plants and animals. They have suggested that the site be elevated to formal reserve status but as ever there is no one out there listening.

This is the land of Pear Tree Farm. Its barns and farmhouses have been upgraded and extended to become a Welsh Government Highway Depot, a storage for traffic cones and road salt. Through a security fence I can see great heaps of this winter essential stacked waiting for the next freeze.

Next door is Welsh Water's Pear Tree Depot, filled with valves and trunk mains. "What exactly do you do here?" I ask two guys in hi-vis vests unloading equipment from a van. "Don't know," replies one in a strong Polish-accent, "we work on telecoms." He points towards the collection of O2 and 3 phone masts sprouting among the trees. Beyond I can see container lorries at speed, their roar muffled by the all-engulfing green.

Both SABRE – The Society For All British and Irish Road Enthusiasts and the Roundabouts of Great Britain Appreciation Society enthuse about this place. Well, they would. It's more gentle than Spaghetti Junction, easier to navigate than that whirligig monstrosity in Swindon, and nicer to look at than the duck pond roundabout in Otford, Kent. It's the biggest in Wales and there's little to beat it in England either. They should sell postcards. Maybe they soon will.

Walking through it there's a sense of otherness little experienced elsewhere in this city. The paths are largely deserted, constantly buffeted by fenced or concrete-walled road, complexly interminable, sliding the visitor unknowingly from district to district without stop. Morganstown, Rhiwbina, Radyr, Whitchurch, Coryton and Tongwynlais all meet here. Where the boundary lines are, where that spot is where you can stand and be in all six posh north Cardiff suburbs simultaneously is anyone's guess.

Just to the south, (I would have walked through its grounds had the chain-link not prevented me), stands late Victorian Coryton House. This was originally the residence of shipping magnate and great grand Cardiffian J. Herbert Cory[3] (1857-1933). The house was built in 1900 replete with majestic gardens and went on to give its name to the whole district. Cory's original plan was to develop the area as a garden village in the style of the one at Rhiwbina but the outbreak of the Great War put paid to that. After his death Cory's house languished. It was used by Civil Defence until 1952 when the GPO took it over and made it their Welsh HQ. When the GPO was divided into the Post Office and BT both concerns sold off their land. The BT portion of the grounds ended up in the hands of Belway Homes who have developed a compact complex of new town houses in what is now known as Whitworth Square. Coryton House itself was sold to Orbis Education who extended and rebranded the property as Tŷ Coryton. This inelegant mix of Welsh and Anglo-Saxon where both t and ton mean the same thing could be unkindly translated as Cory House House. The complex is now home to a residential school for autistic pupils.

I'm on Pendwyallt Road now, reached through a Coryton Gyratory underpass. This area once held great cold war significance. Hard to believe now that all that's history. The Cardiff War Room, one of thirteen regional command and control centres created by a frightened UK government in 1952 was near here. In the early sixties I'd bought the CND pamphlet, hastily cyclostyled, which identified the UK's hidden places of future war. Top Secret, it said on the front. Given the Cardiff War Rooms' location on the edge of a built up area I doubt that. Not shouted about might have been nearer the mark.

The Rooms were located sunk into the ground at the rear of the Wales and the Marches Telecom Board HQ. They remained operational until 1958 when they were replaced by a Regional Seat of Government located at Brecon. My CND pamphlet didn't mention that.

I turn off from Pendwyallt and onto Pantmawr Road to check if anything is left but absolutely nothing is. The Rooms were located on ground between present day Springhurst Close and Gerddi Ty Celyn. Redeveloped as upmarket housing, the dormitories, teleprinters, maps and signals equipment trashed.

Behind me the Gyratory hums. I walk south, back, now that ROF Llanishen has been built on and the submarine Z-berths in the Bay abandoned, to our nuclear-free city.

Coryton Roundabout Species Listing

yellow parsnip
bee orchid
nipplewort
bird cherry
field horsetail
twayblade
mcNuggets value pack
agrimony
dryad's saddle
larch bolete
cinnabar moth
six spot burnet
plume moth
green shield bug
long-winged conehead cricket
syrphid hover fly
halford's essential 13" wheel trim
funnel web spider
cynipid wasp

ROALD DAHL'S CARDIFF NORTH LEY

I catch the train at Cardiff Central. This is the City Line which began in the city's north east and now, after looping in a great U through the city's heart is about to head north again. I'm in the two-car Sprinter and I'm standing. Every single seat is occupied by pupils from Bishop of Llandaff High School. Kids, bags, blazers, headphones, chewing.

The windows stream as the train steams. Around us is railway land, an industrial cityscape full of rail sheds, engine bays, carriage washeries, repair shops and assembled new track in stacks like a giant train set. This south west of the city on view from the tracks is the capital with its guard down. Backs of mosques, tottering streets, unkempt gardens, the yards of Brains brewery, warehouses stacked with building materials, and even more open and right now empty rail beds. It reminds me of London, how the land looks as you reach Paddington or Waterloo.

But it doesn't last. After the carriages have disgorged a hundred uniformed school kids at Fairwater, the cuttings emerge, wooded banks and scrub masking the housing above. It's leafy suburbia giving an impression of empty countryside. A green west Cardiff, a place that doesn't change.

It's freezing. This is January. The train has reached Radyr where it will rest a while before returning the way it came. I'm off, up the footbridge steps, plastered thickly with Network Rail road salt. No one but no one will slip and sue here. In a previous, smaller, steam-filled incarnation, the Radyr train would have served Roald Dahl's father, Harald, who did a daily commute in to what was then called Bute Road Station. His ghost is there on the platform now, eye glasses, three-piece suit, white starched collar. He looks like a disapproving headmaster. His railway season ticket was found inside his expensive leather wallet when he died in 1920. That was on April the 11th. The ticket was valid until the 23rd.

Like most in Cardiff at this time Harald's business was coal. With his partner Ludvig Aadnesen he had established a business as a colliery agent and provider of all that ships docking in the world's leading coal port would need. Provisions, ropes, oil for their lamps, food. The profits flowed.

In 1917 Harald had bought Tŷ Mynydd (Mountain House), set on rising ground a mile north of the Radyr rail station. As befits the successful businessman Harald was, here was life on a grand scale. 150 acres of land, outbuildings, cottages, a piggery, lawns, formal flower borders, terraces, its own electricity generator and an enormous Victorian house.

In photographs it looks like part of Hogwarts. It had multiple chimney stacks, mock Tudor gables, a tiled roof larger than most churches' and greenhouses to the side to rival those of Dyffryn

House, to the west of Cardiff. This is the place Roald, the great author, remembers with nostalgia, recalling the fields full of shire horses and dairy cows. There are photographs of him as a four-year-old out on the lawns and terraces, in the fields among the sheaves of corn, sitting on the wall of the piggery and of the house itself, which is resplendently decorated with both the Union Jack and the Norwegian Flag. No Welsh dragon in sight.

Like Cefn Onn, Tŷ Mynydd also had railway connections. The house had been built in 1883 by George Fisher, Director of the Taff Vale Railway. When he died in 1891 the property passed to his son, H. Oakden Fisher, Chair of both the TVR and the Cardiff Gaslight and Coke Company Ltd, although his real interest lay with the military. He was Lieutenant Colonel of the Glamorgan Volunteer Artillery. Harald bought the estate in 1918. When he died in 1920, his second wife, Sofie Magdalene, moved to smaller premises back in Llandaff. Tŷ Mynydd then became the property of the architect Sir Beddoe Rees, MP and for a brief time in the 1930s was turned into St Maur's College, a small private boarding school for girls.

In 1967 the house and most if its outbuildings were demolished. This was the first full-blooded rush at clearance following the war. Cardiff was expanding. Property developers had no interest in the preservation of inefficient, draughty piles such as Tŷ Mynydd. On its lands a whole housing estate could be build. It had to come down.

I take the road up out of the station's gully. Already the old shunting yards and waste ground lining the river have been populated with high density brick town housing. There's little public space. Most structures are distinct from each other, laid at angles as if thrown there like dice. Room for breath is restricted and corners are rounded. Access is on turning roads named after De Clare, Norman Lord of the City, Aradur Hen, an ancient local croft that gave us the name *Radyr*, and Goetre Fawr, the farm that once worked these lands. Behind the aptly named Junction Terrace is a field replete with three grazing llamas, tall-necked beasts which, despite the ll of their name, are about as common in Wales as kangaroos. Food To Go which has signs offering coffee and warmth is closed. I head up along rising Heol Isaf in the direction of the Village of Fire.

In 1841 the ten cottages of Pentre Poeth (Warm Village) were all that existed of what is now Morganstown, upper Radyr – that part of Cardiff north of the M4's périphérique grip. This is where the workforce of the developing fire-filled ironworks at Pentyrch lived, an element of Cardiff's lost industrial heritage. Heol Isaf was and still is the main road to Tŷ Mynydd. It's no distance to cover. In my ears I've got Emmylou playing through the buds. 1970s country, when what she sang was the edge. Alabama down home. Dahl wouldn't have stood for this. He preferred Beethoven.

The Tŷ Mynydd estate has been built on; the fields are gone. The line of the original entrance path running up from Tŷ Mynydd Lodge has been preserved in the rising bends of Maes Yr Awel. The detached late-sixties houses along it turn eventually to a U-shaped cluster of apartment blocks. Cwrt Tŷ Mynydd is the appropriately named first; after that the developer gave up and resorted to names with a strong English resonance – Norfolk Court, York Court, Windsor. It's a marketing thing. Here, near the eastern edge of Wales, where the language thins, the Anglo norm dominates.

Beyond the apartment courts, circled like a residential wagon train, there's a copse, ancient pine trees, all that remains of what once was here. For the Dahls of the nineteen teens this would all now be virtually unrecognisable. A local walking his young daughter to the primary school at the former estate's southern end tells me, yes, he knows about Dahl and the great house. He points me back towards the still extant Tŷ Mynydd Lodge which faces Heol Isaf. And there it is, the gatehouse preserved, doing time now as an up-market B&B. The Llandaff Society have installed a celebratory plaque above the front door. Over the years since Roald would have known it the building has been much extended. But there's enough original left for the Dahlian spirit to soar. I can see him outside, short pants, laced leather shoes, hat, overcoat with enormous buttons. Mama holding his hand.

Back at Radyr Station, Food To Go is still closed. Clearly, they don't do mornings here. I decide to hike it back along the bone of this Dahl route I've found. With the llamas once more on Junction Terrace I find the entrance to Radyr Woods which I last visited a decade ago when I was researching the first *Real Cardiff* book. What I was interested in then – the Radyr Burnt Mound, a scheduled ancient monument known locally as the Junction Terrace Cooking Mound – remained elusive. I couldn't find it anywhere, although I did not let this failure prevent me from writing up the whole experience. That's part of a psychogeographer's life, hunting for the lost, the invisible, the once was, the unfound. Staring at void space, the absences above playing fields, the gaps between trees, the undulating lie of vacant land. Not there today but used to be. Shimmering in empty air.

Today I find the Radyr Mound by simply walking up to it. It is a grass-covered two-meter-high dump of once heated rocks and animal bones. This was our ancestors' version of Macdonalds. It is described on the woodland interpretation board as an Iron Age hearth. I photograph it with my phone but it comes out looking like nothing more than a pile of grass and earth.

The paths are empty and even in the leafless winter foggy dark. They run across a duckboarded wetland of pond and drainage ditch before rising steeply up Beechwood Bank. There they follow the ridge first below Radyr Comprehensive School and then below the splendours of the Danescourt Estate. These woods and their paths are old. Roald could well have walked through them. Could this be the Forest of Sin where the Whangdoodles, Hornswogglers, Snozzwanglers and Vermicious Knids hang out? If it is, then they are uncharacteristically quiet today.

Woodland doesn't normally lend itself to the kind of poetry I engage in but with Dahl's narrative lines clouding my creativity today I decide to glory in the contingent prompts of the postmodern. As the sound poets taught me, anything can be poetry, it's merely a matter of application. I attempt to read the letter shapes discerned in the path below my feet. I use them to launch phonemes from which I can build poetic structures. This all might sound esoteric but it does have a solid basis. The concretist Paula Claire showed me how when in the nineteen-nineties she sliced leeks into fragments across the floor of the Oriel Gallery and then performed them in a sort of verbi-vocal tea leaf-reading exercise. Concrete poetry as future diviner, leaves that speak, the sounds of the other world.

The letters come up like a chant by that greatest of verse innovators, the American poet Jackson Mac Low. *Kness the real. Tell whole hing lankness an't. Contradictions cover. Re pen remember were. Yu ions range.* I'd driven Mac Low near here once, in the early seventies. Llantrisant Road, not too distant. But we hadn't stopped. We'd gone for an interview at the BBC. 'Poet visits Cardiff' was their line. The interview had made it sound as if they never did. After this, Mac Low had fancied seeing a bit of the Welsh countryside before returning to the grubby room above a pub in Cardiff Central's Frederick Street where we were running the No Walls readings. Poetry mostly soothes, but with its angular stops, elisions and restarts, never Jackson's.

Mac Low employed systematic chance operations as the core of his working method. Like John Cage, he was a twentieth-century giant in this form of poetic and musical practice. Where others would fail from the sheer boredom of the process, its testing duration, its multiplicity of arbitrary conjunctions, Mac Low ploughed on. His output was prodigious. The results were often grey and foggy, but just as often sublime.

By contrast, Roald Dahl waited for the lightbulb moment. His process relied entirely on using his life experience as a jumping-off point and then allowing plot lines to flow from that. When he had an idea he wrote it down before it vanished and then, if he decided to run with it, took at least a year to push it into shape. Stop writing only when it's going well, always leave somewhere to move on to, never return to face a blank page, that's the worst thing in the world. Keep going. Write every day. With Dixon Ticonderoga pencils, a tray on your lap and corrugated cardboard over your knees.

As the path rides up and on, Danescourt begins to intrude from the far side of the restraining fence. There is graffiti much of the way and then a crop of lost cat notices. Bimbo, white and black wearing a collar, nervous, went missing from Blethin Close. Phone 07970 264672. No indication of when. Could the cat still be stuck up a woodland tree? I look but there's nothing.

The alien-sounding portmanteau name Danescourt derives from the two great houses that once stood in the fields on which the present 1970s Wimpy housing estate was built. The powerful Radyr Court and the lesser Danesbrook House. Memory of the Court continues in the Radyr Court pub, a Victorian structure built on top of the remains of an earlier great house of the same name that was destroyed by fire at the start of the nineteenth century. Its foundations are still there, below. Dungeons, runs the local legend, but I doubt that. Of Danesbrook House no one is quite sure. Lost Radyr Isha and Radyr Ucha, both manorial seats, are celebrated in the local histories. The Danes, who locals believe never actually reached here, are not.

Sils ap Siôn, amateur bard, feckless drunkard, a fool carousing from fair to fair, once lived in this place. In the sixteenth century he spent time at Radyr Ucha, now subsumed by the houses of Heol Aradur. His fame was for beating the professional bards at their own game and doing so while pissed. Iolo Morganwg celebrated him. He was a soldier, merchant, wanderer, farmer, leader of a wild life. It's good to see that here in Radyr that tradition rolls on.

Making it up from the wood through the winding post-Radburn Danescourt is like entering a maze. The housing stock is uniform brick, still new enough to lack pollution stains and multiple owner-applied alterations and amendments. No assorted front doors and mixed replacement windows, colourful extensions and sagging gates yet. I check a wheelie bin to work out just where I am. I climb through De Braose onto Timothy Rees Close and then out onto Danescourt Way. William de Braose, one time Lord of these lands. Timothy Rees untraced, but patron of a cul-de-sac in what is, according to the 2011 census, one of the least deprived areas of Wales. Parked with Clios and Fiestas. Statistics tell you what you want to hear.

The geographic centre of the Danescourt reaches of Radyr remains the medieval parish church of John the Baptist. It has a thirteenth-century chancel arch and aged corbels that once held a rood screen. It stands in what was once the heart of a Norman buffer zone holding back the Welsh to the north, much as the M4 now does, keeping Morganstown distant and distinct from the real Radyr. I'm here because this is where Harald is, dead of a broken heart. In February 1920 his eldest daughter, Astri, died suddenly of a burst appendix. Infection, peritonitis. Harald never got over it. He, too, died in 1920. They are here together in the graveyard of St John's.

Up against the burial ground's western wall, mock Tudor houses beyond, watching the pub and its business due east, is a Celtic stone cross, unexpected and dominant. It was erected by Sofie Magdalene – an act that offered, perhaps, a public demonstration of her commitment to Wales, land of Roald's birth and Harald's death. Its base is dressed with creeper and bramble. I pull the leaves back to reveal the inscription. 'Harald Dahl who died at Tŷ Mynydd. 1920. Aged 56. And his daughter Astri aged 7'. Round the side the carved letters continue: 'and His Wife Sofie Magdalene who died 1967. Aged 82 years'. Her ashes were scattered here. With her unbending Norwegian solidity she outlasted her undemonstrative husband by at least another life.

My Dahl trail turns back to pour down the lane leading to ancient Radyr Court Road. This highway predates the Danescourt infill to run alongside the Taff most of the way south to Llandaff. The path tracks the river, the now clean Taff, which would have been fogged with coal dust from the up-valley pit washeries in Roald's day. I pass the rear of the soon-to-move BBC, skirt the rowing club, and descend towards the weir. It's here that the Taffside track becomes Ffordd y Meirw, the road of the dead. Coffins were carried along this route from outlying Whitchurch to the cathedral burial grounds. There are goal posts visible through the trees, set up on the disputed meadow by Cardiff Metropolitan University who insist this land belongs to them. Locals disagree. This is an ancient free green space, common land used for centuries by Llandaffians walking their dogs, maypole dancing and celebrating both the arrival and the passing of Christ with religious and alcoholic zeal. When I pass there are Public Notices attached to the gateposts offering public discussion of the field's future, but I fear the whole thing is now lost.

I hit the southern edge of the cathedral and negotiate the fast and strenuous rise up the Dean's Steps to emerge at the top end of Llandaff Green where the original Cathedral School buildings were. The new ones lie south of the cathedral, embracing the wrecked Bishop's Palace with their educational arms. Roald attended between 1923 and 1925. His biographer Donald Sturrock says the school on the Green was "an elegant three-storey Georgian building

…. an educational institution with a pedigree that dates back to the ninth century", which might stretch its lineage slightly, but whatever, it's now gone. It was demolished in 1958 to be replaced by unobtrusive private residential accommodation. This has splendid views of both the Llandaff preaching cross where Archbishop Baldwin and Giraldus Cambrensis both recruited for the Third Crusade, and the hatted statue of moderniser and benefactor, James Rice Buckley, Archdeacon of Llandaff, 1913-1924.

I stand, staring into empty air again, looking for motes of power which might recall Dahl. There are more here than where I've been so far, for sure. On the corner of Llandaff High Street and Chapel Street is a recently refurbished sleeps-17 holiday let marketed as Roald Dahl's Sweetshop. Until recently this was the Great Wall Chinese Take Away. I have memories of queuing here for egg foo yung after some dull poetry reading held in a nearby pub. Rain outside, windows streaming. According to the Llandaff Society's blue plaque this was originally the place where Dahl carried out the daring mouse plot as celebrated in the somewhat imaginative *Boy*. On Roald Dahl Day, the author's birthday, the Llandaff Society would fill the take-away's window with pictures of sweets from the twenties: Fruit Gums, Peppermint, boiled sweets in screws of paper, Rowntree's Motoring Chocolates, Aero Chocolate Bars, Dairy Box Selections. The present owners say they want to keep up the Dahl connection. Will this mean more sweets? We shall see.

The ley is roaring. Around the corner on Cardiff Road is no 47, the onetime home of Ludvig Aadnesen, Harald Dahl's business partner. His building is long gone, replaced by a sixties stone veneered concrete monstrosity housing Barclays Bank, the Cathedral School shop and Darlows Estate Agents. No one there has heard of Aadnesen, but Roald, yes.

Crossing the main road I turn from the true path south to walk along Fairwater Road. This heads away from Llandaff towards Cardiff West. The main attraction out here is Villa Marie, the birthplace. This is a spot that should burn a hole in the Dahl continuum. If this was America, then by now we'd have paid money to get in, marvelled at the Dahl exhibits, engaged with the multi-media display, watched the films, and would be eating Dahl burgers in the extensive gift shop. As it is, Villa Marie has been renamed Tŷ Gwyn (White House) and is up for sale for a price approaching a million and a half. Viewing strictly by appointment.

Don't knock, ring up. Its eaves slope groundward in arts and crafts style, simultaneously grand and demure. For the Dahl centenary in 2016 a plaque has been installed. Roald marked, at last, at the place of his birth.

Is there more? There is. Inside the walls of Howell's School, as it turns out. I'll visit there next.

HOWELL'S – INSIDE THE WALLS

In the fabric of the city some names repeat. Howells Solicitors. Howells, Photographers. Howell's Removals. Nigel Howells, Councillor. Clive Howells, who sold me my first car. Thomas Howell Liveryman of the Draper's Company. James Howell, the man who started a department store empire on St Mary Street and built both James Howell House with megalithic folly on West Grove and the Mansion House a few yards further along. They sound like the same family, textile merchants, men of clothes, of trade, a Cardiff dynasty, but they're not. James Howell, who ran the shop, came from West Wales. Thomas Howell who was responsible for the school behind the wall on the dark road north to Llandaff came from Bristol.

Thomas Howell was a Tudor merchant. He had only a distant connection with Wales and hardly any at all with Cardiff. He never came here. He spent his time exporting English cloth from London to Spain and to Portugal. His business went so well that in 1528 he moved to Seville. In 1537 he died and his will, written in Castilian Spanish, left 12,000 ducats to pay for the provision of four dowries annually for destitute orphan maidens. He was a Christian, as most men were in the sixteenth century, and doing this charity was a Christian thing. For three hundred years suitable recipients, when they could be found, were helped to the tune of £21 a time. By the nineteenth century interest on Howell's endowment of ducats had generated significant capital. New ways of spending it were sought. And being the Victorian age of culture and morality it was decided that education rather than marriage might be a better way of fending off destitution.

Could schools be built? They could. The Trustees decided that there would be two. One in Denbigh and the other in Cardiff. Both would open their doors to deserving female orphan boarders. To be an orphan in the nineteenth century you only needed one of your parents to have died. There would be thirty scholars chosen by application. Their needs would all be provided for. They would be joined by a second thirty all of whom would have free tuition but have to pay for board and lodging and their indoor clothes.

Howell's Boarding School for the Education and Advancement of Deserving Maidens was built off the turnpike, the road to Cardiff, just south of Llandaff Cathedral. It might not have been quite what Thomas Howell had originally intended but it fairly glowed with goodness. It opened in 1860.

At this time Llandaff was an insanitary village with streets where the past still clung. It had not yet been incorporated into booming, working class, Johnny come lately Cardiff. But things were changing fast. Merchants and the well-to-do were arriving. Transport was good. God was on hand.

I'd taken little notice down the decades, passing the forbidding Howell's School entrance, always on my way somewhere else. Behind the gates stood buildings that might have reminded me of Oxford, if I'd bothered to look. After years of unknowing I decide to request an exploratory tour.

The school could not have been more helpful. They allocated me time, presented me with a copy of their lavishly illustrated and finely written history[4] and got the school archivist, Janet Sully, to take me round. A school with its own museum and in-post archivist is clearly one that operates outside the arms of the state. This is an independent school. It is not a private one as Janet is at pains to point out. Profits are not taken, they go back in. You can get a bursary to come here but most children pay. A year's fees can cost as much as a car.

Howell's sits well in twenty-first century. No one boards here anymore and there are boys in the sixth form. The campus is large and labyrinthine. Centrepiece is the original 1860 building designed by architect Decimus Burton and subsequently amended by the Draper's Company's surveyor, Herbert Williams. This edifice in light grey stone complete with domestic Gothic clock tower is described impishly by Janet as "a mixture of medieval ecclesiastical, Tudor, Gothic, Rhineland castle and French chateau". This should make it a Disney disaster but instead the place has an air of grace and studious age.

High on the walls are the coats of arms of the Drapers' Company (who managed the endowment) and of Thomas Howell himself with his name mis-carved as 'Rowell' by a sloppy stonemason. This original building has been adapted, extended and restructured many times. Stable blocks have become classrooms, walkways have been covered, doors have been blocked and windows added. Additional buildings, contemporary and original, spread out across the green and air-filled site.

By contemporary standards the grounds may be large but they were once much more extensive. In 1896 portions of the seven fields on which Howell's sits were sold off for development. More than half of the estate went to speculative build on Llandaff (now Cardiff) Road, Palace Road and Howell's Crescent.

But twentieth century Howell's fought back. Nearby Victorian houses – Oaklands, Hazelwood, Cumberland Lodge, Bryntaf – have been purchased and converted into accommodation for the school. The pastel shaded S-shaped new build block of the Junior School, known as Tŷ Hapus, stands between them. Structure is perfect. There are no broken parts, no graffiti, no bust-up equipment. Not here.

The Nursery Department occupies Cumberland Lodge. The house actually sits on Cardiff Road, in sight of Llandaff's Cathedral School, with front bedroom windows that gaze out at the expanse of Llandaff Fields. It was here in 1920 that author Roald Dahl's mother, the newly widowed Sofie Magdalene, moved with her six-strong family. Cumberland Lodge was smaller than the Dahls' previous house at Tŷ Mynydd but it was still vast. Long corridors, great drawing rooms, a soaring hall lit by a magnificent stained glass window, multiple bedrooms and a tennis court. Roald lived here until 1927 when he was 11 and his mother sold up to move to Oakwood in Bexley, Kent.

From outside the school, there's nothing to tell you this building was once Dahl space. It stands dark and half hidden by perimeter walls. Three stories of red brick intact, decorative bargeboards and gables, and, despite the extensions, largely unspoiled. It turns out also to be resolutely Dahl. It is surrounded by the nursery playground, animal fences, play huts, climbing frames, slides, model giraffes, and child-friendly fencing. There's a blue plaque put up by the school which celebrates the fact that Roald lived here. There's also an outdoor display panel showing his letters sent back home to his mother, signed "BOY" in a scrawly hand. "Please could you send me some conkers as quick as you can?"

Inside, I narrowly avoid getting sucked into the Nursery School's St David's Day eisteddfod, an exercise that would have been alien to the author and poet who once lived here. Dozens of three and four year-olds dressed in Lady Llanover-created Welsh costume, miniature stovepipe hats, tartan skirts, shawls, most of them with daffs fixed about their tiny persons, are gathered in what would have been the Dahls' drawing room. They sing and recite and dance.

The walls carry Dahl quotations. "If you have good thoughts they will shine out of your face and you will always look lovely." "And above all, watch with glittering eyes the whole world around you because the greatest secrets are always hidden in the most unlikely places." There are exhibition panels showing Quentin Blake's Dahl illustrations and further Dahl boyhood letters, a school report, and a photo of Roald and Mama in the grounds of Cumberland Lodge.

We leave through a painted iron gate bearing the silhouette likenesses of the six great previous Howell's School heads. Much is made here of those who were once in command. Schoolhouses are named after them. Baldwin, Lewis, Kendall, Trotter. The photographs of these stern ladies and their potted histories adorn the walls.

Janet tells me the story of one of the lesser heads, Edith Knight, who ruled from 1937 until the bombing of Llandaff Cathedral gave her a nervous breakdown in 1941. She was replaced by Margaret Lewis, the sternest-looking of all the nine heads and one of the longest serving. She steered the Howell's ship for thirty-six years, dictating its uncompromising flavour and its unfashionable style. She might have begun as a dynamic and energetic leader but things did not last. "While the world outside moved on, she did not" Janet says.

We've walked in past a life size replica Chinese warrior from the Terracotta Army and a Harry Holland painting of a (clothed) woman assembling a corrugated cardboard mannequin. These are both art works which the regressive Margaret Lewis would have undoubtedly had removed immediately from display. Her rules were what gave the school its ferocious reputation as throwback from the Victorian disciplinarian age. No ponytails. No hair dye. No eating of antisocial oranges. No aeroplane stories at table. No talking in the corridors. No speaking to members of the opposite sex. There were so many rules that it was impossible for girls not to break some. Misery often prevailed.

I'm shown the progress of the great fire of 1932 which devastated many of the buildings. We track the corridors, enter the light filled Stone Hall, then the Great Hall with its painted scenes from Shakespeare. Beyond are rooms where great flurries of present day pupils mill. They sell cakes and sweets to raise money for climate change. The school is promoting bio-diversity and building a bee hotel.

The school governors' board room doubles as the school museum. Here among the documents, ancient plate, inkwells and framed photographs of the faded, scratchy past are a series of dummies. They wear school uniform, as it was, as it now is. During the legendary Miss Lewis' era above the knee hemlines dropped to two inches below. This co-incided with the arrival of the mini skirt in the world outside. "I think she did it deliberately," Janet tells me. "Queen Victoria had no legs," Miss Lewis is reported as saying at the time. "So we at Howell's will have no knees."

In a glass case sits a huge three-volume Bible, which had belonged to Howell's first headmistress. "Re-acquired," says Janet. An earlier clean sweep head had decimated the original library by banishing the past and selling off many of the school's treasures. So much went, as I well know. Back home is my complete set of John Hobson Matthew's turn of the century, limited edition set of *Cardiff Records,* bought at great expense from a local book dealer. These red, leather-bound repositories of the city's history formerly graced the shelves at Howell's.

Up north the Denbigh Howell's, architecturally a semi-replica, is now no more. Following a period of poor management and falling numbers the operation closed in 2013. Questions were asked and cases for wrongful dismissal brought. No such disapprobation attaches itself to the Cardiff operation. Here propriety reigns and reputation is solidly secure.

Famous former pupils: singers Charlotte Church and Jem, Julie Morgan MP, broadcasters Lucy Owen and Claire Summers, SF writer Jo Walton. Up north: Nerys Hughes. Before I leave I check the walls of the dining room where school photos hang, spread out by the decade. The earliest shows thirty orphans from 1860 and the most recent, a strip longer than your arm, depicts more than eight hundred. They are serried and uniformed with horse chestnut trees and an edge of grey stone behind them. I peer closely looking for faces I recognise. Don't find one.

THE SLOW EROSION OF JOHN TRIPP'S WHITCHURCH

Heol Penyfai is a real threshold. Appropriate for the residence of a poet. It's geographically Whitchurch but it could just as well be Mynachdy, Birchgrove or even The Philog. The main road to Merthyr gets briefly called that before returning to its original name opposite the dry cleaners. Heol Penyfai is where the borders are fluid and tropes are born. It's all mid-1930s bungalow, flower-filled gardens, well-trimmed shrubs. The place has a faded retiree charm.

I'm with Ifor Thomas. We are looking for traces of the poet who lived here most of his life making himself famous in the annals of Cardiff's outrage-filled literary world in the process. John Tripp (1927-1986) might have been born in Bargoed[5] but he spent most of his life in a Cardiff suburb. He lived in a bungalow with his father, Paul, retired blacksmith and royalist. John was a determined Welsh Nat. Paul Tripp had made the iron gates for the entire road and renamed the bungalow *Pendarves* after his home in Cornwall. Outside in the wet concrete an eight-year old JT had placed his feet. The prints were still visible when Nigel Jenkins went there researching his book on John Tripp for the University of Wales Press[6] in 1988. But like the house name plate and most of street's ironwork time has now seen them off.

It's not been long. 1988. Poetry slams raging across literary Cardiff. Pubs stay open all day. Michael Jackson plays the Arms Park. Paul Gascoigne signs for Tottenham Hotspur, the world's first £2m footballer. Piper Alpha burns. Thatcher rolls on. The current owner of the bungalow is Bruno Moreni, who is having an extension built. He's been here since 1999 and can't recall ever having seen footprints. Is he a Tripp reader? He shakes his head. We walk over to Ararat Baptist built on a mound on the corner of Whitchurch Common. When JT died supporters paid for a memorial bench to stand outside. Why here no one knows, JT never attended. But anyway it's gone. The woman running the playgroup says she's never seen it. "Come inside if you like," she suggests pointing to a riotous interior, "all our toys have just had new batteries installed."

Crossing the Common, where the Americans camped during World War Two, Ifor and I discuss the fate of performance poetry, what we do, or did. He's hung up his performance boots, nothing left to prove. Did he ever perform in Whitchurch? "I read at the church once." That would be St Mary's, the 1883 Eglwys Newydd[7] on the corner of Church Road. The white church it replaced, old St Mary's, is memorialised in a gardens half way down snaking Old Church Road. "It was at the funeral of Lester Lewis. I read Lowell, that one about suicide and all our fists clutching a locked razor[8]."

We pass the pubs JT drank in and then got thrown out of, more in number than a twenty-first century Cardiff suburb should these days be able to support. The Three Elms, the Maltsters Arms, the

Royal Oak, the Plough, the Fox and Hounds round the corner and then the Maltsters again.

Heading up Penlline Road, still Whitchurch, and the sun beating, we pass the British Legion Club where through drunkenness a friend of mine once got himself banned from his own wedding reception and I had my long fought for membership card withdrawn. JT was there, far worse for wear than the groom, but somehow survived. The Tripp traces even in memory become fainter by the day. The annual John Tripp Award For Spoken Poetry, won spectacularly one year by Ifor, seems to have been abandoned. The last show as far as I can track was in 2011.

Ifor was famous for introducing the petrol-driven chain saw into poetry performances. He had a poem that included a riff on Stéphane Mallarmé's "The flesh, alas, is sad, and I have read all the books". To demonstrate this actuality Ifor would chainsaw into two a stack of hardbacks, paper and book-dust flying. The books were supplied by Alan Beynon from his shop, Pontcanna Old Books. The fragile and aged hardbacks, a world's literary endeavour, were actually damaged stock from which prints and maps had already been removed. Half books jumped through the air. Covers flew. Ifor would put on this performance at schools, roaring to circles of cross-legged pupils, chain saw waving like a sword. Health and safety had not yet arrived. You could do those things then.

The red-brick library, which is about as far from John Tripp's bungalow as you can possibly go and still be in Whitchurch, looks a little bit like a bungalow itself. Inside they appear puzzled when we ask about the John Tripp plaque but then recall that it's there, on the wall directly opposite reception. Paid for by the Rhys Davies Trust and the Welsh Writers Trust the plaque was unveiled by JT's surviving partner, Jean Henderson, in 2006. Any JT on your shelves? Yes. A single copy of *Passing Through*, last borrowed in 2012.

How much of JT is left in the landscape? Precious little. Time washes, what else would it do?

THE GREAT HEATH

At the gallows fields there's no green. Not a bush nor tree. Death and distress for centuries and now car pollution and traffic lights at a place where five roads meet. This is Death Junction, half way between the Longcross and the Crwys, where the gibbet stood, where thieves and cut-throats were hanged from poles until they died. Where their bodies were dumped in unhallowed plots. Where weeping made no difference. When we did things like that.

The fields, four of them, had what is now Richmond Road running down their centre. They were named: Gallows Pit, Defiled Pool, Cut Throats, Putrid Field. This was the most southern point of that swathe of common land known as The Heath. It ran back from here to the Cefn Onn hills. It's on the early maps like a green tongue. The Little Heath first then the Great Heath. Rough pasture. Copse. Molinia grass in tussocks. Gorse. Sphagnum moss. Thistle.

Of the Lesser Heath, Y Waun Ddyfal, nothing remains. The city build has been total. But of the larger tract, the Great Heath, there are still traces. In Welsh this land was known as Y Mynydd Bychan, the little mountain, and even if the land has changed beyond recognition the mountain still stands, Caerphilly beyond it.

For centuries The Heath was common ground used for the grazing of pigs, goats, geese and cattle. Turf for fuel was cut here. George Yates' map of 1799 shows how large it was, marking both what he calls The Little and The Cardiff Heaths as well as the town gallows. After the Heath Enclosure Act of 1802 a lot of the land was fenced and sold, although there had been numerous great landowner incursions before that. Much of The Heath was then sold off by the Corporation and three farms were created: Allen's Bank, Ton-yr-Ywen and Heath. The Corporation retained an open swathe which eventually became Heath Park. The switch from farms to housing was largely a twentieth century phenomenon in response to the City's need to expand. Much of the district's core was built in the late fifties.

I'm walking it with John and John, Briggs and Osmond, two fellow urban explorers keen to see what's left and experience what might have been. Our starting point at Death Junction is auspicious. The Roath Brewery, the second one[9], run from a shed somewhere at the back of Colchester Avenue, has been experimenting with locally themed ales. So far they've produced three – 'Antarctic Pale Ale' after Captain Scott, 'Mill Garden', a wheat beer, and 'No 3 Tram', a lager that celebrates the famous route from the Pierhead to Roath Park Lake. Today they are launching their fourth beer – 'Death Junction', a dark oatmeal stout. I've got a celebratory poem on the back of the label.

Death Junction itself is not full of dark death but bright light. The day is crisp enough for the haze of traffic fumes to be made visible. They hover above the plaques that mark this place as a death spot for Fathers Philip Evans and John Lloyd. They were executed in 1679 for practising Catholicism at a time when the British Crown felt this inappropriate. The pope canonised the pair in 1970.

There's a giant yellow dragon painted on the wall of Mashup's Jamaican restaurant with a string of other unlikely animals decorating the sides of the bridge over the Rhymney Railway. John Briggs, born in the state of Minnesota, has recently been back. He's been visiting Hibbing and Duluth on the Bob Dylan Trail and has photographed the celebrated northern reaches of Highway 61. By contrast today it's Crwys Road with students on their way to lectures and locals setting out for the low cost Co-Op. John regales us with musical tales. He once lived with his first wife Cathy in rooms near here, he says. She hated it. On the back of John's Mothers of Invention album, *Mothermania* with its hit from the edge of psychedelia, 'You're Probably Wondering Why I'm Here', she'd added the words "or the Ballad of 65 Mackintosh Place". The accommodation was dismal. Hot water from a geezer. Lino. Drafts. Dripping taps. Houses here are largely unreconstructed original Cardiff Victorian. Evidence of an earlier great urban expansion.

At Fairoak Road where the refurbished local library faces St Monica's Church In Wales Primary School we turn into Cathays Cemetery. There are more than 150 years of the honoured Cardiff dead in this place. Everyone from Jim Driscoll to Ernest Willows and William Reardon Smith to William Tatem, First Baron Glanely. We cross via heart-shaped paths, no route direct, getting lost more than once and needing to Google Earth our location on my 4G. The gate out is up beyond the memorial to the Irish Famine. Despite the prevalent green the sense of great heath is about nought.

Allensbank Road leads to Heath Hospital. The risen land here, literally a bank, was named after Allen's Bank Farm which stood opposite the main cemetery gates in the back gardens of what is now Inglefield Avenue. The hospital grounds, once Allen's Bank Woods, expose us to patches of green. But the sense of heathland remains distant.

John O is in full George Thomas memorial mode. He had a vague family connection to the much-reviled Viscount Tonypandy, the obsequious Speaker who lived for his mam. This was the man who told the grieving at Aberfan that they needed to fund the tip's removal themselves. He earned himself one of the most honest obituaries I've read. This was in the form of a poem by the late Nigel Jenkins, 'An Execrably Tasteless Farewell to Viscount No' which appeared on the front page of the *Guardian* shortly after Thomas' death in 1997. "A white man's Taff ... may his garters garrotte him ... the Lord of Lickspit, the grovelsome brown-snout and smiley shyster whose quisling wiles were the shame of Wales..." the verse ran.

Reporting for the *Western Mail* John went to interview him in his semi on Heath's King George V Drive. The walls were covered in photos of the sycophantic politician shaking hands with the world's great and good, from Harold Wilson to the Duke of Edinburgh. "Did you get a decent story?" "Can't remember."

Heath Park is large, wooded, once held a World War Two US Army Camp, now a car park. There are tennis courts, children's play, a miniature steam railway and great expanses of football fields. The stream, Nant y Wedal, has been canalised. The woodland is dense but not ancient. The ryegrass mix of the sports pitches is not original. These grounds are actually one of 400 British fields established in memory of King George V. At the far extremity there remain the not unimpressive four metre high brick gate posts, hidden in the trees below King George V Drive North where Heath

Woods and Heath Farm once stood. I try hard to imagine the wild and desperate heathlands, full of thieves and ne'er-do-wells, of commoners down on their luck, of goatherds and pig farmers, of low ponds and hummocks, of the past stretching back hundreds of years. But I get nothing.

North of here lie the streets of the Heath that were built as the century got up speed. Lower-cost housing with air and space and metal-framed windows. The streets are first named after the farm fields that stood here – Tair Erw, Pedair Erw, Pum Erw – and then saints – Edwen, Bridgid, Asaph, Ina, Isan, Cadoc, Denis, Brioc – all of them Welsh. Centrepiece, invisible unless you stumble on it, is Llwynfedw Gardens. This is half bowling green and half tennis courts plus a brick community centre where a nursery operates. The sign outside asks parents to "teach your child the words to 'Away In A Manger'" for this year's Christmas play. Another warns that this area of the park "is designated for the quiet enjoyment of bowling only", a game that breeds silence among noisy men.

Nearby is a parked white van operated by a provider of full volume party equipment including sumo suits, rodeo bulls, UV bubble generators, foam makers, surf simulators, bouncy castles and karaoke. No one among us has ever experienced a fully-fledged evening of foam or similar unbridled excitement although John Briggs does recall a court case recently in his home town of St Paul where a slap party got out of hand and the police had to be called. I must remember those for my next big bash.

Our long march up Ton Yr Ywen Avenue, named after a lost northern section of the Wedal brook, eventually hits Maes y Coed. This is a road that follows the line of the original Cardiff racecourse where nags and champions galloped for a hundred years until racing transferred to a new course at Ely in 1855. I'd come here in 2008 with historian and turf fanatic Brian Lee and we'd toured the places where the starting box had stood and where local landowners had gathered cheering their horses on. Any mark left? Like almost everything else lost from Cardiff, no.

On Maes y Coed Road itself we skirt what was once the Gnome factory[10] and is now a giant Lidl to turn right facing the site of Cardiff's controversial bomb factory, ROF Llanishen. John Osmond had been here covering the 1980s campaigns when women padlocked themselves to the fence and built benders in replica of those at Greenham Common. John had been there too, writing the protest up for *Arcade*[11]. The women's march to this proposed site for American Cruise missiles had set out from Cardiff in 1981. In those days we all imagined that the world would soon face a nuclear end. ROF Llanishen had been taken over by the Atomic Weapons Establishment in 1960. It manufactured nuclear bomb triggers until the 1990s when the site was cleared and the ground decontaminated. No marker left to what once was.

That the Heath also ran here is today difficult to imagine. Caerphilly Road is traffic overkill. But there is one exception: Hill Snook Park. This is set alongside the Coryton railway. It is named after former Cardiff Mayor and benefactor R.G. Hill-Snook. His bust at City Hall depicts him as a Victorian – wing collar, handlebar moustache – although he died in the 1950s. The park, unexpected and to most Cardiffians little known, would have been on the original Heath's fringes. At its western end lies a section of ground given over to Cardiff's Pollinator Project which abandons mowing in favour of a return to the wild. Here are marsh grasses and the reappearance of Molinia tumps. In this small stretch there's just a touch of uncouth wildness. The real Heath, the ancient heath, the past returned.

The rail station here on the City Line is Birchgrove although where we are feels more frontier. This is a place of change, a malleable Heath meets Llanishen spot where developers have competed with their own district names: Parklands, Ty Glas, Llys Enfys, Watkins Square. None of them really stick.

Beyond the tracks is Ffordd Mograig. There could have been a councillor Mograig, I suppose. Or a developer with that unlikely name. The nearest to it on the old maps is Castell Morgraig, the half-finished castle at the back of the Travellers Rest car park up on the mountain. Still there. Mor graig. *As rock.* The new houses here all sparkle. On Tatham Road there's a new stretch of deep green, an unvandalised play area, grass manicured flat.

John Briggs catches up. He has dawdled for most of the trip, taking shots from behind bushes, getting locals he passes to pose, discussing music with two Irishmen wearing Munster jerseys encountered outside the tax office, photographing a café owner proudly wearing her poppy. He's pleased, he says, that at his age he's managed the walk thus far without failure. He's my age. Hell.

He talks about morris dancing, a preoccupation of his. He's one of the oldest members of Isca Morris. Teams dance together. The Men of Sweyn's Eye. Heb Enw Morris. Carreg Las Welsh Northern Morris. Cardiff Morris. Morris dancing as a traditional sport. In Wales of all places.

Going north, forever onwards, we cross Tŷ Glas Road. Here, west of the tax offices, we access the northern stretches of Llanishen Park via Whitebarn Road. The park entrance straddles the site of Tŷ Glas, the farm after which the roads and buildings here were named. The Tŷ Glas pub, the Tŷ Glas government buildings, the Tŷ Glas leisure centre, and then a whole Tŷ Glas shopping mall.

Arriving at Llanishen Park, as wide as anything else green we have in the city, is like reaching Gwynedd from the capital. Crossing it is like traversing the Yukon. Distance engulfs you. Parkland, playing fields, paths and then the expanse of Coedcochwyn Woods. The Heath that once existed ran out here. Northwards the land rises towards that line of Norman castles, motte and baileys, that ran from Cardiff to Caerphilly via Radyr, Whitchurch, Rhiwbina, Castell Coch, and Castell Morgraig. A Maginot line to protect the city's prospering immigrants from the much wilder natives.

There's a strip of Cardiff left before the motorway – North Llanishen, Thornhill – what were once the fields and woods of Llwyn Crwn Ganol, Coed Evan-Bychan, and Llwyn Crwn Fawr – but remnants of The Heath, if they ever ran here, are now gone.

Notes

1. Finch, Peter, *Real Cardiff Two – The Greater City,* Seren, 2004. – 'Canal North' and 'Canal South'
2. Bob Cobbing 1920-2002, sound poet, a man fascinated by accents, dialogue and language.
3. Sherriff, MP, Baronet, director of at least 35 companies.
4. Sully, Janet, *Howell's School, Llandaff 1860-2010 A Legacy Fulfilled*, Howell's School, Llandaff (GDST), 2010.
5. "I was born in Bargoed in 1927 and I want to know why" – John Tripp's regular refrain when in his cups.
6. Jenkins, Nigel, *Writers of Wales – John Tripp*, University of Wales Press, 1989.
7. *Eglwys Newydd*, the Welsh name for Whitchurch lit *new church*. The white church it replaced could well have been the source for *Whitchurch*, the district's English name.
8. "We are all old timers / each of us holds a locked razor 'from Waking In The Blue' in *Life Studies*, 1959.
9. The first Roath Brewery was operated by SA Noel and Co at the turn of the century from premises in Bedford Place. The operation merged with Fred Dunkerley's Black Lion Brewery on St Mary Street in 1903.
10. Gnome was an independent company founded by Heinrich Loebstein. It manufactured cameras and other photographic equipment on the site from 1940 until 1994.
11. *Arcade*, Wales Fortnightly, was a cultural and political review that ran from 1980 and 1982. It was edited by John Osmond with the support of Robin Reeves, Ned Thomas, Dai Smith and others. It was the first vehicle I'd encountered that genuinely mixed the cultural world I occupied with the political and social ones that made up the rest of Welsh life. There's been nothing quite like it since.

WEST

CAPTAIN VIDEO LANDS IN KINGSLAND ROAD

I'd been sold the idea of moving to the west of the city with the promise of a new bike. Trevor said I'd never get it and he was right. He was one of the few friends from Roath who bothered to keep in touch. The east of this city and its west rarely mix. You stick with what you know, it's in the blood. My mother, ever determined to better us or at least to give that impression, had begun with our address. She would have none of this Canton stuff. We live in Victoria Park, she declared, standing there in her hair net, bristling. Years later, when I checked the history, I uncovered the fact that until 1897, these lands were part of undrained Ely Moor. Hell on a bike, it's a good job my mother didn't discover that.

I was duly enrolled in Lansdowne Road School, a vast and rambling Victorian structure that had space for 1474 pupils. I could walk there from our house, which was a bonus but as I knew no one I felt totally lost. In the rumbling rush for morning assembly, the school's daily mass indoctrination of Christianity, I noticed a small gaggle of boys sitting to the side reading comics. Marvel Man, Superman, The Justice League of America. I joined them. "Why are you here boy"? asked a passing teacher. "Are you Jewish?" I wasn't but I nodded anyway. "Right," he replied, striding away, the good book under his arm. During my time at Lansdowne I read a lot of comics. Religion is a wonderful thing.

Trevor and I were both space fans. The fifties were the age of ray guns and space helmets and men who could travel by rocket to Mars. Cowboys with their ridiculous hats were passé. We preferred sensible headwear, like space helmets. Trevor cycled over most weekends. We played in the third floor attic rooms of Kingsland Road where I had created a space base from which we could control the universe. My mother had abandoned this floor as undesirable. Instead she spent what little resource she had on making the front room as perfect as it could be. Once finished, new carpet, new sofa and new and gleaming cream paint she banned everyone from going in there. "We'll keep this door shut," she said, slamming it. I have no memory of ever entering. Not once.

My space fixation centred on *Captain Video*[1], a Columbia Pictures serial shown in multiple cliff-hanger parts at the Saturday morning cinema matinees. Trevor and I attended the Gaumont on Queen Street. The Gaumont was huge. It had opened as a theatre in 1887 and was initially called Levino's Hall but changed its name to the Cardiff Empire in 1889. It presented music hall, melodrama, opera and had its stage frozen for an ice show each Christmas. Down the years everyone from Fred Astaire to Gracie Fields and Will Hay to Charlie Chaplin played there. It seated two and a half thousand and was often full. It was converted to a cinema in the thirties and hosted promotional visits from many stars. Gloria Swanson, Cary Grant, and Kenneth More all appeared here. In 1954 the cinema was rebranded as the Gaumont.

By the time I came to attend the stars had largely abandoned Cardiff. Instead we got the yo-yo boy who could walk the dog and hop the fence with two yo-yos simultaneously, a bloke dressed as a red Indian selling pop guns, hula hoop promotors, and a man in a shapeless suit who tried to talk about the evils of drink but was defeated by the booing. Gaumont matinées impressed their audiences. In the days of the cowboy I'd always galloped home shooting passers-by with my imaginary revolver. But now it was the space age. Travel was instant and ruthless dictators could be atomised from great distances with ray guns.

Captain Video: Master of the Stratosphere held our attention. Video wore a motorbike crash helmet, fighter pilot boots, baggy trousers and had pouches full of futuristic devices strapped to his waist. His ray gun could do everything from open locked doors to demolish mountains. Each week he and his Rangers saved the universe.

Video episodes were true cliff-hangers. At the end of each the good Captain would be left in an impossible to survive situation: frozen solid, thrown off a ship into deep space, smashed to atoms by dastardly diathermic impulses. And each week following he would be saved by the revelation of a previously unseen action. Something in our fear for his life we'd failed to spot. He'd set in motion a defrosting device slipped from a waist pouch just before the polarised freezing ray took effect. A second ship would scoop him back from space free fall. It wasn't he who was atomised in the first place but an evil double.

Science in these episodes was on overdrive. This was the soon to be arriving future. It was full of vapour bombs, gravitational decelerators, cloaks of invisibility, sonic air cushions and isotopic radiation curtains. There were robots, space ships, interplanetary journeys, and the triumph of the new over the old. It was the space age. We were enraptured.

Viewing these episodes again fifty years on the magic has largely turned to dust. In Captain Video episodes there are no video screens.

Observations are made through tubes. The robots all wear metal fedoras (they were actually recycled by the studio from a 1930s Gene Autry serial). The surfaces of alien planets look like Texan canyons (which is, in fact, just what they were). Everyone, apart from the Captain and his Rangers, was as fashion-conscious as your father, moustachioed and overweight. The evil Vultura, Dictator of the planet Atoma, appeared more like a cigar-smoking banker than an enemy alien. Everyone looked old. Youth had yet to arrive.

Episodes were written by George H. Plympton who had previously been responsible for the serialising of much similarly enthralling tosh including *Flash Gordon*, *Tarzan* and *The Green Hornet*. Video himself was woodenly played by Judd Holdren, a tall and handsome man of his time. He'd gone on to star in Columbia's *The Lost Planet* (1953) and *Commander Cody: Sky Marshall of the Universe* (1953). In both of these he'd wielded a ray gun while wearing a crash helmet and goggles. He committed suicide in 1974.

None of these failings were visible to Trevor and me. With the innocence of the young we remained perpetually enthused. From our base in my Kingsland Road attic we too regularly saved the universe. Had to be done. That universe is still here. Video must have been on to something.

Captain Video ran to a mere 15 episodes. By the time he'd done TV had taken his place. *A for Andromeda*. *Quatermass*. The Gaumont's matinées faltered and the cinema itself closed in 1961. C&A, cheapo clothier to the masses, opened on the site. Today, up here in the even more distant future even that has gone.

IKEA AND THE GRANGETOWN GAS WORKS

There was a gas light on the dining room wall at Kingsland Road. A thin pipe with a knob on it emerging from the plaster. It was topped with an ornate glass shade. Inside was what looked like an off-white bandaged thumb. This was the bit that you set fire to – the incandescent mantle. "We're not using that," warned my father, fearful the gas was still connected. "Absolutely not," agreed my mother. "There'll be no gas in this house." Town gas, apparently, had a reputation for smelling, staining things and ruining ceilings. In houses my grandfather had owned it had escaped and whole floors had to be lifted tracking it down.

I wouldn't have known. I was too young. While my parents were out I naturally tried out the banned gas lamp by turning it on and waving a lighted match underneath it to see what all the fuss was about. Nothing. Following my mother's instruction my father had disabled the supply at the mains with a hammer.

Gas had been made in Cardiff since 1821 when the first gas-holder to supply 48 street lamps was erected in the Parish Clerk's garden near what was to become the fish market on The Hayes. This great industrial leap forward was more or less where St David's Hall is today. In later years the fish market site had been used as a showroom for the Electricity Board and after that as a branch of Habitat. Furniture and displaced industry is a theme here, as we'll see. Today the neo-Georgian building houses the city's second Miller & Carter Steakhouse which for a time had a branch of Burger & Lobster stuck on upstairs. Its basement had originally housed the town centre's electricity transformers. Supply had come from the council-owned generating station at Roath. The Hayes buzzed with power.

For much of the nineteenth century gas-making was a boom industry. Initially to light the streets and then as illumination for housing. Electricity with its glowing bulbs which no one understood was a Johnny-come-lately which didn't get a hold until the new century had well turned. Inside houses town gas burned, flickering yellow, marking the furniture, ruining books, turning white clothing khaki. The enterprise on The Hayes with its single gasholder was soon outgrown. In 1837 the new Cardiff Gas Light and Coke Company (CGL&C) opened a works on Bute Terrace. Where the Big Sleep Hotel now stands, right next to St Mary's National School. The all-pervading smell that town gas manufacture created worried no one. Smells and choking fumes were how it was in nineteenth century industrial age Britain.

The demand for gas rose as Cardiff grew. Houses began to be supplied through a meter rather than via the earlier system of being charged by how many burners you had. Gas was also made available during the day rather than just between dusk and midnight. The coal, the raw material from which town gas was produced, arrived at the cramped Bute Terrace works in growing quantity. As the increase in demand showed no signs of slowing a new and larger works was built on Cardiff's West Moors on land adjacent to the Grangetown Iron Foundry. Supply was connected to Bute Terrace with an eighteen-inch main.

As usage continued to increase so too did the size of the gas works. When the iron foundry next door closed in 1881 Cardiff Gas Light and Coke expanded onto the site. Complete production was transferred to Grangetown in 1907[2]. At its height the CGL&C had five gasometers and carbonised 400 tons of coal daily. It occupied the land presently used by Ikea and ran south almost as far as the art work at the top of the Iron Age fort-like prominence of Asda Hill, otherwise known as Grangemoor Park.

As the twentieth century advanced so too did the shift from wavering, unsafe gas lighting to the much cleaner, more flexible and by now significantly brighter electrical bulb. The Grangetown gas works began a slow and progressive decline. The arrival of natural gas from the North Sea in the nineteen-sixties put the cap on it. Gas production ceased in 1997 and the works were dismantled.

A single gasometer still stands, town gas's last memory. It's Grade 2 listed which gives it some protection, a circle of 16 cast-iron Doric columns scratching the Grangetown sky. Around when I visit it lies polluted desolation with security fences, concrete blocks and iron mesh all blocking passage. You can't touch it which makes it rather like Stonehenge. The central dome is missing as are the metal container sides but the 1881 Florentine superstructure, built by J. & W. Horton of Smethwick (it says so on the side) remains glorious.

On the land south of here, the whole reclaimed gas works site almost as far as the river will soon see new housing. Five hundred homes with a further hundred on the now removed embankment that once carried the Penarth Harbour and Dock Railway along the back of Clive Lane. Thousands of new residents will arrive to use central heating boilers that burn gas tapped somewhere deep in North Sea Doggerland hundreds of miles distant.

The heart of what was once Cardiff gas production is now occupied by the Swedish yellow and blue furniture giant Ikea. You say *Ee-key-ah*, apparently, rather than *Eye-kee-a*, much in the way you are supposed to say *Leydle* rather than *Liddle*. But no one in the UK does. Ikea opened in 2003 in a three story 25,950 square metre box, surrounded by parking for 1200 cars. No one walks here, Marketing Manager Allyn Burford tells me, there's little passing trade. But with Cardiff's soon to arrive new Grangetown housing, not for long.

The rumour of Ikea's imminent Cardiff opening was confirmed when, in early 2003, promotional slogans were spotted painted across the grass of fields alongside the motorway and 250 bright pink plastic Klimme easy chairs appeared in the streets of the city. Passers-by looked in puzzlement at first but soon recognised a freebee when they saw one. The chairs vanished at speed.

The brand Ikea is an acronym from the name of the company's founder, Ingvar Kamprad, his childhood farm, Elmtaryd, and his village, Agunnaryd. Its ownership which we'd all love to be eco and simple is actually Euro and labyrinthine. Kamprad's book, *The Ikea Story*, includes an ownership flow chart that would put Kafka to shame. Foundations own holding companies which in turn manage service operations. Up there at the top is a box labelled *The Kamprad Sphere* and the words "Simplified summary of the organisation". I'd hate to see the full diagram.

Kamprad, who died in 2018, continued to be involved. He visited the Cardiff store twice, for last time in 2008, arriving by bus in true egalitarian, green culture style. The Cardiff store has 300 co-workers, all of them till trained and able to assemble a wardrobe at a moment's notice. I'm sitting in the co-workers restaurant talking to Allyn and his assistant Chris. Nothing on the menu here is expensive. Highest price today is 90p. Quite often chips are free. The feel is Silicon Valley. Brightly lit, primary colours, a corner fenced off and artificially grassed, populated with garden furniture.

Chris tells me that the chain's bestseller is the Hemnes daybed. Cardiff shifts a shed load. Local turnover is £50m annually from a range of 9500 products. Stock holding is minimal, most kept out there in the racks themselves or 'in the air' above them. Design is entirely Scandinavian although manufacture is now largely not. The stuff comes in by truck daily from Ikea's warehouse in Doncaster. Ordering is automatic, managed by algorithm. Items sell and then replacements show up a day later. Humans only intervene when something goes wrong.

Do staff laugh at the strange names products are given? Dombas wardrobes, Pysslingar bed storage boxes, Prickig microwave accessories, Stenklover quilt covers, and the famous, and now apparently withdrawn, Godis Skum marshmallow sheep. They don't, I'm told. Internally products are generally referred to by their numbers.

Ikea's unfathomable product names have their origins in a system initiated to help with the founder's dyslexia. Kamprad found numbers difficult to remember so he chose places instead. Dining furniture is named after towns in Finland. Bathroom kit from Swedish lakes. Garden furniture after Swedish islands. Carpets from places on the Danish map. The notorious *Godis Skum* actually translates as *Candy Foam*, a pretty straightforward name by Ikea standards. Lars Petrus has an online dictionary[3] for Ikea obsessives where he lists English translations for the names of 1362 products. "This site is very much under construction," he points out. It needs to be given the range of available Ikea merchandise.

Despite the perceived bleakness of the economy Ikea continues to grow. There is no shortage, yet, of the operation's target customer – female, 30-45, ABC1, usually with children. In store displays are becoming increasingly realistic. Cardiff Ikea is basing some of its room sets on actual local houses. Prospect Place near the Ferry Road International Sports Village has already made an appearance. Other places will follow. Room sets smell of freshly ground coffee, birdsong drifts in through the fake windows. A sitting area has been lit with a giant chandelier made from six suspended angle-poise lamps.

In this fringe land, an Ikea-artificial world wedged between a worn-down Grangetown and a pacified Severn Sea I've often dreamed of instigating literary interventions: poetry performances among the sofas, dadaesque sonic renderings broadcast between the kitchen displays, Tôpher Mills shouting verse amid the bedding. I've sat here writing too, surrounded by easy chairs, poems plucked from the air, a leather Poäng nearby taking a pounding from Ikea's mechanical look-how-much-wear-this-chair will take demonstrator. No one bothers you.

In the restaurant the £1.50 all-in breakfast is a best seller. Beats the greasy spoon offer on Corporation Road. A few lost souls spend their entire waking days here, dining for a pittance, absorbing the store's warmth and transient company. Mothers' groups, language exchanges, park runners and fan groups all meeting without any involvement with Ikea's raison d'etre. On my last visit I asked a retiree in a faded 2006 World Cup T-shirt what he'd come in to buy. "Buy? I don't buy things. I don't even like this stuff. Too modern. I just come in for the free coffee[4]."

THE CANTON BORDER

South of Cowbridge Road East I am once again in the margins. These are peripheral places where boundaries meet, usage conjoins and the land can't make its mind just where it is. When Cardiff was young with barely a coal staithe to its name and the railways were still plateways in the mind of Mr Trevithick these lands were a barren waste. The moors of Ely were to the north and those of Leckwith to the south. As late as 1880 workers arriving at the new paper mills still talked about crossing a bleak, unlit common, of jumping the channels made to drain water off the fields. These were marshlands on the floodplain between the Taff and the Ely. Damp was everywhere.

I've left hugely popular Victoria Park full of Bank Holiday sun to cross the railway frontier. The district is intersected by two lines – the Cardiff to Swansea main, what was originally Brunel's Great Western broad gauge, and to the south what remains of the Taff Vale. This was once the Penarth Harbour and Dock Railway but is now where the train operator run their Sprinters to leafy Radyr.

Sanatorium Road originally led to the 1895 Cardiff Isolation Hospital. Vanished, apart from a 1934 strip of former observation wards and operating theatres, closed and boarded, abandoned by the NHS. It's a wasteland of former health care, overgrown with buddleia and Himalayan balsam. How our post-Brexit medical futures could well be if we don't look out.

These hospital lands have now been largely covered with a development of new town houses, stacked so closely that residents can surely hear each other breathe. Lansdowne Gardens it's called. "Which district are we in?" I ask a local cleaning his white Merc on his Bank Holiday drive. "Canton". He's sure. He points west towards the link road in the distance, the Cardiff beltway of sliding cars from the M4 into the Bay, "Leckwith starts over there. And up there," he swings his arm, "is Ely. But this is Canton."

The new Gardens are built on land that once held wards full of desperation and diphtheria death. They eventually give way to the freshly cut green fields of what is now Sanatorium Recreation Grounds but were originally the flooding river meadow that surrounded the ever-meandering River Ely. There is a playpark and there are benches but flowerbeds are yet to arrive. West of this strip of imitation countryside flows the river itself, safe now in its flood-proof new cut. The wild lands of Plymouth Great Wood, the real country, rise beyond. The sense of uncertainty could not be stronger. This is liminal space. Purposeless. Ill-defined. Things begun and not yet finished. Use in transition. Everywhere the flickering of change.

My route goes north. I pass the new Welsh-medium School, Ysgol Gymraeg Pwll Goch, and then the edge of the in the process of being developed site of Ely Paper Mills. In the process at the time I pass it anyway. A complete set of show homes at the south eastern end with the rest looking like a war-time airfield after a bombing raid, grey concrete littered with broken hard core as far as the eye will go. The paper mills[5] that stood here for 135 years from 1865 to 2000, employed almost the entire district. In their place Tirion Homes are building 800 new houses in what they term an urban village to be called The Mill. Bright brick, new people. The developer's web site sparkles with reference to the provision of training academies and community halls, flood defences and riverside parks. A highlight is pedestrian footbridge access to vibrant Cowbridge Road East. Not how I'd describe it. But it does have a funeral directors, a Spar, a new chip shop and a creperie.

Along the edge of Paper Mill Road older concerns linger. Builders, car fixers, tyre replacers, Ninja Martial Arts, a micro-brewery. Things advertised with hand painted signs. A litter of bust metal and waste ground. Nature and its summer bramble is half way through reclamation. On Cowbridge Road East, when I return to it after going both under and over the rail tracks, stands St Luke's Church. There's a flood mark[6] on the wall celebrating the 1927 Ely bank breaking. Was that when Billy the Seal swam down the four foot waters of the road and was given beer at the Corporation Hotel?

At St Luke's I once gave a talk on the Severn's edge to a pensioner's group. I'd recently published *Edging The Estuary,* a book about my coastal ramble. I made the talk entertaining with anecdotes about readings that went wrong at Chepstow, getting chased by security guards at Port Talbot and the Elvis convention at Porthcawl's Coney Beach Pleasure Park. I did well, I thought. But some members of my audience neverthless went to sleep and after a cup of tea and a garibaldi at the end I managed to sell absolutely no books.

The road here rises towards another of Cardiff's frontier intersections. This one where Western Avenue reaches its destination and Cowbridge Road West, the Ely artery proper, begins. Pwll Coch, the famous pool formed from a bend in the River Ely and which got its name from the blood of the dead lost here in the Battle of St Fagans in 1648 has long been filled. The pub named after it, Ty Pwll Coch, closed in 2012. It's been redone as city apartments and still retains some of the Tudor look of the original. Old photos, though, show the black half timbering and ancient-looking portico to have been a 1930s addition. We did gentrification even then.

On the roundabout the traffic is intense. Ely Bridge and its roaring river is below. The route to Grand Avenue ahead. Hoardings advertise Wellman Vitabiotics, patio heaters, and Suppleform Protein Blend. A kilo bucket costs as little as £19.99. Body builder territory. Hard men inhabit the frontier. Always have.

I'm back where I began at Victoria Park which opened in 1897, the year of Queen Victoria's Diamond Jubilee. Plans to call the pleasure grounds Ely Common Park were dropped in favour of something more patriotic. Victoria, Queen of Great Britain, Empress of India and ruler of a third of the world was an obvious choice. If opening today the grounds would be known as Parc Frank Hennessey or Bob Derbyshire Gardens.

Things are not as they once were. The park's Victorian bandstand might have been simply repaired with aid from the Heritage Lottery but elsewhere the park has been totally transformed. A whole Costa del Sol waterpark, known as the splashpad, with spinnakers, spraying pipes, fountains and giant emptying buckets has been built where the Victorian zoo and paddling pool once stood. Water, in Cardiff it's everywhere.

THE CROSS AT CULVER

This one, if it's a cross at all, is a Celtic one. A nimbus of circling cars intersected by north-south and east-west highways, the whole construct interlaced with slip road, intersection and crossway. Flow is controlled by lights and hieroglyphic markings in white on the carriageway surfaces – decide now which road you want to follow and get in lane. If you don't know its number then all hope is lost. Your fellow motorists – children-hassled saloon drivers, busmen, blokes in the high cabs of liner-sized artics – they'll never let you back in.

Culverhouse Cross in Cardiff's far west is where the writ of dynamic Cardiff runs out and the steady conservatism of the Vale begins. Signs mark the border. Cardiff is twinned with Hordaland, Lugansk, Nantes, Stuttgart, Xiamen and somewhere now crossed out. The Vale of Glamorgan, still home of the National Eisteddfod 2012, is twinned with three European places no one has ever heard of and quite friendly with a couple more. As you navigate the intersection it's hard to tell where the border actually is, the western edge of the Cardiff Link Road as it turns out, not that this matters amid the cuboid warehouses, fast-food outlets and brick and curved roof superstores that populate this place.

Walking this circuit of intersecting roads I'm the sole pedestrian in a sea of seated riders. In their cabs their rear view mirrors are festooned with objets d'art, fluffy dice, humorous figurines of bunnies and frogs, beads, crosses, the Qur'an on CD, flowery things that smell of fabric conditioner, good luck charms. They dangle and swing.

There's a sense here of otherness of the kind prevalent in airports and rail stations and places where populations arrive, leave or change direction. It's a melancholic dislocation, a sense of not belonging, Baudelaire's alienation writ large. I track the road edge and encounter no one bar a man in a blue anorak stringing a laminated notice to the barriers of a road island. *Weight Watchers Because It Works* it says.

There are five distinct retail parks here, each with a nose touching the main roundabout. Three have name boards: Valegate, Brooklands, Wenvoe Park. They house the vast empires of B&Q, M&S, Tesco, Homebase, Bensons Beds, Comet, TK Maxx, Mothercare, Dreams, Carpetright. The same lexicon of stores that inhabit road junctions throughout this British part of the western world.

Slivered between the fourth and fifth parks with its own drainage lake softening the pollution is the Copthorne Hotel. I don't enter although I did once, years back, for a postcard and coin-sellers fayre when I was the entertainment performing rhythmic slices from *Real Cardiff*. Psychogeography as history, although nobody called it that. My audience stood dumb, coffees in hand, wondering what this literature stuff had to do with old banknotes and the flogging of sepia cards showing Cardiff Castle in its former existence.

Culver comes from the Middle English word for a pigeon or dove. There was a Culverhouse farm with a dovecot on this site in the turnpike past. The cross would have been the roads running from Cardiff to Cowbridge intersected by the route from St Fagans to Wenvoe. Christ's version is absent, far as I can tell. For the last part of the twentieth century Culverhouse Cross was home to HTV's independent and edge-pushing studios, demolished now with the site developed for housing by Bellway.

East of the trees as I circumnavigate the interchange and beyond B&Q sit the distant houses of Caerau, Ely's southern twin. That's the nearest real Cardiff gets to this realm of the consumer on speed. The north, Ely proper, is dominated by the long pointed finger of Western Cemetery. These congested lands of the dead opened in

1936. They are serried with marble grave markers and deeply felt memorial assemblages of toys, stone dogs and balloons. Some are rich enough in sentiment to rival the George Jones concoction that I spotted in Nashville, TN: an overkill of marble guitars and fretboards, musical notation and memorial vases. At its western end the cemetery has a section of simple, white headstones maintained by the Commonwealth Graves Commission – Cardiff's Imperial War Graves – last resting place of soldiers and sailors lost in the world's two great conflicts.

On the hill rising up from here are more dead. The world belongs to them after all. In the outlying grounds of the grade one listed neo-classical Regency villa of Coedarhydyglyn at the top of the Tumble are the natural burial meadows of Cardiff and the Vale. Here the dead lie in sustainable and secure surroundings – free from embalming chemicals and imported headstones – decomposing naturally in handmade shrouds and wicker coffins.

Below is the now blocked mile-long tunnel of the Barry Railway Company that once brought coal and iron down from the valleys at Trehafod. The line ran across the vanished Walnut Tree Viaduct at Taffs Well to finish at David Davies's Barry Docks. The tunnel opened in 1898 and was closed after the Beeching cuts in 1964. It's still there, caged and leaking, with a water main taking an easy route along its bottom. No tracks, no access, unless you are a Cardiff subterranean and fancy your luck[7].

I circle on and find myself in sight again of where I started. Little has changed, why would it? Same blue X1 bus in the car park, same hi-vis vests rolling lines of trollies. Culverhouse Cross as time machine.

NINIAN PARK

I could never figure football. Running across the schoolyard shouting out the name of the bighead with the ball only to be ignored as he passed it to someone else. What was this game about? My father had for years valiantly bought me Roy of the Rovers annuals and books about Stanley Matthews but to no avail. Although I tried I just couldn't get myself interested. The final straw came when I was given a pair of real boots for Christmas. What did I want with these? They were in brown leather, utterly inflexible, and came up high over my ankles. I applied dubbin as I'd been told to, put them on, and then clattered on unfamiliar studs over the road to the Roath Park Rec football ground. New boots. Real boots. I was bound to be taken seriously now.

On the pitch, however, things did not work out as I expected. Everyone else was kitted out in better boots than mine. All the kids who dribbled the ball magnificently towards opposing goals, and even my friends who were not quite as good, they all wore the new Bobby Charlton Brazilia Continental. Lightweight, below the ankle, white speed flashes on the side, guaranteed a whole season, full of contemporary style. I was from the past, from the pre-War land of huge laces and pigs bladders. I gave up and went home to read my Marvelman comics instead.

Since then football appears to have taken over the world.

You don't need to support your local team anymore. You can support anyone you like. Manchester United. Liverpool. Real Madrid. It doesn't matter that you've never been to these places. Few of the team players come from them anyway.

These days the Cardiff City fan-base runs throughout south Wales. This is despite Swansea often doing much better than Cardiff does. You can support Cardiff if you live in Barry or Merthyr or Carmarthen or Ponty. Many do. This is tribalism by self-selection. Like being Welsh, I suppose. You are Welsh if you say you are. Unless you come from Gwynedd, that is. There you don't need to say, you just know.

Walking out towards where the Cardiff City home ground of Ninian Park once stood is a trip into the past. These were levels, moors, and tidal fields that, until they were drained, swamped and sank. Here Grangetown finishes and the western homelands of Leckwith and Ely begin. Here are corrugated sheds and industrial sweatshops, repair depots, storage facilities, bus washeries, train yards, and wrecked ground. Everything has seen better days. They used to make bricks here, they tanned hides, wound ropes, and manufactured gas. Coronation Park, opened in 1953, a sometime City FC Sunday squad ground and now home to Grange Albion Rovers, was formerly a coal yard. It's in use as I pass, youths darting and shouting, testament to the game's omnipresence.

Further on was where, in 1910, they opened a pitch with stands for the new Cardiff City football team. The ground, a former rubbish tip, was named after Ninian, the second son of the Third Marquis of Bute who donated the land. Ninian was killed in the

Battle of Loos in 1915. He'd been MP for Cardiff for five years. There is a statute of him in Gorsedd Gardens. Most people today haven't a clue who he really was yet his name still resonates. It once meant something. Its history is real. So much better than the streets to the far east of the city with names like The Shires, The Meadows and, even after all my lampooning down the years now actually in use, Mallards Reach. A street where no mallards ever flew.

When I came to view my first City game in about 2006 it was deep winter, ice blowing through the concrete stands. Blokes bought coffee just to warm their hands. I watched the game, a desultory exercise producing no goals, amid constantly shouting fans, arm thrusting Hitler salutes, chanting about the Ayatollah, sheepshaggers, fear, derision, the inability of the opposing team and *%&*$! everything else. Everyone smoked. You could suffocate. The ban had only recently started and in this Bob Bank open enclosure was impossible to enforce. There was no joy, I remember that.

The game had a ball which moved and bounced. Men with slick and swift feet and clever boots would catch and spin the thing, knock it like a shooting star, arcing through the air. That pitch has gone now. It lasted until 2009 when the replacement stadium opened on the wasteland opposite.

Ninian Park had a shop in which you could buy extruded plastic models of the players, a foot tall, objects for the mantelpiece. They made one of Sam the Man, Sam Hamman, the notorious Lebanese building contractor and club owner at the time. Sam was celebrated for walking onto the pitch while games were in progress, striding among rival fans waving a Welsh flag on a long pole and standing provocatively with his white hair and camel coat right behind visiting teams' goals. This was the era of Cardiff's notorious Soul Crew, rival fan bashers of the first order. Hooliganism was allowed or, at least, tacitly endured. How many fans bought their Sam model for display in the front windows of their terraced houses nobody knows.

Ninian Park is now houses. Cardiff City, a club constantly up against the financial edge, sold the site, jammed between Canton rail sheds and Cardiff Bus's main depot to Redrow in 2009. There are now 142 houses in place of the stands and the goal-filled grass. The houses snake in crisp and compact moderness along Bartley Wilson Way. In the middle they have created a sort of decorative garden where kick-off pitch centre is marked with a plaque.

Bartley Wilson was the football club's founder. A Bristolian litho printer and soccer enthusiast. He came to Cardiff in 1895 and formed Riverside AFC as a way of keeping local cricket players fit during the winter months. After a decade of progress the Riverside club was allowed to change its name to Cardiff City. The newly arrived city status for the coal dark town of Cardiff was a huge civic boost. The club moved from its inadequate ground at Sophia Gardens to the new Sloper Park, as Ninian was originally going to be called. Cardiff City FC. Players in the Southern League. First match a 2-1 defeat of Aston Villa. The Bluebirds were on a roll.

The Cardiff team began in chocolate-brown and gold, chequered like harlequins. In 1908 they switched to a blue shirt and white shorts. The Citizens, as the team were colloquially known, then became The Bluebirds. Belgian playwright Maurice Maeterlinck had a play called *The Blue Bird* running at the New Theatre at the time. It's a link, stranger things have been true.

In 2010 billionaire Vincent Tan bought the club. He was at the head of a Malaysian consortium bent on world football domination. He wanted to bring back Cardiff's 1927 form when they beat Arsenal at the Empire Stadium to win the FA Cup. Done it once, do it again. Tan invested, extended the stadium's capacity, built new training facilities, and in 2012 dropped the club's century old blue strip for a new world-beating red. Why did he do this? Because he wanted to make his mark? Because red is lucky in the east? Or because this was a national Welsh colour? If Tan also replaced the pacific bluebird with the warlike dragon wouldn't the world see his Cardiff FC as the Welsh team? Premier League, helicopters, owners' boxes. Tan's Cardiff replacing Manchester United as the world's first football choice. You'd see him there on TV with his new red Cardiff top stuffed into his formal trousers, forever smiling.

Red didn't work. The fans hated it. There were sunless years of kit burning, Tan-distributed red scarves and red hats left strewn along Sloper Road, pitch invasions, the threat of mass ticket ripping, fans refusing to attend, the end of football as we knew it in the capital city. What made it worse was that the team itself fell from grace. Through mismanagement, bad player purchase, and maybe even the superiority of their opponents, the team slid back from the Premier League. Cardiff went through a run of managers, all of them moved on or sacked, to arrive where they are as I visit again. Contenders.

Blue, however, is back. Tan has acquiesced.

I'd last come to the Ninian Park replacement in April, 2015 for the unveiling of a memorial plaque to poet and life-long City uber-fan Dannie Abse. We'd stood in the cold sun, the stadium the equivalent of a Welsh pyramid isolated in the centre of a vast empty car park behind us. Tony Curtis, Cary Archard and Mike Jenkins made speeches. Nick Fisk and a few others read poems. The old Ninian Park gates had been preserved and hung as memorials on new pillars just behind. Dannie would have walked through them hundreds of times. Is that then end of poetry at the club? I doubt it. Poets Mike Jenkins and Nick Fisk attend every game. Lloyd Robson would too if he wasn't in New York.

Today though there is no sun. This is Friday night with the game under lights and kicking off at 7.45, a time decided by Sky, the broadcaster, who press the financial peddles. There's a new manager, Neil Warnock, and a mighty amount of spin and razzamatazz. His beaming face is on the front of the programme, Ken Dodd hairline, Frankie Howard nose.

Cardiff are playing old rivals Bristol and there's a large crowd. I witness the longest queues I've ever seen for KFC and inside use what has to be the most capacious urinal in the world. The atmosphere is buzzing. There are tribal chanting supporters, kids in

City hats, blokes with scarves and more women than I imagined football could ever attract. In the supporters shop, a sort of Bluebirds Matalan, everything in the world that is brandable has been and is being resold at twice the regular price. Cardiff City chocolate, beer mugs, key rings, tooth brushes, clocks, hats, garden gnomes, duvets. You can buy yourself a lime green goalie's outfit if you like the idea of standing out from the crowd at the pub.

In the stand we sit. On the pitch players are parading kids wearing Cardiff FC kit. This, it turns out, is the escort experience and costs £175. If you have it done with City mascot Bartley Blue, a man in a sort of knitted costume resembling a cartoon bird, the price unaccountably rises to £250. Half-time you can come on and play an 8 minute game of soccer for £40. Nothing in football is cheap.

The game itself is exciting. The combination of a new manager and ancient rivalry makes it so. In the Canton Stand the fans chant and wave their arms for the entire game. Up behind them are drummers beating out time. The Bristol fans are corralled in the Ninian-Grange End corner. Lines of visored yellow jacketed security staff and columns of empty seats separate them from everyone else[8]. The home fans demand the world do the Ayatollah and most of us do. This beating of the head in grief mimics the action of Iranians at the funeral of Ayatollah Khomeini in 1989. It's been a Cardiff activity now for more than 25 years. Pain transformed to joy. Neil Warnock does it and the crowd go wild.

Cardiff win. Bristol's only goal is scored while a Cardiff player lies injured and is therefore a matter for contention. Cardiff's two in contrast are both full-on victories. Gladness permeates the air. Is this the turning point? Will I come again? Might.

THE LIDO AT LLANDAFF

Visiting the lido in the dark Seventies after a long night in the Conway had never been a good idea. I'm in the bushes at the northern extremity of Llandaff Fields, almost as far as you want to walk in the company of a taggle of bards and poetasters full of beer. The poets are led by Arthur Callard[9] who has surprised me with the speed with which he has divested himself of shoes and jeans. We have climbed the small fence, negotiated our way across the back of the changing huts and are now frolicking in Llandaff's outdoor lido. This is the seventy-foot pool which was declared the best open air swimming baths in the country by Chairman of the Corporation Parks Committee, R.G. Hill-Snook, when he opened it in 1923.

Forty years on when I return to remind myself of how late night literature originally felt I find the changing rooms gone and the pool itself filled and full of ornamental trees. With the avenue of great horse chestnuts marching up the Fields' path you've just walked you'd never know such a legendary leisure facility had once existed.

Before Cardiff's first attempt at a by-pass, Western Avenue, opened in 1933 the land here formed part of Court Farm. Llandaff corn mill stood where Llandaff Rugby Club now is. In the middle distance, if you knew where to look, was the meandering Taff with the great house of Gabalva standing on its banks.

Today the mill leat has been filled and its sluices, spillways and millponds lost. The Prichard Bridge, which crossed it, linking the old with the new graveyards of the cathedral, has been restored by the Llandaff Society. The leat's westward run on to a second mill has been subsumed by local allotments. Taff alluvium now grows beans. In the nineteenth century this fulling mill[10] and its associated cottages were used as a home for fallen women, The House of Mercy. They still stand. They have been restructured as the Cardiff

Riding School with a restored grade two listed miller's cottage next door, now used as a private house.

At the bottom end of the WJEC's car park, however, beyond a security fence and in a sump of laurel and ivy, a small section still exists. "When the weather gets bad it fills with water," Jonathan tells me. This is Jonathan Adams, encountered earlier at the Sherman Theatre (see page 24), the man who built the WMC and more recently the WJEC's castellated gateway to the west or east, depending on which way you are driving, at the end of Western Avenue.

The WJEC, the Welsh Joint Education Committee, has been here since 1948. Until recently its offices were housed in a knockabout rehash of a nineteenth century domestic house and the nearby former studios of early commercial TV entrepreneurs, Teledu Cymru. The studios, not really the best place from which to run a UK national educational organisation, were known as the black box. "I used to feel a sense of menace when I thought of the WJEC," Jonathan says. "But they were also guardians of something that needed to be deferred to." An exam board, a maintainer of scholarly standards, the people who set those dreadful papers everyone had to sit when they were in school. Still available, I learn later. Early scripts, marked and going back many decades, are housed in storage off site. If you had the patience you could return and see just how clever your younger self really was.

Today the WJEC is doing well. It provides, marks, and maintains qualifications in use by educational institutions right across the UK. The fact that post-Assembly Wales has diverged from the English path has doubled the WJEC's market. Manager Lucy Hopkins tells me that their Eduqas brand is a world beater. Educas means learning. In its mangled form this Latin word crosses boundaries that Welsh will not.

Jonathan sketches the ground plan of the building into my notebook. He has bent the north-facing front walls round into the heart of the structure as if this were a sardine tin – a giant T with an elongated tail. Here décor-softened externals are visible inside the atrium foyer. Conference rooms and milling areas beckon. The WJEC building majors on meeting spaces. Your security pass gains you access through electro-locked security doors much as a chip-operated cat flap does. Except, while I'm there, half the visitors appear to stumble and need to be helped. The future can be a difficult place.

The ideas at work in the building's design overlap. The north-facing front is clothed in protective metal cladding with visible castellations, "a sort of Ninja castle from which legendary warriors spring to surprise you," says Jonathan. I had no idea he harboured such aikido leanings. The cladding panels are shaped to recall the multi-coloured construction of many nineteenth century Cardiff buildings. Jonathan has limited himself to three polygonal shapes cut from a single aluminium sheet. These permutate right across the frontage and then reappear inside.

The metal castle stands on a plinth constructed entirely from found river cobbles. Dug out of the site when constructing the foundations. The builders, Willmott Dixon, had a hard time getting their heads around the idea of material for free. But river cobble use does link the construct very firmly with the site's history. Builders have always done this. Reused material from earlier structures, made the best of what was available immediately to hand.

The south-facing aspects of the building are hung with warm clay tiles. Inspiration comes from viewing the way domestic buildings lean against town walls, the kind of thing you can see in Chester and in Tenby. There are vents near the roof to allow bats to gain access. "There were bats in the attic of the original mill house,"

Gareth Pierce, the jeans-clad CEO, tells me. We are standing in the roof garden unable to peer over the parapet because building regs require it to be more than two metres high. Not that the space is actually a garden yet either. For now it remains an easy to drain terrace dotted with chairs, a place to go to smoke. The grass and potted trees have yet to arrive.

There is a local activist who complains that the WJEC's tree cover in the park beyond is not dense enough yet. Jonathan's warm clay walls are still too visible, as if that were something detrimental. This is actually a splendid structure. Its design concepts have been realised with such style. It's a post-modern place that does not unsettle. How many polygon shapes are there on its walls? Do they really recall ballast reused as building stone as seen in the walls of Ebenezer in Charles Street? They do. The cobble plinth is emulsioned safe as it walks past the WJEC's ground floor bookshop. But below the surface it's still in touch with its river origins. The clay tiles look just like the kind of thing we'd make in Wales but in reality although ordered from a supplier in Ruabon they've been shipped here from the Caribbean.

Upstairs the shape and size of the admin spaces are derived from ISO 216[11] paper sizes. Window ledges accurately accommodate A4 stacks of exam papers. A4, A3, A2, A1, and A0 repeat everywhere you look. Most of the windowsills I see however contain not papers but family pictures in frames, ornaments, tubs of biscuits, coffee cups, mini jungles of spider plant and cacti. The WJEC's menace is slipping.

I go outside, to the immediate south, to photograph the place where the poets once drunkenly bathed. I do a lot of this, visiting absences, locations where only the motes shimmer. Around me locals perambulate, exercise dogs, push prams. Western Avenue's gateway traffic snarl is hidden by trees. The fields are full of engulfing green.

Notes

1. *Captain Video: Master of the Stratosphere*, Columbia Pictures. Release date: 27.12.1951 but shown in British cinemas right through the 50s.
2. The Bute Terrace site continued to be used to house Gas Company and later Gas Board offices right up until 1999. Snelling House, a modernist all-glass high rise set of offices were built in 1963 and eventually sold and converted to The Big Sleep Hotel in 1999.
3. http://lar5.com/ikea/
4. Available Monday to Friday to anyone signing up to Ikea's *Ikea Family* loyalty scheme.

5. Ely Paper Mills was founded by Brown and Evans in 1865 and vastly expanded by Thomas Owen in 1877. By the turn of the century the mill was the largest producer of newsprint in the UK. The company was eventually taken over by Wiggins Teape, later known as Arjo Wiggins Appleton. The mill closed in 2000.

6. Two feet, four inches.

7. The tunnel runs from a gully accessed from the north east corner of Tesco's Culverhouse car park. It emerges 1867 yards later near Alps Quarry Road. Check Roger Newberry's blog at http://rogernewberry.com/2014/06/24/adventure-is-out-there-the-wenvoe-tunnel/

8. Post-game violence on the roll home along Sloper Road included setting off flares, and punching both stewards and each other. Six arrests.

9. David Arthur Callard, 1949-2006, author of the literary biographies *After Pretty Good for a Woman: The Enigmas of Evelyn Scott* (Norton 1987) and *The Case of Anna Kavan: A Biography*, (Peter Owen 1992). His early poetry was published, alongside that of Geraint Jarman, in *Zutique* (Second Aeon Publications, 1969).

10. *Fulling* otherwise known as *tucking* was a process in the production of woollen cloth. Wool was cleaned of oil and other impurities and then thickened. Fulling mills used water-driven hammers to pound the material. The Welsh for a fulling mill is pandy, a word often encountered in place names.

11. ISO 216, the international standard for A, B and C paper sizes.

SOUTH

THE COAST PATH

On the far side of the gypsy camp on Rover Way there's a track. This is a designated component of the Wales Coast Path which runs 870 miles right round the edge of the country. The travellers are not keen. And you can see their point. Rucksacked and walking pole-bedecked family groups, chattering and map waving, are not what you want outside your windows. This Wales Coast Path is not quite what it seems either. For at least 20 per cent of its length it deviates from sea-facing to meander inland avoiding those sections of the trail where land owners have refused permission or there are other obstacles. Not all of Wales' edge is cliff top and beach. A fair slice of it is industrial slum, rolling mill, disused dock, quay, warehouse, sewage works, power plant, scrap metal dump or land given over to the storage of everything from disused caravans to clinker.

The Cardiff component, this trail around the flat southern edge of the capital, is no exception. Finding it is the first challenge. I've parked at Tesco Pengam Green. The store itself has been built on the site of the short-lived Rover gearbox factory which occupied the land from 1963 to 1984. British Leyland, which owned Rover, was once thought of as Cardiff's work-providing salvation. These moorlands, formerly the tidefields of Pengam Farm, began their modern life as Cardiff Aerodrome in 1931. The inventor, Ernest Willows, had flown his early Willows airships from here in 1905. The levels flooded regularly even then but when seawalls were built in the 1930s air traffic increased. The airport became a Spitfire and Hurricane base during World War Two and a target for German bombers. It closed to aviation for the longer runways of Rhoose in 1954.

When I was here as a schoolboy in the 1950s there were wrecked fighters, a burned-out oily Messerschmitt, and the remains of a control tower. Today there's nothing although the flatland I cross, now that I've escaped the crisp order of the supermarket car park, has the remains of tarmac there deep among the grass. Runway.

The Coast Path among the bushes, bunds, drainage ditches and the thundering grit of Rover Way's non-stop and mostly industrial traffic is pretty resistant to discovery. For a publically-funded facility and jewel at the centre of the government's public health policy you'd expect a sign or two. But there are none.

Skirting the traveller's camp to the east, avoiding a cluster of corralled cockerels and stumbling through the remains of several fires, blackened wood and sundry clinker everywhere, I reach sea's edge. Could be the path. There's nothing else. Locals have helpfully marked passage by towing several cars here and setting them alight. The way for two hundred metres at least is blocked by broken glass and the remains of burned-out vehicles. Seawards is a sewage outfall and a sheet of glutinous mud. Gulls circle. Well they might.

The path, for this it has to be, improves as it rises heading west. On maps as recent as 1950 the land here didn't exist. This whole salient of coastal Cardiff south of Rover Way is reclaimed. All of Tidefields Road, the Tremorfa Industrial Estate, the clinker dumps, the traveller's camp, Sim's scrap metal yards, Cardiff Reclamation's fireworks stores and the Foreshore MXC's motor cross park were once tidal estuary. The land retreats in Preseli. Here it bulges and returns.

At a point somewhere to the centre of the seaward prominence I sense something you rarely experience in this city – silence. I'm out of sight now of both the traveller's camp (behind me) and the Cardiff Waste Water Treatment Works (to come). There may be bulldozed piles of waste from Celsa's arc furnace but there are also yachts in the distance circling Flat Holm like a flock of gulls. The water below has lost its look of estuarine sludge to become maritime instead. Cardiff on sea, at last.

Ahead lie the water treatment works in a coast-hugging line. Sludge is caked here, water filtered and digested. You can smell the ripe edge of these processes humming in the air. Globe-shaped gas tanks stand like something out of 1950s SF. Mars invaders lurk within. Quatermass is on his way by Landrover to investigate. Seaward there are moulded hunks of GKN-era steelworks clinker in use as a palliative against coastal erosion. The path turns, landward, towards the edge of Ocean Way.

There's a beach nearby which I visited once in the company of Brendan Burns, hunting for a local replica of his then obsession, Pembrokeshire's Druidstone. It wasn't the same. I'd come also with a team of amateur photographers hunting for great things to shoot. Everyone snapped like fury, taking in the boulderfield of waste revealed by a retreating tide.

Today the tide is in and the wrecked glory that is this combination of main sewer outfall and drainage reen, Cardiff's final beach, is largely hidden from view. I reach the road again, traffic blaring. The official Coast Path now trails inland through the business park splendour of Ocean Way. Artics and cars thrash towards Splott and the city centre. The coast itself bends on towards the heliport and what remains of APB's still working Cardiff Port. Warehouses stand behind security fences. Signs warn against entry.

I slog back along the side of Celsa's steel maker, the furnace recycling scrap metal in a renewable roar. The dust on the pavement resembles that on the moon. Robot trains move on the steel maker's track towing ingots towards the mill. Red heat rises. There's little to choose between the never-ending thrum of the traffic and the perpetual thunder of the furnace. I wipe motes from my eyes. Then suddenly Tesco appears again. White and welcoming. Café inside. I almost break into a run.

THE CROWN PATENT FUEL WHARF

Harold Pinter is on the platform being asked about *Mountain Language*, his latest play. In his answer he's prevaricating, just as we expected he would. Ron Knowles, his interlocutor, is doing his best. Knowles has written a book[1] on understanding the absurdist playwright so he's well placed. But Harold is holding on.

This is the Cardiff Literature Festival, 1994, back in the days when big lit in Cardiff roared. We are assembled in the Captain Scott Room at the Royal Hotel on St Mary Street. The walls are mahogany panelled in elaborate Victorian style. It was here in 1910 that the ill-fated British Antarctic Expedition held its farewell supper. Trevor Jones, Chairman of the Chamber of Commerce, proposed a toast. There were copious cheers. The Expedition officers drank to the monarch. The room was known as the Alexandra Room then, named after the wife of the king. Music was provided by F.G. Roberts' String Band who opened with 'The Hero of the South'. The 100 diners present ate fillets of beef *Terra Nova*, followed by soufflé Capt. Scott and then finished their meals with South Pole Ice Pudding. This was the 7/6d officers menu. The crew, slightly more boisterously, ate at the Barry Hotel lower down on St Mary Street. There the menu cost 2/6d.

The Captain Scott Room, as the venue was subsequently renamed, was on the first floor. It had an antique plushness redolent of Empire endeavour. The wooden walls gave the impression that you were dining while sitting inside a walnut. It had been hired down the years by a variety of organisers of literary extravaganzas. R.S. Thomas had read here in one of his rare forays back to the city of his birth. So had Nigel Jenkins, Robert Minhinnick and John Tripp. It had also been used for civic society meetings, chambers of trade round tables, union bashes, 21sts, 18ths, bar mitzvahs, wedding receptions, engagement parties and all kinds of other celebratory wallops that involved eating with alcohol.

In the new millennium when the Grade Two listed 1860 hotel was comprehensively refurbished the Scott Room was moved up a floor and provided with a new mahogany wood bar. You can't see the joins. When I visit it is full of eastern European waitresses bustling in preparation for a corporate banquet. A glass case in the corner displays Robert Falcon Scott memorabilia, photographs, contemporary newspaper cuttings. I ask a woman with striking orange hair, bearing down on me with a set of silver serving spoons, what she knows about Scott. "They do it every year," she says, "the Scotts. They have the dinner. They eat the same things. They do it all over again." The Scott Society in a Groundhog Day loop forever.

The Cardiff Scott connection is scattered all over the city. In the National Museum, or more likely its store, they have the restored wooden figurehead stripped from *Terra Nova* when it returned to Cardiff in 1913. This stood for decades in debilitating rain on the promenade, then known as the dam, at Roath Park Lake[2]. The ship's binnacle is on display at the National Assembly's Pierhead building. There's a memorial plaque, paid for by what appears to be a group of reluctant Cardiffians, on display at City Hall. There was a Captain Scott bed, once, in the Bay's Hamadryad Hospital (closed 2010, now apartments). Latest arrival, 2003, is Jonathan Williams' *Antarctic 100*, a fractured larger than life-size ceramic memorial to Scott and his crew. It stands in Waterfront Park, outside the Norwegian Church. Cardiff keeps its Scott connection going.

On the west side of Roath Park Lake's prom, just down from the Terra Nova Café stands Elfed Evans' Chelsea Flower Show silver medal-winning garden. This was created in honour of Scott for the centenary. It's been rebuilt here after a stint at the RHS show in Bute Park. Gardens that travel are how it now is. Centrepiece is a pillar reminiscent of a ship's mast. It stands on a map of Antarctica engraved into paving. Behind is a purple grey fence with porthole cut-outs. There are a few shrubs. You don't walk in it, you gaze. But as horticulture it makes its point.

The Scott memorial that has become a city icon is the Lake Clock Tower. This is the famous white-washed lighthouse structure shown on all the postcards: three floors high, balcony, slit windows, locked and blue painted wooden door, accessible only by boat, model of the *Terra Nova* as a weather vane on top. It stands, just out of reach, among the thrown bread and squawking ducks half way across the prom. This monument has already been offered for sale on Rightmove replete with cod photographs showing a vast interior, a lounge with panoramic underwater views, a bedroom big enough for a harem and with windows showing sheets of water and passing rowboats. It was a 1915 gift to the city from F.C. Bowring, Chairman of the Liverpool shipping company which first sold Scott the *Terra Nova*. Bowring was not as altruistic as this gift makes him sound. He was at the time prospective Liberal Parliamentary candidate for the Borough of Cardiff.

You'd think from this plethora of memorials that Scott's Cardiff connection was rock solid. *Terra Nova*, Cardiff ship. Half the crew born in Grangetown, the officers in Penylan and Scott himself in Cyncoed. Despite reports to the contrary in contemporary newspapers none of this is actually correct. The association with Cardiff was driven by local shipowners, notably Daniel Radcliffe, and by the *Western Mail's* enthusiastic editor, W.E. Davies. They were the ones who raised the expedition's funding and talked local companies into supplying the ship without charge. The expedition was in receipt of complimentary barometers, crates of Stone's

Ginger Wine, cooking utensils and tents and sleeping bags. The Crown Patent Fuel Company gave 300 tons of their compressed coal dust and bitumen briquettes, fuel that being cuboid would stack neatly. And weigh less.

The *Terra Nova,* a constantly leaking former whaler, was loaded to sinking point. It was decked with Welsh flags donated by generous Cardiffians. A few wanted the Draig Goch run up the South Pole, when Scott got there. Others asked for pieces to be chipped off the pole as souvenirs. Earth science was not an Edwardian strong point.

Before she sailed *Terra Nova* had been tied up at the Crown Patent Fuel wharf[3] where locals were charged half-a-crown for a tour. Only a hundred bothered. Understandable when you translate 2/6d into contemporary money and find that it comes out at £20.50. The wharf is at the western end of the Roath Dock, one of the Port of Cardiff's two remaining operational docks, and totally empty of shipping when I visit. The land that once held the Crown Works has been cleared in advance of development. As a hotel it says hopefully on the billboards. At the edge, through a flimsy wire fence, you can see the bollards that once held Scott's ship firm. Ghosts drift in the heat.

The ship lasted until 1943. She'd been redeployed from decades of Arctic seal fishing to war-time work supplying allied bases in Greenland. Sea water had breached the hull and swamped the boilers. The crew were rescued and the ship set alight. The burning hulk was ingloriously sunk by gunfire. The leaks for which she'd become famous finally became unfixable.

HODDINOTT HALL AND THE WMC

Coming through the Bute Tunnel I hear Alun Hoddinott's *Clarinet Concert*[4] on the radio. Its fluent neoclassical rhythms fill the car. How many others could recognise this music from the few bars I hear? But chance is on my side. These recent weeks I've been researching the work of this great Welsh composer. He was a master of the brooding, of the rhythmic and of the dark. I want to know why he has a concert hall named after him in Cardiff Bay. Breadth of vision, prodigiousness of output, tenacity, age? You can get famous by always being there. But for Hoddinott this has been more than simply turning up. By the time he died in 2008 his back catalogue had reached national treasure proportion – 6 operas, 10 symphonies, 20 concertos. In total it was more than 300 pieces strong.

Welsh music, it seems, occupies similar territory to that of Welsh writing – a sparsely populated place given to acres of the worthily mundane occasionally illuminated by flashes of the profoundly great. Sometimes I wonder that in performance its sheer seriousness is the thing that's holding it back. Participants dress formally and silence between pieces prevails. Is there no way out? "We try to include the popular," Chris Painter tells me, "The BBC Proms with the Pet Shop Boys in the programme, perhaps. Pity is that the Pet Shop Boys never return the compliment."

Chris is a composer and a former pupil of Alun Hoddinott. He's currently music librarian at the BBC and just the man to show me round. We pass the entrance to the building's get-in yard where it was originally proposed to hang gates illuminated with new bilingual poetry from Ian Davidson. The hinges would play snippets from Hodd's clarinet masterpiece as they moved. But, as so often happens in Wales, decision makers had a crisis of confidence and we got a roller shutter instead.

The Wales Millennium Centre (WMC), the artistic centre of Cardiff Bay, first opened in 2004. The building was already much addled by financial restraint and difficult compromises but even in its amended form the architect's vision for a truly Welsh cultural focus shone through. En route things had been lost. There was no Welsh national art gallery, no multi-cultural centre. There was also no central indoor plaza onto which all artistic residents would face, no place where art in its many forms would mingle. Yet the WMC's auditorium, its poetry adorned frontage and its astute referencing of the matter of Wales through the materials of its construction was a brilliant achievement.

What many did not know, after the inevitable what is it for philistine razzamatazz had died down, was that the WMC was not actually finished. What we had in 2004 was just Phase One. Phases Two and Three, when resource would allow, would follow. Hoddinott Hall, the BBC National Orchestra of Wales rehearsal suite, recording studio and concert hall was to be Phase Two's centrepiece. The BBC Governors loved the idea. Their facility would be in permanent view of the Assembly's Senedd building next door. Assembly Members in charge of broadcast funding streams would pass the BBC's illuminated signage on a daily basis.

Except they didn't. In the cause of design excellence Millennium Centre management had banned all external signboarding. The BBC was reduced to a glass panel on their get-in yard entrance door. Invisible unless you had already arrived.

Phase Two which also included office suites for the Arts Council and the WMC itself opened in 2009. It was late and achieved not without difficulty. The aspect of the hall itself was changed by the architect to make it fit available space and to avoid having more than one public entrance. Tim Green, the man responsible for the Hall's interior, then sought synergy with the idea of the Welsh Victorian chapel and in this he has succeeded. Timber with masonry above, the big seat out front, an acoustically silent space where even your breathing sounds holy.

Up on the third floor is the Grace Williams Studio, an acoustically high-end space for the recording of smaller groups. The chapel-like wooden acoustic lining from the main hall continues here. We gaze out of a high and rare Hoddinott Hall window onto the still vacant lot south of the multi-story car park outside. In the distance you can see the space ship curves of Viridor's Ocean Park waste incinerator. Chris points. "You could have moved the whole of the BBC there – Roath Lock Studios, Hoddinott Hall, that facility they are building outside the rail station. Everything in one place. But someone decided that wasn't to be."

To the east, angled at the junction of Pierhead Street with Bute Place is the site for WMC's Phase Three. Forgotten about temporarily but still there. The Pod as it was once called. An egg-like tower reminiscent of Norman Foster's London City Hall in one sketch I've seen. What could this place hold? Restaurants, accommodation for the First Minister, an official residence as Ron Davies wanted the Pier Head Building to be. A true National Gallery for Wales maybe? A reflight of that Roald Dahl Children's Centre once on the cards. A docks museum. A club with lights and chill-out, space and smoke. My guess is that it will never be any of those. High-end apartments, more likely. A hotel. Or an empty dome of shimmering air to hang on for further decades until the time is right.

Back in the sleek acoustic splendour of Hoddinott Hall Chris shows me where the Chorus sits. High up, near the lights, where the air gets thin. "Someone usually faints," he tells me. The Hall's public programme always includes a fulsome slice of Welsh material. The works of Daniel Jones, John Hardy, Hilary Tann, William Mathias and Hoddinott himself all feature in this year's programme.

How hard is it to enter this world? Chris's own work – symphonies, concerti, opera pieces – full of brooding and melodic roars follow the trajectory travelled by Hoddinott, his mentor. "You need determination. Having a conductor onside helps. Alun Francis did my *Third Symphony – Fire In the Snow,* a commission for Orchesta Filharmonico de la UNAM in Mexico City. It was a great success. Broadcast twice on TV to a million viewers. Full coverage in the Mexican media. But back here in Wales, not a word."

Chris shifts his amiable bulk, and moves on, work-day shorts and large man sandals. Years ago he gave me a CD of an early violin concerto. Loan me something typical of your style, I'd asked. I put it into the car player from where it revealed its uneasy and edgy form. I played it twice and then to my consternation couldn't get the reject button to work. It played for most of the following week until I eventually hauled it out with a pair of long nosed pliers. "Ah, the technique worked," said Chris. One way to ensure an audience for your output I suppose.

Outside, in the Millennium Centre's airport check-in foyer the crowds are surging. It's mid-August, Cardiff's Bay Beach and Fun Fare is in full swing outside in the Oval Basin and there are visitors everywhere. Fifty or so sweep past on the behind the scenes tour. At Mrs Pratchett's sweetshop recreated in the space once occupied by the Touch Trust and looking a bit like a branch of Mothercare the Dahl books are stacked. This is the centenary and Welsh claims on the Norwegian's allegiance are high.

When I came here at the end of last year hunting Dahl traces for a commissioned piece of anniversary psychogeography[5] I couldn't find a single Dahl title on sale anywhere. Now the Bay is full of them. Dahl, true Cardiffian. Check the real name of the Oval Basin – Roald Dahl Plass. Redesignated in 2002 by Russell Goodway, Council Leader and friendly giant in the company of both Liccy, Roald's second wife and the Norwegian Ambassador.

On my way back, driving north, the Millennium Centre's poetry helmet recedes to become a piece of fun fare architecture in my rear-view mirror. It's not really part of us, the Bay. It's still a destination rather than a component. A place to go to. A Cardiff satellite glowing in the dark.

Music Listened To Immediately Following Hoddinott's Clarinet Concerto

Cage, John, *Second Construction (1940) For Four Players* performed by the Roath Ensemble For The Greater Good.

Albinoni, Tomaso, *Concerti a Cinque, Op. 5,* Anna Maria Parc Cathays *violino* avec Bois y Blacbord

Schwitters, Kurt, *An Anna Blume¸* (vcl) nach oben in den Vier Bars, Castle Street, Cardiff

Shostakovich, Dmitri, *String Quartets Nos 14 & 15,* Brodsky Quartet, chorus Cor Cochion Caerdydd

Meazey, Peter, *The Grangetown Whale*, Llandaff Cathedral Choral, Reid, D. *bass*, Stephens, Meic *spoons*.

WHERE THE A470 FINISHES

At Bay's rim with the red brick of the Pier Head to your side and the impounded water of the inner harbour out front there's a bronze ring. A giant affair you can walk under and hide inside. It's large enough to anchor dreadnoughts, a Celtic torque wearable by a giant, pointing its open end out across the breadth of Wales. This is Harvey Hood's *Celtic Ring*, installed in 1993. It's a work that has blended in so well with the Oval Basin that most visitors think of it, if they think at all, not as art but as street furniture, a wind break, an artefact left over from the docks, something to do with shipping that they don't understand. Inside its rim you can read Hood's bronze embroideries – maps of the dockland, the flotsam of cargoes in low relief, sails, compasses, echoes of dock buildings that once were, churches, warehouses, even the front of the cigar-shaped Cardiff Bay visitor centre that was dismantled in 2010.

Hood's artwork is as much a beginning as it is an end. The A470, the Welsh road that links the north with the south, starts here, or finishes. You can track it back up Lloyd George and on to Pontypridd, Merthyr and the further reaches of those parts of Wales of which most Cardiffians know nothing. That art sits at one of the most psychogeographicaly significant places in the city seems more than appropriate. If Cardiff were meditating then this would be the place where the in breath stopped just before the out breath began again. A place of stasis, of past and of future meeting.

The Bay itself, in redevelopment at a rapid pace since at least the arrival of Hood's masterpiece, has become much more than a seat of government, a hot spot for the upwardly mobile and a visitors' dining destination by the water. It's also a huge, open, and publicly accessible art gallery. Start to look and you'll encounter works everywhere. Constructs, castings, bas-reliefs, dialogues, representations, abstractions. Art works. Quite early on in the process a centrepiece of Bay expansion was the requirement for developers to offer a percentage of their project budgets for art. 1%. Small beer. But it's bought a lot.

This most significant of recommendations was enshrined in Vivien Lovell's *Strategy for Public Art in Cardiff Bay*, a document published by the Cardiff Bay Development Corporation (CBDC) in 1990. Suddenly there was art where previously there'd been dark. The extreme recommendations of the report suggested a total art budget of £30m, which was never reached. The Barrage, however, did end up as an artist inspired snake rather than the straight line originally preferred by engineers. And visible and usually touchable art right across the Bay arrived in abundance.

I'm touring with Wiard Sterk, Netherlander, sailor, bicyclist, and public art entrepreneur. He was the last head[6] of the Cardiff Bay Art Trust (CBAT) and its successor, Safle, the organisations largely responsible for matching the sometimes recalcitrant percentages for art with the works themselves.

Before CBAT's intervention public art in Cardiff was either seen as a remnant of the industrial age (statues of the Butes, John Cory, Lord Aberdare, John Batchelor, Viscount Tredegar on his horse, and others, mostly done in bronze by Goscombe John and placed on plinths near City Hall). Or some misguided latter-day intervention, erected with little consultation (but often dramatic effect) such as the great spray of coloured plastic fragments that adorn the Gabalfa flyover underpass. These appeared pretty much at the same time as Eastern Avenue did. Suspicion as to their creator points towards a student relative of one of the engineers.

Until the establishment of CBAT Cardiff had no policy. Our public art arrived by scattergun, often at the whim of then men at the helm at the time. A lot of it still does. Wiard points to the run of bronze figures of women, miners and children that now adorn Queen Street. Statues purchased in a job lot from the sculptor's yard having already been rejected earlier by Milton Keynes. This still happens, Wiard complains. Bad art gets installed while no one is looking. There's an incongruous peace sculpture on the bayside beyond the Pierhead and then a dreadfully composed figure of Ivor Novello with a pointy leg sitting on a bronze chair in the wind outside the Wales Millennium Centre. To this list should also be added the woman holding a seagull in the air on Kingsway along with some of the sculptures in our parks. Why are these things where they are? They are all a bit like the line of sea-facing cannons on the former dockside just along from the *Celtic Ring*. What did those things shoot at? What wars do they recall? Outside what was once the HQ of the Taff Vale Railway just what did they once defend?

The successes of CBAT and its sustained policy of careful and sympathetic intervention are by now obvious. Art in the public realm of Cardiff Bay is as natural as it is striking. CBAT's first triumph was *Secret Station*, Ellis O'Connell's piece from 1992, on a roundabout in Pengam, the eastern gateway to the Bay. This was quickly followed by Brian Fell's *Merchant Seafarers' Memorial*, the half face, half boat that lies on its side outside near the steps to the Senedd. Wiard points to this as the best there is. Established against the might of architect Richard Rogers who, when building the Senedd, said it was in the way. The seamen themselves originally wanted a cenotaph, a plinth with names on but were persuaded that a book of remembrance was more appropriate and less likely to be defaced.

Out east at the edge of Splott is the third of CBAT's greatest hits. The Magic Roundabout. That's its colloquial name, proof of acceptance by the public at large. This is Pierre Vivant's *Landmark* from 1992, a wild assemblage of road signs on a grass road island which the artist wanted to have removed after time had worn them. But when public art enters public consciousness that can't happen. The work was refurbished in 2017.

The failures, Wiard says, are the works that never made it beyond the drawing board. The ones that never happened because of developer intervention, lack of nerve, or both. Typical would be the mirror to *Secret Station*, a welcome *Western Gateway* on a roundabout near Asda in the western Bay. New Yorker R.M. Fischer, an artist with an international reputation, had designed a work of steel towers but the developer, aided by Council Leader Jack Brooks, shot the project down. "It will look like a bunch of illuminated chimneys" was the main criticism. "The people want statuary" was a phrase often heard. Conformity won the day.

We do a tour of the central Bay, the inner harbour as the Council boosterers like to call it, a half an hour ramble in what turns out to be freezing air. From Brian Fell's *Merchant Seafarers' Memorial* we walk to the *Celtic Ring* and then up into the Oval Basin. The basin was built at the same time as the Bute Ship Canal, later known as the Bute West Dock, in 1839. It was filled in using slipped slag and slurry recovered from Aberfan in the 1960s. On its western rim stands *Deep Navigation*, Stefan Gec's pair of rusty columns from 2000. These were made from recast scrap – one from material recovered from Tower Colliery and the other from debris found in the centre of the Oval Basin. The project structural engineer warned that they wouldn't last. "They'll be all rust in 500 years," he said. As Gec desired, they corrode beautifully in the Cardiff damp. One bears a list of all the collieries that sent their coal out through Cardiff. The other has a list of the world destinations to which it went. Cardiff the port at the centre of this enormous industrial exercise. No sight of coal anywhere now, not a cinder.

In a tower up above the first floor of Mermaid Quay's Signor Valentino's Italian restaurant, in a place technically known as Tacoma Square (but try asking for directions from your average Cardiffian), is Andy Hazel's *Willows Clock* from 2000. This assemblage of spinning hands celebrates the dirigible flights Captain Ernest Willows made from Pengam in 1910. Willows became known as the father of the British airship. National fame. But nothing in his home city beyond the Wetherspoon's on City Road and this splendid clock, no longer working. No budget. We move on.

Brian Fell's work appears again in a large metal slab next to the stall selling tickets for boat trips out to the Barrage. It runs the words of John Masefield's three stanza lyric poem 'Cargoes'. Masefield, Poet Laureate until his death in 1967, had no Cardiff connection. He was born in Ledbury. His poem, however, sums up the kinds of things ships sailed with on the seven seas: "ivory, and apes and peacocks, sandalwood, cedarwood, and sweet white wine", "diamonds, emeralds, amethysts, topazes, and cinnamon, and gold moidores" and then "Tyne coal, Road-rails, pig-lead, Firewood, iron-ware, and cheap tin trays". We turn round the corner into Lower Bute Street and there they all are in steel replica, more than twenty, hanging from the sides of buildings, up above eye level. Every one of the items Masefield mentions realized by Fell and fixed to the brick. It's a brilliant trail, unmarked, undirected, a Bay secret in plain sight.

Back at the Wales Millennium Centre where the heaters work and the air seems easier to pass through we regroup. Like many of the buildings of Cardiff's Portland stone Civic Centre[7] the WMC is also adorned with public art, has art on its surfaces, its glass, its DNA. Writ huge is Amber Hiscott's startling *Colourfall* that burns down three floors of glass bulkhead at the northern end of the Centre's booking hall, an area officially known as the Angorfa, the anchorage. On a circuit of the building outside Hiscott's wavering line etched on the glass serves as a reminder that the glass is there. It follows the skyline contours of the Welsh coast, top to bottom, flailing and soaring.

The CBDC was wound up in 2000. Formal art agency planning and delivery of public art ended a decade later. We're on our own now. We'll get new statues if the developer likes them and new art in the built fabric if the right kind of planning mind considers it. The A470 heads north from where we sit. Onwards to where the sea is again, at Llandudno.

MOSQUES

During the time I worked in Butetown the mosques never made a sound. Not that I heard. Even on Fridays. There were no muezzins wailing from the minarets nor recordings of the Qur'an played over loudspeakers to summon the faithful. It was not like this in Turkey or Egypt or especially in Indonesia where the call to prayer ran loud through the night as competing mosques vied to become the most holy. In those places it was if something had to be proved. But maybe here, in one of Britain's earliest Muslim conclaves, we no longer need to bother.

In the Bay populations pass through each other without touching. The Somalis, the Yemenis, the Asians, the Afro-Caribbeans, and the working-class whites rarely mix with more recent arrivals – the middle-class professionals in their water-facing apartments. They don't interact. They rarely speak. The old town, Tiger Bay, the Docks, Butetown, remains a place apart.

In the enclaves behind Bute Street where the teeming tenements of Victorian Loudoun Square once stood the Sixties slum replacements have themselves been replaced. New block walls, new bathrooms, new doors. The tower blocks have been tidied with new communal entrance halls, new shops, new grass, new pavements on which to park your car.

Cardiff's Muslims go back centuries. This was once a coal port, a starting point on the Empire's mainline to India. Sailors from the Yemen and Somalia worked the ships and settled here. In the 1930s they established a mosque, Cardiff's first, in a row of terraced houses on Peel Street.

During the war the Peel Street terraced mosque was bomb damaged. In 1946 the local Muslim community built a replacement on the same site. This was a two storey whitewashed, square turreted structure. It was erected behind a white wall and had an Arabic arched entrance. It stood until 1988 when the street was cleared.

A short distance south, on Alice Street, another mosque was erected in 1967. Redeveloping the site of Stewart & Lloyd's iron tube warehouse Cardiff's new mosque offered a radical shift in design. It had a circular prayer hall with an offset rectangular residence and entrance lobby. It was as distinctive as it was non-traditional and it didn't last either. It was demolished ten years later in 1977.

Its successor is the much grander and very much still extant Masjid-e-Ziwiyah, the bronze-domed and red brick minaretted Yemeni[8] Mosque of the South Wales Islamic Centre. You can see it if you peer down Hannah Street. It's not a structure you'd traditionally expect to find in a Welsh city. The design, by the Davies Llewelyn Partnership, is classical Arabic. There are stained glass windows and a great dome. The minaret is topped with three brass balls and a crescent moon. It stands with its back onto Canal Park, the grass space that's been made of the drained canal basin that was once here.

Inside, in a space smaller than I had expected, calm perfection rules. The racks of religious books are ordered, the walls illuminated with Arabic script, the carpet lit by daylight filtering in through the coloured windows of the dome above. The community centre outside offers further space for education and gathering. There are plans to extend upwards although build is yet to start.

Things change rapidly, Azim is telling me. Abdul-Azim Ahmed is of Bangladeshi origin, Sylhet, although you'd be hard put to tell that from his accent. He's the Assistant Secretary General of the Muslim Council of Wales but with his jeans and distinctly non-Islamic-looking beard he could easily be a doctor, a performance poet or a financial advisor. "I deal," he says, "with Anglophone Islam." He's made a study of Cardiff mosques[9] and has concluded that there are four types: the house mosque, the converted church or chapel, the community hall with additions and the purpose built. His 2011 survey counted eleven in Cardiff. Muslims in Britain[10] who have an online mosque map show in 2017 there to be nineteen. Azim says he's sure there are others.

Mosques usually establish themselves for a single racial community. There are Bangladeshi, Somali, Yemeni, Iranian and Pakistani managed centres in the city and, although technically anyone is welcome at any mosque, as with churches, the faithful tend to stick to what they know. But with more than 30,000 Muslims in the city and with the vast majority of those being under 25 ethnic differences are inevitably becoming less apparent.

At Noor ul Islam, on Canal Parade just south of Callaghan Square and in sight of both the twin towers of St Mary's Church in Wales and the high dome of the Greek Church of St Nicholas, the Somali[11] Mosque is a style free brick cube. Its facilities are much larger than those at Masjid-e-Ziwiyah and it even has a glass-sided roof light in the shape of a low dome but no coloured glass. But it lacks Yemeni finesse. By comparison things here are more informal.

The core language is Arabic, like Latin once was with Roman Catholicism. The imam understands and directs. The faithful follow. The only place in the world where this isn't so is post-Atatürk Turkey where Arabic was banned in favour of native Turkish. A progressive act. But under Recep Erdoğan even this is now fading.

Given its long Muslim association is Cardiff a particularly spiritual place? Azim says it is. Spaces habitually employed for prayer become holy by usage. In Islam rhythm and recurrence are both significant. Timing is essential. You pray five times a day and the timings cycle. The festivals Eid-al-Fitr and Eid-al-Adha spin through the calendar. "The next time I will need to fast through the long hot summer days where nightfall is as late as ten o clock will be in thirty years' time," says Azim. "I'll be old."

With so many mosques taking over the spaces once used by now redundant churches I ask if conflict of faith ever manifests itself. No. The reverse. Spirituality adheres to place. Belief persists, a mark made in god's endless continuum of space and time. Former churches are easy, their prayer spaces always faces east. That's the direction of the second coming, of Jerusalem, and also of Mecca. If you say God's name somewhere often enough then that the place itself will become holy. "Although," warns Azim darkly, "some of the ubers might have trouble with that idea." "Ubers?" "The uber Salafi, particularly stringent Saudi Arabia-inspired Muslims." I understand.

We visit the Dar Ul-Isra mosque on Wyverne Road, a converted community hall with extensions funded by the Assembly Government. The building was originally erected in 1940 as St Teilo's Parish Hall and sold to the Muslim community in the 1980s. It's a storefront mosque. From the outside, other than by reading the signboard, you'd have no idea that this wasn't a warehouse stocking hairdressing supplies or car parts. There's no Islamic adornment. In this hall a local scout troop once met. "We keep that tradition on," says Azim. "The First Cathays Al Huda scouts use the space now. Same tradition as the one established by Baden-Powel."

Azim is surprisingly open when showing me his spiritual practise. He demonstrates ritual cleansing before prayer and then prayer itself. The space around me in the first floor prayer hall, thick carpet, no shoes, little adornment, resonates. Around are notices in Arabic, quotations from the Qur'an, details of a women-only Pilates class, a Twitter feed through which subscribers can receive daily calls to prayer, a silent and personal contemporary version of the muezzin's wailing song. Near the shoe racks is a sign showing a red bar diagonally across a mobile phone with the words "No call is more important than the one from him". There are also a number of bilingual signs directing mosque users to the prayer hall and the office. English and Welsh.

That language issue wasn't one I'd expected to meet. Azim explains that it's more to express this place's wider Welsh identity. Wales not England.

Scores of Qur'ans in many editions are stacked on shelves at the side. Most are in Arabic. Some have commentaries in other languages. A few in English. None in Welsh[12]. Half a dozen on the bottom shelf are in Bangla. Arabia's writ is inordinately strong.

At an Interfaith evening held in the prayer hall later the same week I'm offered mango juice and a chair. The event is centred around the three great Abrahamic religion's responses to the refugee crisis. The three speakers, Stanley Soffa from the Cardiff Reform Synagogue, Canon Aled Edwards from Churches Together in Wales and Sheikh Ali Hammuda, an imam from the Al Manar Mosque opposite the Sherman Theatre all make pleas for peace and toleration.

Palestinian Sheikh Ali is a magnetic orator. He moves his hands in a twisting swirl as he talks. He switches fluidly from Arabic to English, his tenor voice pulsing with conviction and hwyl. He uses no notes and speaks without pause or stumble. He is the nearest thing here to a Christian revivalist. I hear small gaps of 'yes' pulsing in the air behind me as he expounds belief. Call and response. As if this were Pentecostal prayer. Sheikh Ali is dressed as I expected a traditional mid-Eastern educated imam to be. Endless beard, flowing robes. Hard core with an attraction all of his own.

The messages all three offer converge. We are all immigrants. We are welcoming people. We should help to the maximum. And then we should do more.

The canon tells us that shortly he will walk from Bethlehem to Egypt to raise support. I am incredulous until I discover he means Bethlehem in Carmarthenshire and Egypt in Denbigh[13]. Still impressive, nonetheless. We get chapatis and samosas and rice which we eat while smiling at each other. We have agreed no plan of action but we do know that others feel as we do. In some places there's a world which cares.

Outside the other world returns. Street life. Empty air. I'm out of the bubble where we all speak to each other and back in that place where, all too often, we don't.

THE BAY AND BALTIMORE

Crossing the Bay from where the train has dropped me is a delve back into the past. The station is now called *Cardiff Bay* rather than the earlier and more prosaic *Bute Road*. This was all my front room five years back when I occupied an office eyrie in Mount Stuart Square. It had a round portal window which let in the rain. Through it I could see dockland housing. To the west was a buddleia-riddled brown field waiting for the bulldozers. Mount Stuart Primary hovered like a landing flying saucer. Techniquest's blue dock crane broke the skyline. The newly impounded Bay waters glistened beyond. At the millennium's turn the rate of change around the inner harbour was exponential. Each day delivered something new.

Today improvement has visibly slowed. The white heat of change has moved to Porth Teigr at Roath Dock with its new digital media and drama village, apartments, hotels, and the BBC Roath Lock studios looking like a Moroccan fort.

The Bay has been in redevelopment since at least 1986 when the pagoda-like new County Hall opened. A bright spark with influence had visited Baltimore on the United States' Eastern seaboard and liked the mix of waterfront redevelopment on the site on that city's old and run down docks. Here were now museums and convention centres, new hotels and high income apartments, sports stadia, art galleries, eateries, retail plazas, public parks and promenades. Baltimore sparkled. American, sure, but we could do it here, couldn't we?

Jack Brooks[14], Council Leader, took up the idea with passion. South Glamorgan Council were stuffed into tight accommodation in the Hodge Building on Newport Road. Against strong staff resistance Brooks fronted the move to the old dockland. Clerks would have their lunches with the seagulls. Accountants would scuff their shiny black shoes on the post-industrial ground. The deed accomplished, Cardiff tilted. Secretary of State Nicholas Edwards, aware that the city needed more done than the Council alone could provide, proposed a major new development initiative starting with a barrage to impound Cardiff's massively high tidal waters and to eliminate the mud flats. As a delivery mechanism Edwards founded the Cardiff Bay Development Corporation (CBDC). Former soldier Geoffrey Inkin was made chairman and, keeping the local world on side, Jack Brooks became his deputy. To sleep easy Brooks secured the board appointment of his protégé, future Council leader and all-round booster king, Russell Goodway. The mix was in place. CBDC would reunite the city centre with its waterfront, promote the creation of a superb new environment, attract residential and commercial development, achieve the highest of standards in design and build, stimulate opportunity, and establish the whole area as "a recognised centre of excellence and innovation in the field of urban regeneration". Hell, that's a brief. Could it work? We would be a Welsh America reborn amid the wreckage of our steel making and dirty, coal exporting past. Not for the first time in its history Cardiff boomed.

Picking Baltimore, a Maryland city of twice Cardiff's population might have at first seemed fanciful. But there were similarities. To begin with Baltimore had, in its day, been the second leading port of entry into the United States. It was well used to immigrants. It had a history of heavy industry. Its docklands had had their fair share of abandoned warehouses and post-industrial wreckage. It was a great brewing city. It was here they had invented the six-pack. The local accent was called *Balmer* and it sounded quite unlike that of most American east coast states.

This was a Cardiff fit. Brooks was convinced and so were a good many others. A trade in research and familiarisation trips to Maryland flourished. By the start of the nineties if you hadn't gone then your grip on power was lacking. We sent out the BBC Welsh National Orchestra on a goodwill visit. Our great and good courted their civic leaders. We rang the Baltimore bell. In 1991 Rhodri Morgan, then MP for Cardiff West, told the house "If one lives in

Cardiff, is involved in politics and has not been on a trip to Baltimore, one has not lived." Cardiff, capital of Wales, twinned itself with Baltimore, the eastern American heavyweight.

In 1994 Inkin and Development Corporation CEO Michael Boyce went to the harbour at Baltimore on a factfinder. They told the local paper, *The Baltimore Sun*, that Cardiff intended to outdo the American city. Cardiff would have visitor attractions of grander design and in greater number than Baltimore. Cardiff would build a world-class infrastructure including an opera house to the revolutionary designs of Zaha Hadid. Most significantly the Welsh capital would also avoid Baltimore's mistake in failing to link the old city centre with the new. Cardiff's main connecting highway, boulevarded and truly triumphant, would not be stopped by the rail link. It would burrow.

In reality, of course, most of these grand ideas failed somewhere in their delivery. A pub, the Baltimore Arms, featuring John Allinson's jazzy murals, opened at the bottom of Bute Street. A sign went up announcing Cardiff's new twin. We were one with Baltimore; but not for long. In 1999 the Council cabinet decided to relinquish twinning links in favour of pursuing San Francisco and Cape Town. Neither of those ideas came to realisation either. By 2006 the Baltimore Arms had closed and was redeveloped as a letting agency.

The Bay should have been an unmitigated wonder but twenty-five years after it all started with so much drum and thunder, the weaknesses, lost opportunities and failures of courage are increasingly visible. "The most exciting waterfront development in Europe[15]" it isn't. The lop-sided Welsh Champs-Elysees that is Lloyd George Avenue goes nowhere. Rapid transit to the city proper is still yet to arrive and what we do have, the Queen Street heavy rail link, terminates far too early. The tracks should run on, to the WMC, to Mount Stuart Square, to the Sports Village. But they don't. Core redevelopment in the inner harbour could have been urbane and human but instead it's cheap and prefabricated, dealing in dining at the expense of almost all else. In the making of the Bay as a "superb environment in which people will want to live, work and play" critical mass has yet to arrive. CBDC's core objectives wobble.

The Bay, however, does have both the iconic Millennium Centre and the Senedd building next door. Professor of Urban Design John Punter calls this "a model of sustainability and of Welsh parsimony and a stunningly simple form in contrast to all its neighbours". Both the WMC and the Senedd, he says, suffered poor management in their delivery. Punter reckons this "has done serious damage to Cardiff's and Wales's reputation for design standards and patronage[16]." When it comes to change and despite Russell Goodway's good intentions, we all too often falter.

New housing, which has arrived in quantity, certainly provides places to live. But not neighbourhoods. Not really. A lot of the new housing is situated either behind the walls of gated developments or in blocks which have turned their collective backs on the streets which link them. There's little shared community space and scant opportunity for new neighbourliness. Maybe that's less the fault of the developers and more of the world we are now moving into. But walk around. Check the high-rise wharfs and the blocks sitting like hotels at the western Bay's water edge. These places do not feel warm and welcoming.

It can be argued that a lot of what we see is the result of the 2007-2008 global financial crisis and the failure to finish what had so enthusiastically been begun. But now that redevelopment has recommenced Cardiff eyes are on the Ferry Road peninsula with the International Sports Village at its core. Everything faces the water. The Barrage, after all, has been a worldwide success. Despite local opposition, fear of rising groundwater, the roaring forties of Cardiff weather and scaremongering about wild life you can now walk across the water to Penarth in twenty minutes.

Which way next? The two most influential Cardiff political leaders of the past twenty-five years, Russell Goodway and Jack Brooks "resolutely believed that politics was about working for the people rather than with the people[17]", as Kevin Morgan has it. But we are in a new era now. Boosterism, the art of exaggeration and spin worthy of the best of pulp fiction novelists, has run its course. For the future its conurbation and city regions – or maybe we should head back over to Baltimore to see how they've done.

Notes

1. Knowles, Ronald, *Understanding Harold Pinter*, University of South Carolina Press, 1995.
2. The figurehead was presented to the National Museum of Wales by Cardiff Parks Committee in 1932. It was restored to become a centrepiece in the Scott Centenary exhibition *From Coal To Pole: Wales and Antarctica* in 2014.
3. A contemporary newsreel clip of *Terra Nova* leaving Cardiff is viewable on YouTube – https://www.youtube.com/watch?v=RR8aNabrWL8 The City dignitaries and their

hat-wearing wives shown waving from the bridge were taken off by the tug *Falcon* as soon as the *Terra Nova* reached Breaksea Point. Expedition officers did not enjoy their enthusiasm. Captain Oates is reported as commenting "The Mayor and his crowd came on board and I never saw such a mob – they are Labour Socialists" (Johnson, Anthony M., *Scott of the Antarctic and Cardiff*, Captain Scott Society, 1995).

4. Hoddinott, Alun, *Clarinet Concerto* (1950) recorded by Gervase de Peyer with the LSO and available on Lyrita SRCD 330.

5. *Dahl's Cardiff Places* in Walford Davies, Damian (editor), *Roald Dahl – Wales Of The Unexpected*, UWP 2016. An edited extract from this appears as *Roald Dahl's Cardiff North Ley* on page 123.

6. Sally Medlyn 1990-1995. Sue Grayson Ford 1996-1998. Carole-Anne Davies 1998-2003. Wiard joined CBAT in 1994 and became director in 2003. He was CEO of Safle 2007-2010.

7. For me the best adorn the former Glamorgan County Hall, now the Glamorgan Building of Cardiff University. Here massive neo-Greek sculptural groups adorn the entrance steps. These are by Albert Hodge from 1912. They represent Mining on one side and sea-borne Navigation on the other. Miners mix with great horses and Neptune is all flowing robes and trident. On the left one of the miners looks like the late poet Bob Thomas. On the other Neptune's assistant resembles the still living Cardiff poet Jonathan Brooks. Go and study these things, they'll pay you back.

8. Yemeni management but, of course, a mosque open to all.

9. *Visual Dhikr – A Visual Analysis of Mosques In Cardiff* – A dissertation submitted to Cardiff University in 2011.

10. *Muslims in Britain* offers a range resources for Muslims and non-Muslims in Britain to live and work effectively together. It includes a comprehensive searchable mosque map. http://www.muslimsinbritain.org/index.html

11. Somali management.

12. Although I was assured a Welsh translation is contemplated.

13. A sponsored walk – Escape to Egypt – from Bethlehem in Carmarthenshire to Aifft (Egypt) in Denbighshire raising money for Christian Aid.

14. John Edward 'Jack' Brooks, Baron Brooks of Tremorfa, Labour politician, 1927-2016.

15. CBDC slogan.

16. 'Cardiff Bay: an exemplar of design-led regeneration?' – John Punter in *Capital Cardiff 1975-2020* – eds: Hooper & Punter, UWP, 2006.

17. 'Governing Cardiff: politics, power and personalities' – Kevin Morgan in *Capital Cardiff 1975-2020* – eds: Hooper & Punter, UWP, 2006.

JOURNEYS

SO WHICH DISTRICT DO WE LIVE IN?

Market Road is right in the centre of what was originally Canton village. It's still pretty much an epicentre for the whole west Cardiff Cantonian massif. Here I stop a man walking towards me dressed in reefer jacket and desert boots. "What district are we in?" "Pontcanna", he replies. That's what it said in the *Echo*. The Community Boundary Review of 2015 had just been published and Pontcanna had at last been given official status, carved out of north Riverside, darling of the Cymry Cymraeg, and home to more creatives than Greenwich Village. Or at least the residents liked to think so.

Victoria Park was blossoming east to meet it while Pontcanna itself, with middle-class passion, was rapidly heading west. This was a great estate agent powered burgeoning destined to put the economic map right. Working-class Canton fading. White collar Cardiff on the rise.

The boundaries of the districts of Cardiff have been improved and amended almost constantly since the place grew big enough to have districts in the first place. In medieval times Cardiff was in what was known as the commote of Cibwr which itself was in the cantref of Senghenydd. The town had two parishes: St John and St Mary. The Castle in St Johns, most of the town in St Marys. Beyond the walls lay other parishes with villages at their centres. They had names we still recognise – Roath, Llandaff, Llanishen, Lisvane, Caerau, Llanederyn. You didn't mess with where you were. The fields in between places saw to that.

The imperative to change things began with the industrial revolution. South of the town were the tidefields: the West Moors, the East Moors, the Leckwith Moors, the Canton Moors. Splott and Adamsdown touched them and then a whole lost region called Soudrey ran to the sea's edge from the gate at the bottom of St Mary Street. The village of Crockherbtown (now Queen Street) was absorbed early, the leper hospital run by the nuns of St Mary Magdalen at its eastern end abandoned and railways with their attendant stations established instead.

The great build accelerated as Cardiff steadily added outlying villages to its inner core. Roath, Canton, Grangetown, Cathays, and Splott came early. New construction, cheap and fast, added the now lost districts Temperance Town and Newtown. Tredegarville was built east of the Taff Vale Railway. The land between City Road and the old Merthyr Road (now Albany Road) running north from St Margaret's Church filled with workers terraces. Where you lived mattered. The moneyed had houses on the front near the docks. Windsor Esplanade and Bute Crescent. Or if not there then on Penylan Hill from where they could observe their businesses without the dirt of industry adhering. Tredegarville was a place of grand residences, town houses, villas with space and style. Newtown, the town's inner courts, and the tight terraces below Queen Street were where you resided if you were one of the labouring poor. Most of expanding Cardiff was like this. Eight to a room in back to front housing. Water from a shared pump. Streets awash with slurry.

As Cardiff town turned into Cardiff city living here slowly became a more egalitarian affair. Yet for many where they actually lived was never enough. Places needed to be enhanced. Elevated. Upgraded. They began to morph. Newtown to Atlantic Wharf. Canton to Victoria Park. Llanishen to Lisvane. Morganstown to Radyr. The Docks to Tiger Bay. Tiger Bay to Butetown. Grangetown to Grange. Ely to Leckwith. Cathays to Cathays Park. Or in the case of some letter writers to completely new places of which most of the rest of us hadn't heard: Waterloo, Hollybush, Coryton, Sanatorium Park, Maerdy, Tredelerch. Use of this last place name, actually the Welsh for Rumney, allowed for a whole new level of district oneuppersonship obfuscation. Y Rath, Treganna, Y Tyllgoed and Trelai are all traditional Welsh names for traditional Cardiff places. But they don't often appear on the fronts of buses.

In the Bay residents often had their own ideas. Sections of Butetown were sometimes known as Rat Island (the streets between the canal and the river), as Little Athens (the area at the top end of Bute Road) and with some of the streets off James Street known as Little Madrid. At one time a slogan on the rail embankment wall declared the place to be 'Independent Tropical Wales'. But time has moved and it's all Cardiff Bay now.

Over the years the Council made various attempts to corral Cardiffians into giving where they'd lived for years brand new names. Plasnewydd and Waterloo were two that never really caught the imagination. The same fate befell the more recent suggestion that the top end of Penylan should retitle itself Ty Gwyn.

Arriving as I write, however, is the next stage in the city's perpetual fascination with the renaming of its parts. The Local Development Plan demands the erection of thousands of houses on both greenfield and brownfield sites. The names of these places will inevitably be new ones. Some will relate directly to the land they will occupy – St Ederyn's, Plasdwr. Others will be named after the enterprises that formerly occupied the land on which they are being built – The Brickworks (edgy apartments in Trade Street), The Mill (family housing on the site of Ely's paper mill). Beyond that it's a free for all. Cardiff's newly christened places usually relate to sites the precise location of which only their developers are sure. Try pointing these out on a map: Churchlands, St Lythans Park, Parc Tyn y Gollen, Willowbrook West, Castle Quarter, Central Quay, Bayscape, Cardiff Waterside, Cardiff Grove, Cardiff Pointe.

And by the time you read this there will be more, for sure.

NORTH TO SOUTH

Getting a sense of the shape of this city has always been problematic. All roads lead to the centre. Stand in Penlline Road, Whitchurch and look for a bus to Ely. There isn't one. Sit in your car in Rhiwbina and try to think your way along the labyrinth that will take you to the heart of old Rumney. Not an easy task. The railways are no different. They run in their culverts, bent spokes failing to connect. Even the canal, when we had one, took the direct route through the middle. Cardiff's trapezoid resists all alternative crossings.

To get a grip on this city that is simultaneously a place of reassurance and alienation I decide to cross it completely, boundary to boundary, and to do that in several compass directions. I decide on the simplest traverse first – east to west. I get onto the new bus. This is a blue low-rider, so new it still smells of showroom. NAT, New Adventure Travel, is the service operator. Crosscity. X1. *We Give Change*. Every 15 minutes. £3 a go. Cheap as that. Thanks to them I discover that the city begins and ends with supermarkets. Pontprennau's far eastern Asda matching Culverhouse Cross's Tesco in the west.

I'd already tracked the north south route that the docks-bound Roath coal railway formerly took in an earlier adventure. I'd also driven across the city at speed, seeing little, and then cycled slowly around the not quite ring road and seen glorious everything. Now I decide to do it on foot again, riverine, sticking as near as possible to the north south waterway that made Cardiff. The river that was here long before we were, the Taff.

As a psychogeographic escapade this is hardly innovative. The

Taff Trail, a metalled byway running from the Taff's mouth to its source in the Brecon Beacons opened to great and green public delight in 1988. It doubles as the final section of National Cycle Network Route Eight that reaches from Holyhead to Cardiff Bay. Hundreds use it daily, *de rigueur* helmeted, in their twenty-first century lycra. But where there's an alternative I'm going to take it. I'm going to deviate. Muddy track on the left bank when the Trail rushes on the right, inland diversion east when the path goes west, bridges, underpasses, lost tracks through fields. I'm going to take them all. According to the measurements I've made Cardiff border north to its southern extremity in the Bay is seven miles. A stroll.

My companion on this amble is John Osmond, last with me on the Great Heath ramble (see page 140). He's a thinker, author, political candidate and the only man I know who has walked every inhabited street in north Pembrokeshire. Done not for creative but for political purpose: Preseli was his constituency after all. Not that he's actually been elected, of course, or even come near, but he has tried and hard. On the course on which the party sent him, for door stepping voters, they instructed him to carry a clipboard and to always write down whatever voters said, no matter how irrelevant. That way they would feel that their voices had been heard and, as a consequence, might vote for you. Patience of a saint I'd say.

We meet in the chilly car park of Taffs Well station, not the city this, still RCT[1]. The border is a hundred metres to the south. Cardiff's southern and northern boundaries, like those of Wales itself, are both in water[2]. Here the border flies down the wooded slope from Castell Coch to plunge into the Taff opposite the yard of Jasonic Ltd, Builders Merchants and DIY. We stare at its place in the moving river as if a red-dotted line might be there, inked across the bottom. "So, if I want to, I can stand here in Cardiff and piss into RCT," suggests the yard foreman, come out to find what we are doing here so early in the morning. We all agree that, yes, if you want to, you certainly can.

Cardiff is a clean place these days, our heavy work has now mostly fled. Nonetheless there is still a subconscious anxiety that, somehow, profligate industry will return, will refill our air with smog and re-impose coal on our streets. To defend ourselves we riddle our townscape with parks and pathways, with riparian trails and byways, with lakes and ponds, with champion trees and greenscapes that serve to mask the railtracks and the highways that are the real lifeblood of the working city.

John and I find the sole walking route through the gorge with difficulty. Everything heading south has to come this way, stuffed and overlaid in the pincer gap between the twin eminences of the Garth and Castell Coch. Highway, river, canal (once), railway, thoroughfare, path, cycletrack, pipeway, local road, and pavement (just). South of the border it's all traffic at this time of the morning. Everybody else is on rush hour wheels.

We divert, in error, over the nineteenth century Ynys Bridge which once carried the old trunk road and walk into the dead-end of Heol Yr Ynys. This is a land of clutch fixers, wheelie bin cleaners, street lighting maintainers, low grade rambling industrial units filled with plastic sacks of rejected clothing: jumpers, leggings with holes in, ripped shirts. The one we call at is managed by two east Europeans who labour in the unit's cavernous and windowless depths. They yell "yes, no, out that way, no go back" when asked if there's a path south of here. It was the word "south" that did it, I'm sure. Under artificial lighting nobody knows where they are in the world anymore.

Formally the Taff Trail avoids the Taff completely here. It's up above us, zigging its way around the tourist destination of Castell Coch to reach the actual river again a kilometre away below Tongwynlais, Cardiff's northernmost reach, where the line on the

map is drawn. We track down Iron Bridge Road to reach the river opposite Gelynis Farm, still standing, still 1570 ancient. The iron bridge which leads to it and which we do not cross once carried a horse-drawn tramroad which linked Pentyrch Ironworks with Melingriffith Tinplate. Today it carries a Welsh Water sewer main and a footpath wide enough for a bike but maybe not a horse.

The river slides slowly south. Through trees there are glimpses of container traffic on highways, diesel units on rail tracks and endless new housing in crisp orange brick. But nothing intrudes much. The sense of green pervades.

At Radyr Weir Sawnus Construction have built a two and a half million pound hydroelectric scheme which pours the Taff through twin turbines and generates enough power to light most of Radyr. The owners of the project are the Council, pursuing their green agenda. They've been here before. Last century they operated the coal-fired power plant at the back of their Newport Road bus depot, built originally to run the trams. Control your own destiny where you can. It's a good working philosophy.

John, given to encapsulating political theories in single paragraphs, is telling me about the power of the regions and how it was felt for a time last century that the nation state was doomed. Europe has always had its provinces, its subdivisions, its East Midlands, West Midlands, Andalucía, Jura, Upper Austria, West Pomerania, Saxony, Munster, Ulster, Catalonia, Basque Country, Alsace Lorraine. Significantly a number of these regions, Catalonia, and the Basque lands, for example, cross nation state borders as well. A map of Europe with its regions prominent shows up as a far more ancient quilt than the European political heartlands we recognise today.

Power would come down, the plan was, some thinkers' plans, from the European centre to the regional diaspora. Not to the national state capitals. The nation states would slowly wither. The new closer to the people governances would prevail. It sounded leftist, especially with that Marxist word in there, *wither*. But I could see the benefits and the prestige.

John was convinced it could have worked. Wales with its ancient Celtic language mashed by Latin would serve us better than the less-European Gaelic of those other Celtic places where the Romans never reached. "Saunders[3] would have loved this," John insisted. "Power circumventing the nation state. Wales in charge of itself at last."

But despite John's 1992 series of TV programmes on the European borderlands and the convincing pro-regions political theory fronted by Prof Chris Harvie of Tubingen and Edinburgh none of this happened. Europe continued as a wrestling match among its richer components while Wales and Scotland and all those other provincial scatterings floundered.

The river moves on passing Forest Farm, the nature reserve that holds the one still-extant watered section of the Glamorgan Canal. Here, too, is the land that once housed the Melingriffith Tinplate Works, west of Whitchurch Hospital, and now bright brick redevelopment. In the nineteenth century there were eleven rolling mills here. All that remains is the reconstructed feeder pump that once lifted water into the Glamorgan Canal. Made of wood and standing in grass amid clean air. It works, allegedly, but nobody tends it.

Through the trees in the western distance we can see the land rising above Radyr. This place has now has lost all of its industrial age flourishes. Its quarry is exhausted. Its great shunting yards have been replaced with three storey town housing closely packed.

On south, skirting Whitchurch and then Llandaff North, Llandaf itself appears although amid the river-sided green you wouldn't know. Llandaf, the Welsh city known by generations of Cardiffians as *Landaff* but now that we're a real Welsh capital with cymraeg in surge again it's *Llan* and it's *Daf*. You say these words long and falling as if we were deep in Ceredigion, or someplace distant from the English border. The cathedral is there among the trees, its bulk well hidden. We pass it on the far side of the river.

Below us the city surges, you can sense it coming. There are glimpses of the flat roofs of tower blocks, the red light on top of BT's Stadium House, a flicker in the distance of stadium itself, glass and more glass, the sky gradually enlarging to dome blue above. The new city. We love to think, I tell John, that we are so original here in the Welsh capital. That we have replaced the industrial wreckage with new age build, made the centre a rain-defended shopping fantasy, added apartments, clubs, bars, pedestrianised self-indulgences where we can perambulate and ceaselessly party. Coal and steel, pale and mild deleted, varicoloured shots and craft beer sold from drinks lists that read like found poems instead. There are artworks and lights, multi-screens and restaurants as vast as assembly halls. It's ours, unique, Cardiffian, essentially and always Welsh.

But it's not, of course. Visit any of the English cities, Birmingham, Sheffield, Manchester, Nottingham, Leicester and you'll find they've done the same. Their apartment blocks look much like ours, although often they are bigger. "Ah, but they don't have barrages," John reminds me. Despite it all we do have a few things that are uniquely ours.

South of cathedralled Llandaf the great Cardiff parklands spread. The river routes through Bute Park, Cardiff's vast and central meadowland, a much underrated triumph of sense and style, keeping a green sward spread in the city's heart. At the Park's Secret Garden Café, first Taff-side watering hole in five miles, crowds jostle in the autumn sun. The Severn Sea, although you can't see it, can never see it, even from the final dockside, you can now sense is within range.

The barraged, no longer tidal river barely moves. From the suspended Stadium walkway, hung out over the Taff's waters we watch the river taxis ply their trade. If all this were mine I'd build cafés here, edging the river. I'd put bookshops on barges and sell flowers from dinghies. There'd be poetry readings given from floating platforms and tea dancing weekly to a ship-mounted orchestra playing its way from the Castle to not that distant

Penarth. Bogman, the guy who dresses in reeds and tells tales from a rowboat on Roath Park Lake, could be induced to practise his art on these waters.

Right now though, apart from the taxis and the boat that clears the weeds, there's little. We steer a course through Riverside or Canton or Grangetown, whatever this district of workers' housing and backpackers' hotels has today decided that it's called. The city's end is in sight. Somewhere down there where the sea lock once hung, where the land petered and the mudflats began, that's it, the southern border. In the sea, in the water, out at Cardiff's territorial three mile limit or whatever it is, offshore in the still extant mud.

We finish not at the bottom of the Oval Basin where the Taff Trail formally begins, nor at the flourish front of the WMC, the motor car start of the A470. Nor even at the Waterguard, Cardiff's most southerly pub. We sit instead on the wall lining the Bay's wetlands park. St David's Hotel with its seagull roof beside us. You can see John's house on Penarth heights from here, his writing eyrie, the place where he's deep into creating his trilogy of great Welsh novels rolling our culture through the 70s and the 80s. Except that he's not there today, he's here wasting his time sunning on a wall.

TWENTY STATIONS

Northmore and I are on the end of platform one at Queen Street Station. Northmore has on his trademark greatcoat, all itch and huge collar. He's got a handwarmer in one pocket and his pad in the other. There's a 2-6-2 Large Prairie heading three carriages coming in from Cardiff General. On Platform Two there's a pannier tanker waiting to go on to Barry Island. The air is filled with biting cold and smoke.

Northmore is the big train fan, much more than me. He knows all about spotting rarities at St Phillips Marsh outside Bristol and how to get to Green Park, the Midlands Depot at Bath. He's shown me the way to blag your way into Cardiff's Canton sheds and to do the same at the one time wagon works just before the bridge on Corbett Road. He's got into the shunting yards at Pengam and seen the saddle tankers down the docks. He's done all this but never before set foot on Queen Street Station. Or so he says.

We stand and stare at the tracks bending south. At Queen Street little terminates. All trains steam on for elsewhere. "No point in coming here really," says Northmore, "you can see much more at the General[4]."

In the years since operationally nothing has altered much. Trains still roll on towards Cardiff General (now known as Cardiff Central) or return up the valleys from whence they came. I'm there again, on the station, this time in the familiar company of John Briggs. He and Northmore share many features: greatcoats, handwarmers, love of industrial remains, flasks of tea and cheese sandwiches in their rucksacks. Not that John was ever a simple train number collector like Northmore. His interests were much broader.

As a building, however, Queen Street Station is nothing like what it was. The superstructure and platforms have been rebuilt at least twice during the past fifty years; the entrance has been shifted; underground access to the trains has altered. The past has largely vanished. But look hard and you'll find the insignia of the two founding rail companies, the TVR and the GWR, still present in the cast iron ends of platform benches. There's nothing visible, though, to commemorate the other two former users of this station: the Rhymney and the Cardiff Railways. British Rail hangs on with its Gerry Barney-designed crow's feet logo on a pole outside, probably the most famous transport insignia in the land.

John and I are here to test out Cardiff's metro, not that it has one yet. For as long as the city has been a capital dreamers, dopers and politicians have harboured the desire to establish a city-wide transport network using heavy rail. The incoming Cardiff Metro[5] will not be in tunnels like the ones in London, Glasgow, Paris, and Moscow but overground. It will link together the numerous strands of existing track that snake out from Cardiff centre heading north, south, east and west. Many times in the decades between Beeching and now visionaries have come up with plans for the simple linking together of these strands and the building of a few new suburban halts. This would result in a jam-free, endlessly green urban transport system to rival the world. Both business and commuter user would benefit. New shopping malls housing fast-food floggers, jewellery and t-shirt outlets and places where you can get your feet fixed by nibbling fish would infest the stations. Travellers would flock. The roads would empty, existing tarmac surfaces would last decades, flyovers would be taken down, the air would be better to breathe. But so far vested interests (including the owners of threatened properties along the lines of the new trackbeds) and, more significantly, lack of government grit and capital finance have inhibited real progress.

But there's a city deal happening, with cash attached, and for the first time in decades a real chance a fully-interlinked Cardiff Metro transport system will come into being. Electricity will be strung from poles and track extended to new unified transport hubs at M4 junctions. Cardiff Gate, the Coryton Gyratory and Burger King Pentyrch will become great new glass shopping palaces where urban road, rail and motorway meet. Down in the Bay the tracks will no longer terminate at Cardiff Bay but will slide on to new stops at the Wales Millennium Centre, the Senedd and the BBC at Porth Teigr, south of Roath Dock. We may well get new stations at Roath and more in the districts being built to the city's east and north. Connected Cardiff. It's almost touchable.

Already Christian Amodeo's I Loves The 'Diff have celebrated the future with their map of Cardiff's new underground stylised as if it were the London tube. Here they have added new stations at Sevenoaks Park, The Sports Village, Ikea, The Pumping Station, Chippy Alley, City Temple, Juboraj Lakeside, Clark's Pies, St Athan, Welsh St Donat's and Chapter. The proposed start of the Culverhouse Crossrail is marked with a cross. It's the system we'd all love to have.

Briggs and I set off to explore what we currently possess. We will travel on all the rail lines Cardiff operates and visit every station. There are, amazingly, twenty of these. John determines to set foot on every one. How will the city look and feel? Can we get everywhere we want? The train operator has helpfully provided us with complimentary tickets. At Queen Street with its new frontage, crisp booking hall, and London-style ticket barriers the system feels as if it is already part of the future. Even up on the platform first drinking tea at Café Cwtch and then mixing with the hundreds streaming onto the Cardiff Bay shuttle that sense of functioning future city remains.

It sticks with us as we bang around the great U of track that the train operator has, with a sense of prescience, named the City Line: trains every 30 minutes from north west Radyr to Cardiff Central and then rattling on to Coryton in the city's north east. The Radyr section hosts a string of comparatively new stations – Danescourt, Fairwater, Waun Gron Park, Ninian Park – which have all opened during the past twenty-five years. As we reach each one John leaps out to snap whatever he can in the twenty seconds or so that that the train dwells: conductor, station sign, mass of greenery, bemused fellow travellers.

At Radyr where a million-pound rebuild to provide new bridges, signage, access and lifts is in progress. Here we take a break. On the pedestrian bridge over the Taff that connects Radyr with Forest Farm we discuss the art of the shot. John shows me his Rollei 35 film camera, acquired in the 70s and still returning, he insists, better than digital pictures today. He talks about the social documentary photographer who recorded the fall of Ukrainian communism, Boris Mikhailov. Unlike his own, Mikhailov's work reveals a desperate and broken people wandering among urban detritus and failed buildings. The drunk. The damaged. The garishly incoherent. John's own recording of the social mores of today's Cardiff train travellers couldn't be more different. People with tattooed backs, overweight Merthyr youths wearing Jimi Hendrix tees, a woman this hot day in a fur-lined parka engrossed in *The Sun*. He engages with his subjects when he can. He smiles. With his American voice he asks permission to shoot. Hardly anyone says no.

The trick the company in charge of the infrastructure, Railtrack, have not yet pulled off is to make these tracks properly circular. City Line trains down from Radyr return the way they came. To get to Llandaff and Cathays you need to change.

We catch a four-unit high-speeding in from Merthyr. The carriages have prints of Caerphilly Castle on the walls inside. There's a real sense here of the Cardiff Region – that Cardiff is not just a city limited by border. Instead it's a component part of a much larger Wales. As you rocket through in your cushioned seat from the dormitory valleys to scintillating Cardiff by the sea what changes? Little, other than the train operator banning alcohol on everything travelling north of Ponty. Warning signs repeat this prohibition like a mantra at every opportunity. Don't drink, it's bad for trade.

At Cathays students and civil servants dismount bound for Cardiff's heartland. Queen Street, the café culture and Cardiff shopping centre is next. I'm beginning to see that without this Queen Street hub the whole rail system would falter. From the platform's southern end you can view an unrivalled city vista, the old city now almost entirely vanquished. No Cory Hall, Capitol, Dutch Café, no blocks of smoke stained Victorian housing. Instead it's the towers of the Capitol Centre, the University of South Wales, Altolusso, Liberty Bridge, the Premier Inn, the Big Sleep, the Radisson Blu. Among them the walls that surrounded the now demolished Guildford Crescent baths and the back of the Masonic Hall are still anachronistically extant.

We change trains and head west to Cogan on a service destined for Barry. Beyond Grangetown the tracks slice between the west Bay apartment towers and the green rising of Llandough. This is frontier land, west of the River Ely and, when I consult the map, not actually in Cardiff at all. That's the issue with this city. For what it does it's far too small.

Rolling back up to Coryton on the City Line shuttle again just to be sure we cover the whole network the atmosphere changes. The urban city retreats to be replaced with leafy banks and open parkland. These are real suburbs. Ty Glas, Rhiwbina, Whitchurch where the hospital isn't and then end of the line Coryton where it actually is. End of line is how it really feels as well. The passive growth of overhanging greenery leans in to brush to diesel two-car's sides, there are buffers up front and unmanned halt labelled Coryton with the first and only extensive flowering station garden so far seen.

We take a break and walk around Coryton's houses, a cul-de-sac mini-estate sandwiched between the hospital and the golf club. Handy for the trains but full of the noise of M4 and Northern Avenue traffic. When it was first built there was a serious proposal to name the station here as Asylum Halt. Early political correctness prevented that. On the return, station hopping over because we've done them all, John talks about real ale, his second interest, after photography. He's toured the new craft beer pubs of Cardiff far more successfully than I have it seems. He's done The Cambrian, The Lansdown, Hop Bunker, The Rummer, The City Arms and Zero Degrees in one staggering swoop. Did he reach them by train? No, he took the bus.

Have we got the start of a real Cardiff Metro? Hardly. Instead we have a set of scattered randomly distributed stations. They are where the tracks run rather than where people need them. Here they are: Coryton, Whitchurch, Rhiwbina, Birchgrove, Ty Glas, Heath Halt Low Level, Queen Street, Lisvane, Llanishen, Heath Halt High Level, Cardiff Bay, Cardiff Central, Grangetown, Ninian Park, Waun Gron Park, Fairwater, Danescourt, Radyr, Llandaff, Cathays. On a map could you put your finger on each one?

We had other stations, once, in Ely, Roath, Marshfield, Tredegarville, Cefn Onn (see page 116), Woodville Road, Maindy North Road, Clarence Road, Adam Street, Pentyrch, Llandough Platform, Walnut Tree Bridge, and Newtown. And if the money does arrive then maybe sometime soon they'll all return.

LEAVING THE CITY – SOUTH WEST

Now and again it comes on me, I have to leave. The world just has to be larger than the one which ever circles inside my head. There's a song from the time of the Vietnam War that plays and plays. 'We Gotta Get Out Of This Place'[6]. It might have come out of the song writing money machine that was the Brill Building but for a generation stuck somewhere they never wanted to be, it was an anthem. I've left eastwards already, rolling up Newport Road (see page 66). Today I'll travel south west. I want to connect the two eminences that mark this lowland, delta city. I'll walk from Penylan Hill to the headland of distant Penarth.

Penylan has loomed above me since my childhood. I've lived in many houses on its lower slopes and now here I am half way up to its dizzying two hundred foot top living in Bronwydd Avenue. Bronwydd means wooded incline – which this hill used to be, within my memory.

When those trees were just starting to be cut back, in 1952, on the Llwyn-y-Grant allotment gardens which lined the hill's south-east there was a discovery. Miss Remmington, a geography teacher at Cardiff High School for Girls, found the head of a 200,000 year old Palaeolithic hand axe. Evidence of the first Welshman at last. A direct line could now be drawn between today and our ancient Cymric past. Pious hope. This find was a stray, the Museum's archaeology department said, a lump of worked rock that came from elsewhere and had been lost, abandoned, or thrown away here among the Penylan loams. Miss Remmington's finding of it among the cabbage and runner beans did not necessarily mean that it came from this place.

The hill is made of Silurian Mudstone – old by Cardiff standards – a mix of Wenlock and Ludlow sand and limestone. The Cardiff Naturalists Society, which began as far back as 1867 and is still extant – a record for anything in this changing city – has over the years analysed the geology with trainspotter detail. Their 1906 *Transactions*[7] (accessible via the National Library of Wales Journals Online resource) analyse bedrock to surface at the time of the construction of Roath Park Lake. They discuss everything from the district's pale blue clay, hard red grit, decomposed feldspars and purple siliceous grit, to its well-jointed greenish mudstone. Anecdotal evidence shows that this hill is clay and, given a long summer drought, will crack and shrink. Houses will shift, as they did in 1976, and when repairmen were employed for months.

I head for the hill's highest point. Site of the defunct reservoir and the celebrated but lost Penylan Observatory. It's as if the scant history this district once had has been entirely lost in a rush of municipal redundancy. The 1897 reservoir and attendant tower was supplanted in 1920 by a new and larger facility on the Wenallt. The Penylan land transferred to the Council Parks department who developed it for public use: bowling green, tennis courts, paths, railings, seats. On the eastern edge a wooden hut housed the Observatory. Stargazing for the public continued (so long as they had obtained a permit from the town clerk in advance). The enterprise employed a 12-inch reflector telescope. This had been made in the 1870s and, along with an astronomical clock, donated to the city by its owner, Franklen George Evans, a medical doctor keen on the stars and good works.

The Council never planned to operate a municipal observatory. Most councils don't. The donation was a difficulty but for a time the facility was maintained. In 1925 the garden shed-like operation was upgraded to something more substantial. A curator, Dan Jones, was appointed. There's a shot of him in the 1930 *Cardiff City Observatory Handbook* which he compiled. He is seated beside his Newton reflector wearing round glasses, waistcoat and watch chain. He more resembles T.S. Eliot than he does Patrick Moore. By 1979, however, public disinterest and encroaching vandalism led the Council to close the observatory down. They disposed of the telescope and melted down its housing for scrap. The stars had been around for ages. They could wait some more.

The Park today is much less than it once was. There's no bowling green nor tennis courts. Building has encroached on both sides. There's a small wooded area where there was once a quarry, a roundel of grass in the centre, and a children's play area. No observatory, nor marker. The red-brick water tower has been tastefully developed as a private residence. To the garden's south stands the Cardiff United Synagogue, moved here in 2003 from the now demolished Penylan Synagogue on Ty Gwyn Road.

The route down, in the hazy sun, is a stroll of unexpected calm. I pass through the red-brick of Ty Draw Place, Kimberley, Mafeking, Westville and then Sandringham. I pass the school I went to as a boy and some of the houses I lived in. Three of them here. And all numbered 3, our magic digit. I photographed their doors once to show my aged, home-bound mother. She recognised not one. I know this district deep in my bones. I've run my memories of it so often now that nostalgia no longer works. It's like Zen. I've recalled and wallowed, remembered and regretted, and now emerged into a future where the heart plays no part.

The language the place speaks is nothing, a rush of wind, a brook full of weeds, sound of birds. Along Westville Park women throw balls for dogs. In the Mill Park and then Waterloo Gardens summer's growth is peaking. Emerging where the great house of Tŷ Mawr farm was until it was replaced in the mid-1960s by Tŷ Mawr old people's home I find an open, grassed-over space surrounded by traveller-proof bollards. The home was demolished in 2013 to make way for brown field redevelopment. But nothing has been started yet. The weeds waver. If it were up to unregulated me, I'd put a park here, with a fountain and swings.

Over the road, Newport Road, a main eastwards arterial is the place where Splott and Adamsdown rub against each other. Two inner city, working class, terraced districts of early origin. They were built to house workers in Cardiff's burgeoning docks and steel works in places near enough for them to walk to their employment.

Stacey Road School is built on what was originally Island Farm, owned by the Stacey family. It has a blue plaque celebrating football international Fred Keenor's attendance and a welcome board that uses twenty languages. This bloom of multi-culturalism sets the tone as I cross southwards. Broadway, a narrow passage east-west was possibly broad by the standards of its origins (as Green Lane, before the housing got here) but is no wider than a side street today. I can't tell if anyone has attempted twinning with New York's more celebrated version but who out there in showbiz land could you ask? Cardiff's version was once famous for its pubs but now they've mostly closed down.

The cultural mix the place displays today has as much variety as anything in the city (except possibly that already mentioned centre for world dining, City Road). The Ihsan Academy, the Al-Ikhlas Culture & Education Centre, a Polska restaurant, the Persian-Welsh Cultural Society, the Al-Madinah Halal Food Store, Latma Afro-Caribbean Beauty – Braiding, Weaving, Ar Agor/Open, and the Roath Sports and Social Club – £2 a pint. Beat that Weatherspoon's.

Coming out of Iron Street I pass the demolished Great Eastern, the original site of Upper Splott Farm. Beyond, on the corner of

Adamsdown Square, near Kames Place, is the Handy Loan Club, latest iteration of an operation that's been helping the hard up from here for decades.

South of the black bridge over the main London railink language, previously in flux, neutralises. Here, between the magic roundabout and the headquarters of Peacocks, is one of Cardiff's great gateways. This is a place where districts touch and passing drivers roar off into the mist. Splott meets Adamsdown meets the Bay and Ocean Park rolls off to the south in all its unknowingness. Ocean Park industrial estate with Ocean Way as its central highway is the least known area in the whole of the city. Artics bound for it for the first time never find it. Road signs are scant. No Cardiffian, to my knowledge, has ever been able to give accurate directions. Multi-laned traffic swirls.

Leaving, I take the waterside route, climbing a low wall and scurrying through a car park to reach the revitalised and now landlocked East Dock. Weed-stuffed, garbage floating on its surface, still as unmanaged and as badly taken care of as it was when I last wrote about it in 2002. This shallow inland lake, swum across by diving duck, and surrounded by a viable paved walkway should be a city asset. As run round as Central Park, as perambulated as much as Roath Park Lake, as fished from as frequently as the pier at Penarth. But it's none of these things. Railings buckle. Paving slabs lift. Lager cans sit among the buddleia and float on the dark grey water.

When I emerge, south again, beyond where the Wharf Pub once stood, scene of poets Lee Harwood and Chris Torrance's return from the lost during one Bay Lit Festival a decade back, the roads bristle up. Rhodfa Lloyd George, Canolfan Mileniwm Cymru, Y Senedd Cynulliad Cenedlaethol Cymru. The language has shifted again. Now it's in favour of Wales' minority tongue. Inside the WMC[8], the steel helmeted Opera House and arts centre, the child-friendly approach is strained but palpable. The Milipwts await. Ogi, Dyfi, Lecsi and Ponti will entertain you. Not quite Optimus Prime nor Iggle Piggle but they'll do.

Outside, Roald Dahl Plass is hosting a food fair. Lamb burgers, Breton stew, Spanish tapas, and cheese from places you never knew existed. The Plass was once the holding area for Cardiff's first dock, the West. A Bute venture with the same kind of success that Bill Gates had with Windows 3.0. A world-beater at the time. But infilled and built on now, home to Cardiff's secret replica of Venice[9].

The Norwegian Church proudly advertises itself bilingually.

Eglwys Norwyaidd. For the name in Norwegian you need to go inside. Beyond it is the Barrage. This £200m southern Cardiff limit stretches for twenty flat minutes out of the city. It heads towards the Vale's Edwardian, genteel and drowsy town of Penarth. Access is beyond the entrance to Porth Teigr, with its BBC studios and allied creative infill.

The road along the Barrage top could carry cars but it doesn't. The fastest thing you'll see will be the Bay land train with its blue engine and string of slowish toy coaches. Already plantings among the grass park-like edges of this massive structure are flourishing. No mean achievement as anyone who has been blown along here during the gales of winter will tell you. Out among the sea holly, thrift, campion, yucca and tamarix a lone soundstore wind-up audio information point is in action. It loudly discusses, in fluid Cardiff Central Station announcer and utterly comprehensible Welsh, plant and animal life in this heady marine environment. There's no one within a hundred metres listening. Bar the gulls.

The Vale, that outpost of the Anglo-Welsh, begins as soon as the barrage ends. The locks with their Swiss art[10] embellished upon them mark a frontier. Roger Fickling's bronze mermaid in the centre of a roundabout. After this, barring a bilingual sign showing the departure point for boats to Ynys Echni – Flat Holm – monolingualism rules. This is the Vale of Glamorgan, a place where the writ of the invader still firmly runs.

The street signs for Jenkinsvill (with the e stolen or maybe never ever there) point up a slope just as steep as the higher reaches of Penylan. On it is the Headland School. This occupies the Palladian-windowed premises of the onetime airy wonder that was originally the Penarth Hotel. Built by the Taff Vale Railway as a speculative venture in 1868 the hotel never took off. The hoped for travellers arriving on the new passenger line in from Cogan never came[11]. There were no shipping agents, sea skippers nor captains of Victorian industry. Despite offers of billiards, croquet and archery at the five acre site monied guests were as rare as Passenger Pigeons. The premises were converted into a children's home in 1918.

Higher, appropriately much nearer heaven, stands the imposing wonder of architect William Butterfield's St Augustine's Church. Viewed from Cardiff across the Bay this place stands for Penarth. It is its big-boned crown. It is the marker for the Vale town that, despite its status as dormitory suburb and its innate proximity,

is resolutely not of the city. Buried here is Joseph Parry, composer of the most memorable of Welsh songs, the one that outdoes even 'Delilah' – 'Myfanwy'. But I don't visit his memorial today. I sweat on for the top the hill. There I find the lane that leads to Penarth Head Park with its sea views that beat anything Cardiff could possibly offer. I slide, seemingly effortlessly now I'm on a roll, down past The Kymin. Beyond is conformist Beach Road and then the even more traditional Promenade and Pier. Penarth's original waterfront.

The Kymin is a still extant great house dating from 1790 built on the site of an earlier farm. Its preservation is in the hands of the municipality who use it for meetings and rent it out for what it loosely describes as 'leisure activities'. If it had been built in Cardiff then a developer would by now have opted for demolition and put in a dozen exclusive and inordinately expensive sea-view apartments. But this is Penarth.

As I round Beach Road's slow steep bend the sea front comes into view. Penarth as destination, Victorian promenade, pebble beach, ice cream, and the Vale of Glamorgan Brass Band settled around the entrance to the Pier. The band are playing wartime favourites to an audience of passing teenagers, couples with buggies, pensioners, a man in a wheelchair with a breathing tube, and a large woman with a dog. It's 100 plus years since Britain declared war on Germany and World War One began. 'Roses of Picardy', 'Keep The Home Fires Burning', 'It's A Long Way To Tipperary'. The extra wide conductor, dressed in dynamic black, waves his arms. There would have been a time when his audience would have been able to sing along. No longer.

The Pier, like the rest of the town, is a Victorian confection projecting into a cold, slate grey and massively unappealing sea. This, of course, might be part of its success. The Severn Estuary here is about as attractive as a Vietnamese swamp. You think about dipping your toe but when you get close up you run. Getting yourself out above the waters on a pontoon provides the best of compromises. Except this structure does not float. It sits hard on its cast iron screw piers with its many times refurbished wooden decking and its occasionally burned down pavilion. Fires and piers seem to go together. British structures built over water appear to be more at risk of conflagration than anything combustible on land. Penarth's Bijou Pavilion, a wooden building at the Pier's outer end, burned down in 1931. Orchestra leader Leonard Zanoni and his Moonbeams, in action at the time, helped bewildered and sometimes drunken dancers to the safety of the shore. The Pier was subsequently rebuilt but the Bijou was not replaced. The present and much grander landward pavilion has, in its time, served as both cinema and dance hall. In its contemporary and recently renovated reiteration it is again doing time as a restaurant, café, meeting hall and exhibition space.

Instead of the expected collection of sunrises over Cardiff and views of Alexandra Park and the many pebbled beach done by local amateurs the gallery space has been given over to a showing of the work of Aneurin Morgan Thomas (1921-2009). Thomas was the first director of the Welsh Arts Council and a funding strategist of influence. He was also, and this was complete news to me, a talented creator of watercolours. His lifetime's work travels from a sort of post-war British cubism to recognisable Welsh landscapes painted for suburban walls. His talent he kept quiet about during the time I worked for him. He preferred to talk about the cut and thrust of Welsh National Theatre funding or the latest novels which I'd just sold him from the Oriel Bookshop.

Centrepiece of the show is his desk. It is covered with books, pens, manuals, crayons and so little free space that you wondered where he put his hands. No computer. Aneurin came from that earlier era where data lived in distant paper filing systems and you looked your visitors straight in the eye.

I'm done. In the sun this is as far as I am prepared to stretch the capital. The run up the Dingle alongside Alexandra Park to the rail station takes a few minutes. Penarth might be imposingly hilly but it's small. All trains go to Cardiff. "They have to," the lone guard, stationmaster and ticket seller tells me. On board it's only a few minutes journey and I'm there.

I alight and return to the capital's arms. Outside on Central Square there was once an abomination of metal sculpture embellished with seemingly random quotations from Welsh poets but happily the world here no longer rhymes. This space, littered today with travellers, alcoholics, sidewalk surfers, men eating burgers and women staring at their phones is the gateway to Wales. It's ever changing. From drained riverbed to Temperance Town terraces, from big Asteys and the 50s bus station to the present BBC-led corporate glass and glitter upward rush of new buildings it never stays the same for long.

CARDIFF – HOW IT COULD BE

If I arrive in the Cardiff future aboard H.G. Wells' time machine how will it be? Flattened by war, wrecked by pollution, a Mad Max dystopia? Or a place of order and light, full of Dan Dare glass domes with space cars flying between its towers? Already that place where imaginative fiction and progressive architecture meet is turning into reality. In Holland where the polders lie lower than our own Wentloog flatlands houses have been constructed which will float in times of flood. Cities will stand on rails to enable them to be hauled back from encroaching water. They will fly, these future municipalities, drift among the clouds in their cloaks of anti-matter.

If such a future is too farfetched then the much nearer one of meshing interminable conurbation is by no means impossible. J.G. Ballard predicted this in his short story 'The Concentration City' published in *New Worlds* in 1957. Here the surface of the planet had become one endless metropolis, city blocks as high as the sky and then running to meet each other as they encircled the globe. In our Cardiff version Newport and the capital join somewhere east of St Mellons while Whitchurch melds with Abercanaid among the valley slopes just south of Merthyr. This endless city has walls to hold back the rising Severn Sea, their prototypes visible already to anyone who has walked the Wales Coast Path in these parts.

Out beyond the Bay in an estuarine water world criss-crossed by barrages and electricity generating lagoons the new city districts of the monied will spread across artificial islands. West Holm. East Holm. Denny South. Great conductor cables will take the megawatts landwards to our ever-consuming world. A western powerhouse in name as well as fact.

There have been proposals around for decades to build a new Severnside airport on reclaimed land upriver from Newport. Causeways would connect with the M4. Hydrofoils would move passengers between runways. Salmon leaps would keep the project green.

To the city's north the ridge will have gone. Quarried flat to build our new super municipalities. On the land released vast bin-blighted housing estates will merge Tongwynlais and Lisvane with Watford Park and Machen. In this curvilinear maze car transport will be impossible. The new Cardiffian will metro or cycle. Pressure from Sustrans and others has already pushed the

Council into adopting an adventurous Cardiff Cycle City strategy which promises 50% of all journeys to be undertaken on two wheels by 2026. We shall see.

Whatever else happens it is inevitable that Cardiff will see a significant increase in the rate that its northern green belt disappears through the building of further new homes for our ever-burgeoning population. The green belt, which protects open land and restricts new development, has already been downgraded to a green wedge. Its piecemeal dissolution will soon resemble that of the Great Heath. Everything to nothing in a hundred years. Its future looks bleak.

The past, of course, is as littered with proposals for change as the present. Victorian-era piers to access deep water liners steamed here from America. A new canal paralleling the original through the centre of Cathays Park. Colin Buchanan's 1964 vision of motorways-on-stilts criss-crossing the centre. The Corporation and Ravenseft's modernist 1970 Centreplan proposals for an extensive replacement of the inner city. At first floor level there would have been districts for offices, retail enterprises, a church precinct, a central youth facility, an adult education complex, a design centre, a bus station north of Tiger Tiger, killer motor traffic , and acres of car parking east of the prison. More recently it was proposed, although maybe with tongue in cheek, to develop the Bute Dock Feeder into a sort of leisure waterway with rentable barges along Boulevard de Nantes and a subterranean water park with cafes and bathing facilities under the tarmac of Churchill Way.

Access has always been an issue. Tunnel builders have long sought to inter-connect the city with subterranean passages although no one yet has proposed putting railways in them. BT's communication tunnel[12] still exists under Westgate Street. As does the Penarth to Ferry Road subway[13] under the Ely, once regularly used by workers walking to the docks but now abandoned and full of water. Bay developers considered reopening it but were defeated by cost and safety issues. We got the Pont-y-Wern bridge instead.

Cardiff's future continues to be one of constant change. In 2013 a group of young architects including Alex Whitcroft and Stephen Paradise came up with their own new blueprint for a future city. They proposed creating a Costa Del Cardiff by adding a new 2k-long blue flag sandy beach along with affordable housing on land near the Barrage. This would be called Baltimore Village. They would serve their creation with a central Bay transport hub, couple this to a city-wide tram system and have a floating theatre offering a nightly roll of professional productions. Opera for mariners. Waterborne Welsh-language productions of *Macbeth*. Who could turn such ideas down? The *Western Mail* called the proposals 'bold'. The future is often called this. And even if we didn't quite get that beach or the affordable village we may well soon get the trams.

It's the Cardiff past. The end of the 70s. I'm walking back up from the Welsh Industrial and Maritime Museum with the poet John Ormond. We've been to a book launch at the Big Windsor on Stuart Street, bright readings under the high wood panelled roof, books sold, wine drunk. The Museum, darling of novelist and director G.O. Jones, had at this time not yet been demolished to make space for an orange brick block of dining opportunities for visitors known, for some unfathomable reason, as Mermaid Quay. John had read his 'Cathedral Builders'[14] which tells the tale of workmen hoisting hewn rock to heaven, inhabiting the sky with hammers, and working on into the future to get their building done. Occasionally they'd borrow their ladders from site to mend a neighbour's roof. Time would roll. They'd become old, get rheumatism and retire. The work would continue. Others would do it, finish the spire. But then, eventually, the place would be done. They would walk, like a new twenty-first century generation of hard-hatted luminous-jacketed men will inevitably do, down the shining streets of new Cardiff, look up, cock "a squint eye and say, 'I bloody did that.'" Cathedral complete, building done.

Fantasy really. Cities are never finished. They are built and then rebuilt. And after that they are rebuilt again. The process never ends.

Notes

1. *RCT* – Rhondda Cynon Taff.
2. The southern border of Wales starts in the Wye Estuary while the northern border starts in the Dee. See Peter Finch, *Real Wales*, Seren Books 2008.
3. Saunders Lewis 1893-1985 Welsh dramatist, historian and literary critic, one of Plaid Cymru's founders.
4. Cardiff Central Station, the General that was, is covered in *Real Cardiff* (Seren, 2002). Development of the new Cardiff Central is high on the city's lists. Watch this space.
5. When fully developed the Metro would actually be the Cardiff Capital Region Metro (or, better, the South Wales Metro) and extend its tracks from Bridgend in the west to Newport in the east and as far north as Merthyr and Ebbw Vale. The whole south Wales hinterland would be served by one integrated system.
6. 'We Gotta get Out Of This Place' by the Animals. 1965. Written by Brill Building hothouse

composes Barry Mann and Cynthia Weil the song was a huge hit among American Vietnam War fighters.

7. *Geology of the Roath Park* by John Storrie. Prepared from notes made by him and further information added by F.T. Howard. Read before the Biological and Geological Section of the Cardiff Naturalists Society on 29th November, 1906.

8. Wales Millennium Centre.

9. See *Real Cardiff* – Finch, Peter, Seren, 2002. 'A West Bute Dock Walk'.

10. *3 Ellipses for 3 Lock* by Swiss artist Felice Varini.

11. The line in from Cogan to a new station at the foot of the hill was never built.

12. Access restricted by the Official Secrets Act – Simon Fenoulhet – http://-www.simonfenoulhet.co.uk/

13. The Penarth Subway was opened in 1900 and finally closed to pedestrians in 1963. Its designer was Taff Vale Railway engineer George Sibbering. See "The Subway" in *Real Cardiff Three* (Seren, 2009).

14. Ormond, John, *Requiem And Celebration*, Christopher Davies, 1969.

The Cardiff Lost Poem

Abbot's Land, Alyce Hill, Antham, backs, Barnwell, Barrosa, Black Pool, Blind Lane, Boot Croft, Brinder, Bryn Well, Cae Cibwr, Cae Murch, Cawsy Cribyn, Coed Cati Rosser, Coed Sion Hywel, Coquemarel, The Corners Well, Crosham, Dobstreet, The Drying Hays, Eastern Hollows, Ffynon Bren, Ffynon Hoba, Fisher's Bridge, Frog Lane, Freshmoor, The Gallows Fields, Golden Hook, Graham Buildings, Goosleas, The Gowt, Gwelydd Gwynion, The Heaves, High Corner House, Horse Fair, Hungry Hill, Kegdwow, The Linches, Long Dike, Lord's Henge, Lower Layer, Mon Pupit, Muchel Heth, Nant y Gabal, New Patch, The Old Skin House, Our Lady's Service, Pedair Erw Twc, Porridge Lane, Portfield, Porteslond, The Portway, The Red House, The Rich House, Rhyd y Ffagle, Ridge Henge, Rising Sun, Roke's Land, Rowland's Bldgs, Running Camp, Rusham Mead, Sea Furlong, Sokeshay, Sourland, Stiffland, South Layland, Spiremead, Spodomeslonde, Stepaside, Sudcroft, Tir Morgan Hen, Tir Gruffydd Gam, Tir Crwn, Tir Berth y Lan, Townfield, Treasurer's Acres, Walschmenhull, Waterleader's, Weryngtrowes, West Street, Wise Street, Wilderness Well, Ystafell Y Cwn, Endless Zeal.

WORKS CONSULTED

Ahmed, Abdul-Azim, *Visual Dhikr – A Visual Analysis of Mosques In Cardiff*, unpublished dissertation, 2011

Athie, Patricia, *The Burning Ashes Of Time – From Steamer Point To Tiger Bay*, Seren, 2005

Ballard, J.G., *The Complete Short Stories*, Flamingo, 2002

Benjamin, E. Alwyn, *Penarth 1841-71 A Glimpse Of The Past*, D Brown & Sons, 1980

Bielski, Alison, *The Story of St Mellons*, Alun Books, 1985

Billingham, Nigel and Jones, Stephen K., *The Images Of Wales –Ely, Caerau And Michaelston-Super-Ely*, Tempus, 1996

Billingham, Nigel and Jones, Stephen K., *The Images Of Wales – Ely Common To Culverhouse Cross*, Tempus, 1999

Bowen, D.G. & Callow, J., *The Cardiff Trolleybus*, National Trolleybus Association, 1969

Breverton, T.D., *The Book Of Welsh Saints*, Glyndŵr Publishing, 2000

Brook, Diane, *A Short History of Roath Mill*, Morgannwg Vol LVII – The Journal of The Glamorgan History Society, 2013.

Cardiff Council, *Cardiff Public Art Register*, Cardiff Council, 2016

Cardiff Council, *Cardiff Cycling Strategy 2016-2026*, Cardiff Council, 2017

Carradice, Phil, *Penarth Pier 1894-1994*, Baron Birch, 1994

Childs, Jeff, *Roath, Splott and Adamsdown – One Thousand Years of History*, The History Press, 2012

Clarke, Peter, *A Capital Nightlife: The Future of Cardiff City Centre's Licensed Property Market, Highlights Cardiff's Growing Pub and Club trade*, Stephenson and Alexander, 2003

Cocroft, Wayne D. & Thomas, Roger J.C., *Cold War – Building For Nuclear Confrontation 1946-1989*, English heritage, 2003

Crickhowell, Nicholas, *Westminster, Wales And Water*, University of Wales Press, 1999

Crooks, John, *The Bluebirds – The Official History of Cardiff City Football Club*, Yore Publications, 1992

Dale, Peter, *Glamorgan's Lost Railways*, Stenlake, 2014

Davies, John, *A Pocket Guide To Cardiff*, UWP/Western Mail, 2002

Farmer, Shirley & Thomas, David Christopher, *Exploring A Wider Canvas – The Life and Work and Art of Aneurin Morgan Thomas (1921-2009)*, A Wider Canvas, 2014

Foxe, John, *The Acts And Monuments Of The Church*, 1563

Fisk, Nick, *The Blues Are Back In Town*, Parthian, 2015

Friends of Cathays Cemetery, *Cathays Cemetery Cardiff On Its 150th Anniversary*, Friends of Cathays Cemetery, 2009

Gillham, Mary E., *A Natural History of Cardiff – Exploring along the River Taff*, Lazy Cat Publishing, 2002

Gillham, Mary E., *A Natural History of Cardiff – Exploring along the Rivers Rhymney and Roath*, Dinefwr Publishers, 2006

Gledhill, David, *Gas Lighting*, Shire Publications, 1999

Glover, Brian, *Images of Wales – Cardiff Pubs And Breweries*, Tempus, 2005

Gould, David, *Cardiff's Electric Tramways*, The Oakwood Press, 1975

Hall, Mike, *Lost Railways of South Wales*, Countryside Books, 2009

Harvie, Christopher, *The Rise Of Regional Europe*, Routledge, 1994

Higgins, Charlotte, *Under Another Sky – Journeys In Roman Britain*, Cape, 2013

Hilling, John B., *The History and Architecture of Cardiff Civic Centre – Black Gold, White City*, University of Wales Press, 2016

Hooper, Alan & Punter, John, *Capital Cardiff 1975-2020 – Regeneration, Competiveness and the Urban Environment*, University of Wales Press, 2006

Hutton, John, *Taff Vale Railway Miscellany*, Oxford Publishing Company, 1988

Jenkins, Nigel, *Writers of Wales – John Tripp*, University of Wales Press, 1989

Jenkins, Roy, *Twelve Cities*, Macmillan, 2002

Jenkins, Stan, *Llanishen – A Historical Miscellany*, Llanishen Local History Society, 2014

Johnson, Anthony M., *Scott Of The Antarctic And Cardiff*, The Captain Scott Society, 1995

Johnstone, Michael, *The Freemasons – The Illustrated Book Of An Ancient Brotherhood*, Arcturus, 2006

Jones, Bryan, *The Archive Photographs Series – Canton*, Chalford, 1995

Jones, Barbara, *The Archive Photographs Series – Grangetown*, Chalford, 1996

Jones, David, *The Beatles and Wales*, St David's Press, 2002

Jones, Ffion Mair, *The Bard Is A Very Singular Character – Iolo Morganwg, Marginalia and Print Culture*, University of Wales Press, 2010

Kidner, R.W., *The Rhymney Railway*, Oakwood Press, 1995

Lee, Brian, *The Illustrated History of Cardiff's Pubs,* Breedon Books, 2004

Lee, Brian, *David Morgan The Family Store – An Illustrated History 1879-2005,* Breedon Books, 2005

Lockwood, Stephen, *Cardiff Trolleybuses – A Capital City System,* Middleton Press, 2005

Long, Helen, *The Edwardian House,* Manchester University Press, 1993

Lovell, Vivien, *Strategy for Public Art in Cardiff Bay,* Cardiff Bay Development Corporation, 1990

Marsden, Colin J., *Rail Guide 2016,* Ian Allen, 2016

Miles, Malcolm, *Art, Space and the City: Public Art and Urban Futures,* Routledge, 1997

Montgomery, Charles, *Happy City – Transforming Our Lives Through Urban Design,* Farrar, Straus and Giroux, 2013

Morgan, Dennis, *The Illustrated History of Cardiff's Suburbs,* Breedon Books, 2004

Morgan, Dennis, *The Cardiff Story,* D. Brown & Sons, 1991

Morgan, Kenneth O., *Rebirth of a Nation – Wales 1880-1980,* UWP, 1980

Neal, Marjorie, et al., *Rumney and St. Mellons – A History of Two Villages,* Rumney and District Local History Society, 2005

Newman, John, *The Buildings Of Wales – Glamorgan,* Penguin Books, 1995

Ormond, John, *Requiem And Celebration,* Christopher Davies, 1969

Painter, Christopher, Editor, *The Furnace Of Colours – Remembering Alun Hoddinott,* Welsh Music Guild, 2009

Pearson, Mike, *Marking Time: Performance, archaeology and the city,* University of Exeter Press, 2013

Rees, William, *Cardiff – A History of the City,* Corporation of Cardiff, 1969

Roese, Herbert E., *The Town Wall of Cardiff – 16th-19th Century,* Careck, 2011

Shepley, Nick, *The Story Of Cardiff,* The History Press, 2014

Statham, Michael, *Penarth Alabaster,* Welsh Stone Forum, 2017

Sully, Janet, *Howell's School, Llandaff 1860-2010 – A Legacy Fulfilled,* Howell's School, 2010

Thorne, A.R., *Place Names of Penarth,* D. Brown & Sons, 1997

Torekull, Bertil, *The Ikea Story,* Ikea, 2011

Watkins, Alfred, *The Old Straight Track,* Abacus, 1974

Wharton, Gary, *Ribbon Of Dreams – Remembering the Cardiff*

Cinemas, Mercia Cinema Society, 1997

Williams, Gareth, *Life On The Heath – The Making Of A Cardiff Suburb,* Merton Priory Press, 2001

Wharton, Gary, *Capitol Days – The Story of Cardiff's Best-Loved Cinema,* Tempus, 2008

Williams, Jan & Teasdale, Chris, *Cardiff Pride of Place Project,* Caravan Gallery, 2017

Williams, Stewart (ed), *The Cardiff Book Volume Three,* Stewart Williams, 1977

http://www.abandonedcommunities.co.uk/temperancetown.html

A NOTE ON WELSH USAGE

For most of this book I've tried to follow language usage as found. If Cardiff mispronounces or misuses the native tongue then I follow that pattern here. For example: *tŷ*, the Welsh for house, carries a circumflex over its second letter. General Cardiff usage is to drop the circumflex. This can be seen on street signs such as *Ty Draw Road*, *Ty Gwyn Road*, and *Ty Draw Place* and on house and building name boards such as *Ty Gwyn* and *Ty Glas*. However, where the signboard for a building has used the circumflex, as with, for example, *Tŷ Mynydd*, and *Tŷ Hapus*, then I have followed suit.

ACKNOWLEDGEMENTS

Grateful thanks are due to the following, all of whom have given me their time, their advice, found references for me and offered copious support and encouragement: Jonathan Adams, Abdul-Azim Ahmed, Kevin Brennan MP, John Briggs, Kirstie Barker, Allyn Burford, David Coombs, Damian Walford Davies, Grahame Davies, Heulyn Davies, Canon Aled Edwards, Chris Elward, Sue Finch, Glamorgan Archives, Roy Harris, Ian Horsburgh, Jehan & Athar Khatib, Claire Lille, Leo Lyons, Prof Brian Morgan, Derek & Elaine Morgan, the late Rhodri Morgan, Alan Moule, Dan Nichols, John Osmond, Christopher Painter, Mike Pearson, Victoria Rogers and Samantha Heale, Heike Roms, Nichole Sarra, Wiard Sterk, Janet Sully, Ifor Thomas, Amy Wack, Keith Walker, Andrew Williams, John Williams, Matthew Williams, and Emyr Young.

Special thanks go to my wife, Sue, for reading in draft every word of this fourth instalment of what, to her, must appear to be a never-ending project.

THE PHOTOGRAPHS

All photographs including front and rear covers taken by Peter Finch. The full selection of 250 colour shots that accompany this volume can be viewed online at https://www.flickr.com/photos/peterfinch/sets/721576 91514007662

A blog detailing and extending *Real Cardiff The Flourishing City* can be viewed at https://realcardiffpeterfinch.blogspot.co.uk/

THE AUTHOR

Peter Finch is a poet, performer, psychogeographer and literary entrepreneur living in Cardiff. He has been a publisher, bookseller, event organiser, literary agent and literary promoter. Until 2011 he was Chief Executive of Literature Wales.

His poetry has been collected in *Selected Later Poems* and *Zen Cymru*, both published by Seren. His *Edging The Estuary*, the story of where Wales becomes England, was published by Seren in the summer of 2013. His *The Roots of Rock: From Cardiff To Mississippi And Back* appeared from Seren in 2016. His future projects include *The Machineries of Joy,* recent poetry, and *Walking Cardiff*, a guide created in co-operation with the photographer John Briggs.

He edits Seren's Real series of alternative handbooks, literary rambles and guides to Britain's conurbations. His own *Real Cardiff* (in four volumes) and *Real Wales* have appeared in this series.

Since the early 1970s, Finch has been the principal innovator in Welsh poetry.....he deserves a Welsh knighthood. – **Richard Kostelanetz**, Dictionary of the Avant-Gardes

For 40 years he has been the Welsh avant-garde, as inventive and as indispensable as he has been consistently undervalued and ignored...one of the few Welsh writers capable of entrancing young students with his verbal chutzpah, his Crazy Gang of words. Henffych, Peter: a hir oes eto i'ch egni ac i'ch dawn. – **M. Wynn Thomas**

www.peterfinch.co.uk

INDEX

WHAT THE CRITICS SAID ABOUT THE REAL CARDIFF SERIES

This is a marvellous book – one of the very best books about a city I have ever read. It makes me feel terribly old-fashioned – superficial too, because I have never actually lived in the cities I have written about. I skip most of the poems, which I don't understand, but everything else in it is gripping me so fast that I have momentarily suspended my first ever reading of Wuthering Heights. – **Jan Morris**

Native Cardiffians now have the definitive guide to their city...the excitement of being one of the newest European capitals hangs light in the air. – **Kate Nicholson**, *Writers' News*

A wealth of information on the significance of familiar sites for those who live in Cardiff and an interesting insight into Wales' capital for those who don't, Real Cardiff is far more indicative of life in the city than the average tourist guide. – **Cathryn Scott**, *The Big Issue*

The book's great strength is not in the macro but in the micro, in the deep, prolonged engagement with a particular place which has produced a richly nuanced, affectionate and sometimes exasperated portrait of a city. The beauty lies in the detail. – **Grahame Davies**, *New Welsh Review*

Cunningly intermeshed with this cornucopia of useful and fascinating material is an account of how a young man who was something or other in the City Hall became an editor, a publisher, a bookseller, an arts administrator and a poet – the most surreally inventive and provocative writer we have – without leaving the city's limits.– **Meic Stephens**, *Cambria*

In this book, Peter Finch gets the balance damn near spot on, casting the gentlest of aspersions, giving the knife a tiny twist where necessary, but always while staring you unwaveringly in the eye as a true poet. This is not just true poetry, however, it is also travel writing of the sharpest kind....Finch's particular skill is his supreme ability to weave the past in with the present, and to that end his illustrations are often exquisite in their sparseness. – **Mike Parker**, *Planet*

Utterly compelling ambles round the Welsh capital, full of oddball nuggets and with a terrific sense of context and place. – *The Rough Guide To Wales*

Finch's Real Cardiff was one of the most successful and original books ever written about the Welsh capital – Here comes part two, and it's even better than the first. – **Dean Powell,** *The Western Mail*

Well chosen words

Seren is an independent publisher with a wide-ranging list which includes poetry, fiction, biography, art, translation, criticism and history. Many of our books and authors have been on longlists and shortlists for – or won – major literary prizes, among them the Costa Award, the Jerwood Fiction Uncovered Prize, the Man Booker, the Desmond Elliott Prize, The Writers' Guild Award, Forward Prize and TS Eliot Prize.

At the heart of our list is a beautiful poem, a good story told well or an idea or history presented interestingly or provocatively. We're international in authorship and readership though our roots are here in Wales (Seren means Star in Welsh), where we prove that writers from a small country with an intricate culture have a worldwide relevance.

Our aim is to publish work of the highest literary and artistic merit that also succeeds commercially in a competitive, fast changing environment. You can help us achieve this goal by reading more of our books – available from all good bookshops and increasingly as e-books. You can also buy them at 20% discount from our website, and get monthly updates about forthcoming titles, readings, launches and other news about Seren and the authors we publish.

www.serenbooks.com